TO LIVE IS CHRIST

EMBRACING THE PASSION OF PAUL

BETH MOORE

WALKER LARGE PRINT

A part of Gale, Cengage Learning

GALE
CENGAGE Learning

Detroit • New York • San Francisco • New Haven, Conn • Waterville, Maine • London

GALE
CENGAGE Learning™

LIBRARY OF CONGRESS CATALOGING-IN-PUBLICATION DATA

Moore, Beth, 1957–
   To live is Christ : embracing the passion of Paul / by Beth
Moore. — Large print ed.
     p. cm. — (Walker Large Print originals)
   Includes bibliographical references.
   ISBN-13: 978-1-59415-213-9 (softcover : alk. paper)
   ISBN-10: 1-59415-213-6 (softcover : alk. paper)
   1. Paul, the Apostle, Saint. 2. Christian saints — Turkey —
Tarsus — Biography. 3. Large type books. I. Title.
   BS2506.M66 2008
   225.9'2—dc22
   [B]   2007042531

Published in 2008 by arrangement with Broadman & Holman Publishers.

Printed in the United States of America
1 2 3 4 5 6 7 12 11 10 09 08

DEDICATION

To all those who have followed
in the footsteps of the apostle Paul
risking life and loneliness
to take Christ's gospel
to the uttermost parts of the world.

ACKNOWLEDGMENTS

What a treasure God has given me in my friend and editor, Dale McCleskey! He is the reason you have this form of *To Live Is Christ* in your hands. Dale has very carefully and prayerfully reformatted the in-depth Bible Study God gave me by this same title into a more "reader friendly" trade-book version. I am greatly indebted to him for his fine work.

I am also grateful for Broadman & Holman Publishers who unapologetically favor Bible-based books. I am honored to serve them and to serve the body of Christ by their side.

Dear reader, I am also deeply thankful for you. All I want to be is a servant. A bond slave of Jesus Christ. Please allow me to wash your feet with the water of the Word.

CONTENTS

PREFACE 13
INTRODUCTION 19

I. THE FIRST FOOTPRINTS. 21

Chapter 1. Set Apart from Birth . . . 23
Chapter 2. The Childhood of a
    Pharisee's Son 32
Chapter 3. At the Feet of Gamaliel . . 39
Chapter 4. Strangled by the Law . . . 48
Chapter 5. Meanwhile in Jerusalem . . 57

II. FINDING THE WAY 67

Chapter 6. No Innocent Bystander . . 69
Chapter 7. A Sudden Change
    in Plans. 77
Chapter 8. From Persecutor
    to Preacher 85
Chapter 9. A Pried-Open Mind . . . 92
Chapter 10. New Church, New Name . 99

III. MILES AND MISSIONS. 107

Chapter 11. One Blind Sorcerer . . . 109
Chapter 12. A Light for the Gentiles . 117
Chapter 13. A Prudent Pair 125
Chapter 14. Hardships on the
    Kingdom Road 135
Chapter 15. Harder Than It Has
    to Be 145

IV. UNEXPECTED SOJOURNERS AND WIDER PATHS 155

Chapter 16. Divide and Multiply . . 157
Chapter 17. The Birth of a
    Spiritual Son 165
Chapter 18. The Leadership of
    Christ's Spirit 175
Chapter 19. The Midnight Song. . . 185
Chapter 20. The Noble Example of
    the Berean Believers. 194

V. AN UNFAMILIAR ROAD 293

Chapter 21. The Idols of Athens. . . 205
Chapter 22. With Fear and
    Trembling 211
Chapter 23. The Tentmakers 221
Chapter 24. One Stick of Dynamite . 227
Chapter 25. A Great Show
    of God's Glory. 232

VI. TRAVEL TIES AND HARD GOOD-BYES 243

Chapter 26. The Riot in Ephesus . . 245
Chapter 27. A Long-Winded
    Preacher 253
Chapter 28. A Tender Heart 258
Chapter 29. From the Mouths
    of Prophets 267
Chapter 30. A Prophecy Fulfilled . . . 277

VII. A WALK OF FAITH 285

Chapter 31. A Willing Witness . . . 287
Chapter 32. In All Good
    Conscience 294
Chapter 33. A Peculiar Deliverance . 303
Chapter 34. An Inconvenient Gospel . 311
Chapter 35. Man Alive! 317

VIII. THE PATHWAY TO ROME 325

Chapter 36. An Anchor in
    the Storm 327
Chapter 37. An Umbrella in
    the Storm 335
Chapter 38. Island Wonders 342
Chapter 39. Brothers Among
    Strangers 351
Chapter 40. Ears, Eyes, and Hearts . . 358

IX. LETTERS BRIDGING THE MILES . . 369

Chapter 41. Don't Be Kidnapped! . . 371
Chapter 42. A Profound Mystery . . 380

11

Chapter 43. A Ready Warrior 392
Chapter 44. A More Excellent Way. . 401
Chapter 45. A Rare Gem 409

X. GOING HOME 415

Chapter 46. A Sharp Memory . . . 417
Chapter 47. Spiritual Fitness
     in Ministry 425
Chapter 48. Person to Person 434
Chapter 49. Come Before Winter . . 441
Chapter 50. Finishing the Race . . . 449

  • STUDY QUESTIONS 459
    NOTES 479

PREFACE

To Live Is Christ traces the life of the apostle Paul from his presumed childhood to his death, centering on one man's amazing ministry. If you respond to this study like I did, you'll be greatly refreshed by the obvious mercy of God to allow those who have really blown it to repent and serve Him wholeheartedly and effectively. You'll also be amazed by Paul's tenacity, and through his example I think you will find encouragement to persevere in trials. You will also become acquainted with Paul's humanity and perhaps realize he was not so unlike the rest of us — proof God can greatly use any of us if we are fully available and readily cooperative!

I was greatly affected by the study of Paul's life in many ways; but above all, I sense like never before a quickened awareness of the personal calling God has placed on my life. I feel a renewed sense of my purpose in God's plan. I am praying for you to have the same response. You are a Christian in this present generation for a very good reason. Your life has purpose. He planned your visitation on this planet and wants to fulfill 1 Corinthians 2:9 in your life. May these pages enhance your love and devotion for Christ so dramatically that He is freed in your life to do more than your eyes have seen, more than your ears have heard, and more than your mind has conceived!

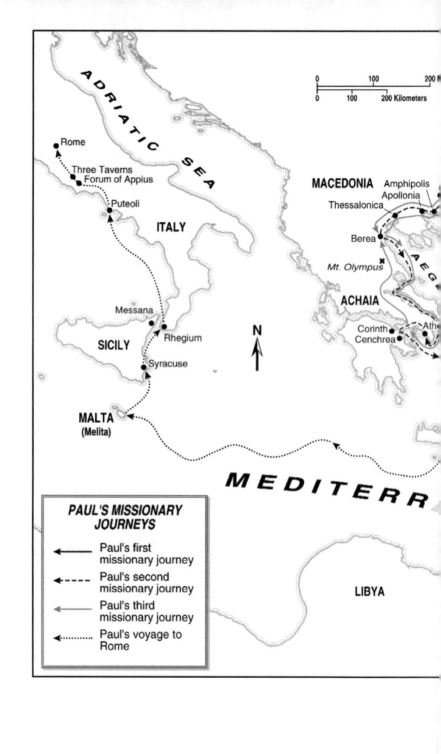

ADRIATIC SEA

Rome
Three Taverns
Forum of Appius
Puteoli

ITALY

MACEDONIA   Amphipolis
Apollonia
Thessalonica
Berea

Mt. Olympus

ACHAIA

Messana
Rhegium

SICILY
Syracuse

Corinth   Ath
Cenchrea

N

MALTA
(Melita)

MEDITERR

**PAUL'S MISSIONARY
JOURNEYS**

Paul's first
missionary journey

Paul's second
missionary journey

Paul's third
missionary journey

Paul's voyage to
Rome

LIBYA

0   100   200
0   100   200 Kilometers

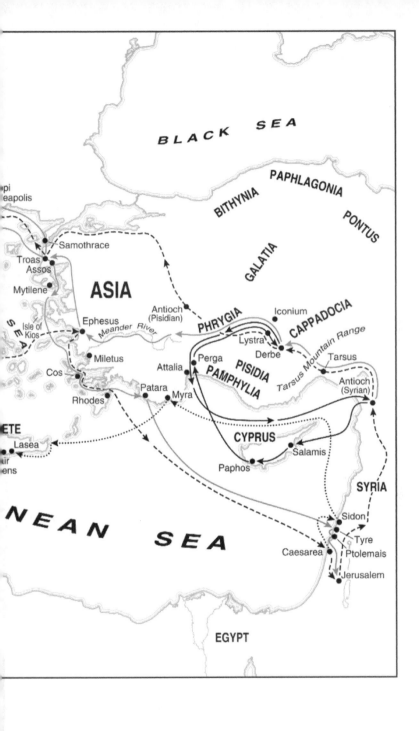

BLACK SEA

PAPHLAGONIA

BITHYNIA

PONTUS

GALATIA

pi
eapoli

Samothrace

Troas
Assos

Mytilene

ASIA

Antioch
(Pisidian)

PHRYGIA

Iconium

CAPPADOCIA

Ephesus

Meander River

Lystra

Derbe

Tarsus Mountain Range

Tarsus

SEA

Isle of
Kios

Miletus

Perga

PISIDIA

Cos

Attalia

PAMPHYLIA

Antioch
(Syrian)

Patara

Myra

Rhodes

ETE

CYPRUS

Lasea

Salamis

air
ens

Paphos

SYRIA

NEAN

Sidon

SEA

Tyre

Caesarea

Ptolemais

Jerusalem

EGYPT

INTRODUCTION

Welcome aboard! I'm so glad you're joining me on an expedition through Scripture with the apostle Paul. Our travels will take us by land and sea to places we never dreamed we'd go. I hope you'll soon agree that the apostle Paul was a remarkable man. His persistence and undying passion will no doubt convince you that he truly encountered the risen Christ. Decades after Jesus interrupted Paul's plans, the apostle's account of the event remained consistent. Something dramatically changed the life of a brilliantly devious persecutor. I pray that the same Someone will also interrupt our lives with His glorious presence as we take this journey together.

I've been a fan of the apostle Paul for years. In my estimation, his writings embody a passion for Christ that is unparalleled in the New Testament. I have accepted many of his words as a personal challenge. "I want to know Christ" has become my plea. "To live is Christ and to die is gain" has become my hope. And to borrow his words once more, "Not that I have already obtained all this . . . but I press on" (Phil. 3:12). I genuinely love Christ, and I am a fan of all those past and present who have loved Him with their whole lives.

Having admired the apostle Paul for years, I was somewhat surprised by a few comments that were made by people who learned I was writing a Bible study on his life. I received questions like, "How can you, a woman, write a Bible study about a man who obviously had no tolerance for women in ministry?"

Sadly the controversy surrounding small bits of the apostle's teaching has often kept students from delving into the heart and liberating theology of the whole man. I think you're really going to like him — once you get to know him. When we've turned the last page, even if you didn't like him you'll have to agree he loved and served his Lord with every ounce of breath and every drop of blood he had. His passion for Christ was indomitable — reason enough to study his life and be challenged by his Spirit-breathed words.

Come on along. Let's get started.

■ ■ ■ ■

PART I
THE FIRST
FOOTPRINTS

■ ■ ■ ■

When a little boy named Saul played make-believe with his friends in a Jewish neighborhood in Tarsus, he never could have imagined the real-life drama that awaited him. As God carefully watched the small child at play, at school, and at worship, I wonder if He thought, *Someday, My child, you will work for Me.* You and I have the opportunity to witness the unfolding of one of the most dramatic stories in Christendom. Our journey begins with some safe suppositions based on chronicles of ancient Hebrew life, but we will quickly move into well-documented scriptural accounts. In this first part of our study, we will imagine what Paul's childhood and upbringing might have been like, then we will set our sights on Jerusalem, where strange twists of events will take place. I hope you'll jump into this journey with both feet. May the pages of Acts and Paul's epistles have our footprints all over them by the time we complete our last mile. It's time to begin. I'll meet you in Tarsus!

CHAPTER 1
SET APART FROM
BIRTH

God, who set me apart from birth and
called me by his grace, was pleased to
reveal his Son in me so that I might
preach him among the Gentiles.
(GAL. 1:15–16)

Paul grew up in an orthodox Jewish home in a Gentile city. The Bible gives us only a few pieces of information about his upbringing; but based on those tidbits, we may draw a number of conclusions.

We know that Paul was reared as closely to the letter of the Jewish law as possible (see Phil. 3:5–6); therefore, based on Scripture and the traditional Jewish code of law, we can describe many details of his young life. We will begin our study of the apostle in the most appropriate place — his cradle.

The following narrative describes the events that most likely took place soon after his birth. The story line is fictional to help you picture the events, but the circumstances and the practices are drawn from Scripture and the Jewish code of law. "For centuries the *Code of Jewish Law* has been and continues to be the cornerstone of Jewish life. Its rules and precepts are the guardians of Jewish custom and tradition and an eternal light guiding Jewish moral, social, and religious behavior."[1] Sit back and imagine the beginning of one of the most significant lives in all Christendom.

"I thank Thee, O living and eternal King, Who hast mercifully restored my soul within me; Thy faithfulness is great."[2]

The words fell from his tongue while his eyes were still heavy from the night's rest. His morning prayers invited unexpected emotion this particular dawn as he soberly considered the honor that lay before him. Eight days had passed since the birth of his friend's son. Today would be the child's *Berit Milah.* He would stand beside the father at the infant's circumcision as the *sandek,* the Jewish godfather, assuming solemn responsibility — second only to the parents — over the child's devout religious upbringing.

"I think they are naming him Saul," said his wife.

"We shall not presume his name until we hear it from the lips of his father," he responded.

He had intended to arrive first so he could assist the father with preparations, but a few members of the *Minyan,* a quorum of ten Jewish men, had already gathered at the door. Normally, the woman of a Jewish household would offer warm welcomes to visitors at her door, but the newborn's mother was treated with utmost care during the days following her delivery. Friends and relatives assisted the father in any preparations that had to be made for *Berit Milah,* a tiny infant boy's first initiation into Judaism.

The small house was filled with people. The father, a Pharisee and Roman citizen, was an impressive man. He was one of a few men in the community who seemed to command a certain amount of respect from both Jew and Gentile. When all had finally gathered, the ceremony began. The sandek took his place in a chair next to the father, who remained standing. The new father was not a particularly tall man, but the sandek couldn't help but notice that his stature seemed particularly stretched today. And why not? What could make a

Jewish man stand taller than a newborn son?

The infant was placed on the sandek's knees, and the father leaned over him with greatest care to oversee the circumcision of his beloved son. He then handed the knife to the *mohel,* the most upright and expert circumcisor available in Tarsus. The father watched anxiously for the interval between the cutting of the foreskin and its actual removal. He could not help but smile as he competed with his wailing son for the attention of the quorum as he spoke the benediction, "Who hath sanctified us by His commandments and hath commanded us to bring him into the covenant of our father Abraham."[3] With the exception of the sandek, all who gathered stood for the ceremony and responded to the benediction with the words, "Just as he has been initiated into the covenant, so may he be initiated into the study of the Torah, to his nuptial [marriage] canopy, and to the performance of good deeds."[4]

No one could deny the blessings of good health God had already bestowed on the infant boy. The sandek had to hold him securely between his calloused palms to keep the child from squirming completely off his lap. His tiny face was bloodred, his volume at full scale. This may have been his first bout with anger, but it would not be his last. Had the ceremony not held such sober significance, the sandek might have snickered at the infant's zeal. He dared not grin, but he did wonder if God was. Tears of joy stung his eyes. The child lying on his lap was yet another piece of tangible evidence that God was faithful to do as He promised. In a society where a child could be discarded as rubbish, nothing was more important to the Jew than offspring. Yes, God had been faithful to a thousand generations.

The circumcision was completed but not soon enough for the master of ceremonies. The sandek cradled the child with a moment's comfort and then handed him to his father, whose voice resonated throughout the candlelit home, "His name is Saul!"

As if only a few could hear, the guests rehearsed the words in one another's ears. "His name is Saul! His name is Saul!" A perfectly noble name for a Hebrew boy from the tribe of Benjamin, named for the first king of the chosen nation of Israel. A fine choice met with great approval. While a great feast ensued, the mother slipped the agitated infant from his father's arms and excused herself to nurse the child.

Custom demanded that the father host a feast to the limits of his wealth. A man who offered less than he could afford at his son's circumcision was entirely improper. If baby Saul's father was anything at all, he was painfully proper. Yes, this would indeed be a child well reared. "I have much to learn from the father of Saul," the sandek surmised.

Darkness was quickly falling when the sandek and his wife finally reached their home. The day had been long but the fellowship sweet. Gathered with those who feared God and worshiped Him only, he had almost forgotten this city was not their own. Tarsus, the city of the Greeks, had given birth to another Hebrew. "Dear wife," the sandek thought out loud, "our Saul seems special, does he not?"

"Dear man," she teased, "he looked like every other eight-day-old infant boy I've ever seen: mad as a wronged ruler!" They both laughed heartily. She prepared for bed as he reached for the Torah, trying to fight off the sleep quickly overtaking him. He repeated the words of the *Shema,* and then he walked over to the *mezuzah* fastened to the doorpost of the house and placed his fingers on it. The Mesusah was a small, longitudinally folded parchment square, containing twenty-two lines, some of the most vital Words of God. He responded to the touch with the familiar words of his own father every night of his life, "The Lord is my keeper."[5] He crawled into bed, remembered their words, and smiled once again. Then he whispered as his thoughts drifted into the night, "I still say he's special. Full of zeal, he is. Just something about him . . ."

No doubt you just encountered some Hebrew terms you had never seen before. Those terms give a glimpse into the Judaism of the first century and shed light on the life of Paul. The *sandek* was the newborn's chosen godfather. The *Berit Milah* was the ceremony of circumcision, performed on the infant's eighth day. The *Minyan* was the quorum of ten Jewish men necessary for a synagogue.

In Galatians 1:15–16, Paul spoke of being "set apart from birth." Genesis 17:1–11 describes circumcision as "the sign of the covenant" between God and the descendants of Abraham. We cannot overstate the importance of Paul's Jewish identity. It powerfully affected his lifestyle in every waking moment. We cannot hope to understand Paul the man apart from the identity of Saul "the son of a Pharisee" (Acts 23:6).

The home of any devout Jew in Paul's generation would have been marked by a mezuzah, which actually meant "doorpost." The parchment inside the *mezuzah* contained the words of Deuteronomy 6:4–9 and Deuteronomy 11:13–21. These Scriptures were the absolute watchwords of the Jewish faith. You are probably familiar with the first passage:

> Hear, O Israel: The LORD our God, the LORD is one. Love the LORD your God with all your heart and with all your soul and with all your strength. These commandments that I give you today are to be upon your hearts. Impress them on your children. Talk about them when you sit at home and when you walk along the road, when you lie down and when you get up. Tie them as symbols on your hands and bind them on your foreheads. Write them on the doorframes of your houses and on your gates. (Deut. 6:4–9)

The father's benediction during the circumcision ceremony was obviously my conjecture based on research. It did, however, express the three obvious priorities of the devout Jew: the study of the Torah, marriage, and the performance of good deeds.

I hope our opening chapter spurred some distinct images of the ancient Jewish home and Paul's probable beginnings. We have so much to learn together. You're off to a great start!

CHAPTER 2
THE CHILDHOOD OF
A PHARISEE'S SON

*Train a child in the way he should go, and
when he is old he will not turn from it.*
(PROV. 22:6)

The familiar utterances of Proverbs 22:6
were not empty words to the ancient Hebrew. The passage represented one of the
sternest commands of God. To the strict
Jew, only one way existed for a child to go:
the way of his father and his father's father.
Theirs was the responsibility to direct the
child in that familiar way. You can be sure
the infant Saul was reared as closely to the
letter of the law as possible. Many years
later the apostle Paul described his home
life in these words: "circumcised on the
eighth day, of the people of Israel, of the
tribe of Benjamin, a Hebrew of Hebrews"
(Phil. 3:5).

A Jew would have known exactly what
"Hebrew of Hebrews" meant. Virtually

nothing but Jewish influence touched him in his early childhood.

Unlike the typical family today, the father assumed primary responsibility for training the child. The *Code of Jewish Law* states, "It is the duty of every father to train his children in the practice of all the precepts, whether Biblical or Rabbinical. . . . It is also incumbent upon the father to guard his children against any forbidden act."[1] As a Pharisee, Saul's father would have assumed his responsibility with great sobriety.

We may have to fight the temptation to automatically attach a negative connotation to the term *Pharisee.* F. B. Meyer's words may help us gain a proper perspective: "The word Pharisee is a synonym for religious pride and hypocrisy; but we must never forget that in those old Jewish days the Pharisee represented some of the noblest traditions of the Hebrew people. Amid the prevailing indifference the Pharisees stood for a strict religious life. . . . Amid the lax morals of the time, which infected Jerusalem almost as much as Rome, the Pharisee was austere in his ideals, and holy in life."[2]

Some Pharisees gave the Pharisees a bad name, just as some Christians give Christianity a bad name. Saul's father was not likely one of them, although a number of scholars wonder if he might have been excessively strict, based on the apostle's words about parenting: "Fathers, do not exasperate your children; instead, bring them up in the training and instruction of the Lord" (Eph. 6:4).

Could Paul's words have been the voice of experience? Did God specifically inspire the apostle Paul to write these words because he had known the injury that harshness could inflict? We do not know, but the possibility certainly exists. No doubt, Paul's upbringing was strict, but to what extent we do not know.

The *Code of Jewish Law* certainly condemned overt harshness in child-rearing. Jewish parents considered children the utmost blessing from God and loved them dearly. The ancient historian Josephus said of the Jew, "We lay greater stress on the training of the children than on anything else, and regard observance of the Law and a corresponding godly life as the most important of all duties."[3] Although young Saul grew up in a very strict home, he enjoyed the utmost devotion of his father to his godly upbringing — something only the very fortunate among our children enjoy.

The rabbinic laws taught fathers to begin teaching their children the ways of God from their earliest understanding. Having been reared in a Baptist church that was famous for hearty amens, I had to smile as I read the words of the *Code of Jewish Law* stating, "It is well to train a child to respond Amen and other responses at the synagogue. From the time that an infant begins to respond Amen, he has a share in the world to come."[4] I can just imagine Saul as a three- or four-year-old responding, brow properly furrowed, with a serious "amen" at the appropriate times in a synagogue service.

As little more than a toddler, Saul learned to say the *Schmone-Ezre* — the primary prayers of the Jews — morning, noon, and night. He learned to pray before and after every meal. He actively participated in the traditional feasts as soon as he could talk. Even today in an orthodox Jewish Passover celebration, the youngest child in the family is the one who asks the traditional questions that prompt the father to retell the rich history of Israel's exodus from slavery.

A child of normal intelligence read Scriptures by five years of age. At six years old, Saul began his education at the school of a rabbi. These schools were ordinarily associated with the community synagogue. The Jewish population was large enough to have at least one active synagogue in Tarsus. Lessons were tedious and teachers were strict, but Jewish children were rarely caught roaming the streets!

Soon after his sixth birthday, Saul memorized Deuteronomy 6:4–9, the words on the tiny scroll inside the mezuzah on the doorway of his home. Far more impressively, he also memorized Psalms 113–118!

Imagine all six of these psalms being seared into your soul in childhood! Being a Hebrew was not just a religion; Judaism wasn't even just a way of life. Being Hebrew defined who you were, how you thought, what you felt. By the time Saul was ten years old, he knew the intricacies of the oral law. Young Saul's mind was thoroughly steeped and vastly stretched with constant memorization. He had little choice but to "meditate on the law both day and night" just to prepare for the following day's lessons.

The years between ten and thirteen are transforming years for any boy, but a particular metamorphosis took place in a Jewish boy's life. He matured more rapidly than our modern-day Gentile boys do. By the age of thirteen, a Jewish boy, for all practical purposes, was considered a man — a milestone he lived for. At thirteen, a boy in our society sometimes seems like an alien. It's "a phase" we often hope they can just live through!

By the time Saul was thirteen years of age, he was considered a son of the law. He assumed all the religious responsibilities of the adult Jew. He started wearing phylacteries, called *tefillin,* during weekday morning prayers. Phylacteries were made up of two black leather cubes with long leather straps. Each cube held certain passages from the Torah written on strips of parchment. Saul wore one of the cubes on his left arm facing his heart. The other cube was placed in the center of his forehead. The leather straps on the left arm were wound precisely seven times around his arm.

The *Code of Jewish Law* prescribed that a Jewish man thirteen years or older was to put on the tefillin at the first moment in the morning when enough daylight existed to recognize a neighbor at a distance of four cubits.[5] These practices seem very strange to us perhaps, but we should appreciate their attempt to interpret Scripture as literally as they knew how.

Exodus 13:9 says the annual observance of the Feast of Unleavened Bread "will be for you like a sign on your hand and a reminder on your forehead that the law of the LORD is to be on your lips." You can see that for the strict Jew the phylacteries were a literal act of obedience.

The left arm was chosen because it was ordinarily the weaker. They were to wear God's Word as a banner and shield over their weakness. We don't practice the outward expression of the Jew, but we are wise to share the inward principle.

Saul would have placed the phylacteries around his forehead and arm in total silence. If interrupted while putting on the phylacteries on any given morning, he would have started the procedure all over again, repeating the appropriate benedictions.[6] You see, a thirteen-year-old Hebrew boy could not even get out of bed in the morning without remembering to whom he belonged. As he wound the straps of the phylacteries around his head and arm, he was reminded of his binding relationship to his Creator. Soberly he assumed the responsibility of one associated with God. The law of the Lord was his life.

CHAPTER 3
AT THE FEET OF
GAMALIEL

"I am a Jew, born in Tarsus of Cilicia, but brought up in this city. Under Gamaliel I was thoroughly trained in the law of our fathers and was just as zealous for God as any of you are today."
(ACTS 22:3)

Although Saul's education in the home of a Pharisee was probably typical, his response was certainly atypical. We might say, "He took to it like a duck to water."

Saul was an exceptional student. Hebrew fathers were not notorious gushers, so his father probably didn't brag on him a lot. Yet, he no doubt considered the wisest approach for Saul's future, not unlike a modern father looking for the best university for his gifted son.

In the search for the best continuing Jewish education, he set his sights on Jerusalem, the homeland — the fountain of Jewish learning. We should take off our hats to the Pharisee from Tarsus for choosing to send his son to Jerusalem. Who would help him with the family trade? If Saul's dreams of becoming a rabbi persisted, who would inherit the family business? Scripture lends some evidence that Saul's father may have made these decisions entirely alone. The apostle made no mention of his mother in any of his writings; but in Romans 16:13, he spoke of the mother of Rufus filling a maternal role in his life. Some scholars suggest Saul lost his mother at an early age.

Mixed emotions must have filled the heart of the young man as he prepared for the journey to Jerusalem. Like most teenage boys, his emotions probably swung to the same extremes as his changing voice. Like any thirteen-year-old going so far from home, he was probably scared to death. Yet, as a Jewish thirteen-year-old, he was considered a man. He packed his bags with articles foreign to us but common to the ancient Jew: prayer shawls, phylacteries, sacred writings, and customary clothing. He probably didn't gaze with affection over familiar contents in his room prior to leaving. The Jew was not given to domestic decor and did not believe in images on the walls.

All his life Saul had heard about Jerusalem. His father probably made the journey often. Three annual feasts beckoned Jewish men from near and far to the city of Zion. A proper Pharisee traveled to Jerusalem for the annual Passover Feast. Saul likely stayed home and watched over the family affairs while picturing the busy streets and solemn assemblies of the sacred city. Saul probably devoured every story his father told about Jerusalem upon his arrival home. Now it was his turn.

Most assuredly, Saul's father sought a Jewish traveling companion for his young son, someone who could provide proper supervision as the young student traveled from Tarsus to Jerusalem. As Saul boarded the boat at the docks of Tarsus, he had no idea just how familiar the nauseating heaving of a sea vessel would ultimately become to him. The boat sailed almost due south as Saul gazed at the ancient coastal cities of Sidon and Tyre in the distance. After several rather unpleasant days on board, he probably arrived at the port of Caesarea with a chronic case of sea legs. There he exchanged rubbery limbs for the peculiar soreness of riding on the back of a beast over rough country. Thirty-five miles later, he caught the first glimpses of the city set on a hill — Jerusalem, the City of David.

Young Saul's eyes beheld a far more cosmopolitan city than had his ancestors. Just a few decades prior to Saul's visit, Herod the Great sought the favor of the Jewish populace by rebuilding not just the temple but the entire city of Jerusalem. The desert sun danced on city walls built of Jerusalem limestone. Saul probably dismounted just before the city gate. The elders sitting at the gate looked up only long enough to notice the young traveler. His dress and manner assured them that he was a newcomer, but he was one of them. No heathen was he. Noting his age, they probably nodded with approval over his father's obvious choice of further education — a budding rabbi, no doubt.

Just inside the gate, Saul cast his eyes on the impressive fruit of Herod's labors: a large theater, a palace, an amphitheater, a hippodrome for horse and chariot races, imposing fortified towers, and perfectly blended architecture. But all this paled in comparison to the structure on top of the hill — Herod's temple. Herod rebuilt the temple bigger and better than its predecessor. Huge, richly ornamented white stones mounted on one another created a lavish feast for the eyes. Young Saul witnessed one of the most magnificent buildings in the entire world.

Saul probably ran up the main street of Jerusalem to the house of the Lord. He surely conjured up pictures of King David dancing down that very street. He hurried up the many stairs to greet magnificent porches surrounding the entire enclosure. Then he walked to a wall, one that held tremendous significance for the Jew, but one that would hold far more significance for a Jew who would ultimately become the world's most renowned missionary to the Gentiles.

When, from a prison cell in Ephesus, Paul wrote that Christ had broken down the wall that separates Jew and Gentile, the apostle was not simply referring to a figurative wall of partition. He was referring to an imposing structure he had faced on the temple grounds as an adolescent many years before. Being raised in a Gentile city, young Saul had no problem reading the notices inscribed in Greek and Latin. This literal middle wall of partition in the temple forbade access of the defiling heathen to the inner sanctuaries of the house of God. As a young man born into a position of religious privilege, he stood a little taller — chest a little broader — as he read those words. What a contrast of emotions he would feel many years later as he came to despise the prejudice of those who would not recognize the walls crumbled by the cross. To them Saul would write, "For he is our peace, who hath made both [Jew and Gentile] one, and hath broken down the middle wall of partition between us" (Eph. 2:14 KJV).

Within days, Saul took a seat in the most impressive classroom in the entire Jewish world. His esteemed teacher was the rabbi Gamaliel, grandson of the great Hillel — names of great importance in the history of Judaism.

Gamaliel continues to be so highly esteemed in Judaism that even the rabbi I interviewed for this writing spoke of him with genuine familiarity. So highly revered was Gamaliel that the Jews referred to him as "the beauty of the law."[1] About one thousand students populated the rabbinical college, also called the House of Interpretation, during Saul's studies in Jerusalem.

One of the most wonderful concepts in the Word of God concerns the plan God has for our lives. In Galatians 1:15 Paul wrote "when God, who set me apart from birth and called me by his grace." God had a plan for Saul from birth. *Nothing* in the young man's life would be a waste unless he refused to let God use it. All of Saul's religious training, his countless hours spent in Scripture and study, his brilliance in spiritual matters would all be parts of God's ornate plan. God would use what Saul learned at the feet of Gamaliel. "Gamaliel was clearly a remarkable man — the first to whom the title Rabban (Master) was given."[2] He was almost liberal in comparison to many of his contemporaries. Big-hearted, wise, and open-minded, Gamaliel had been raised on the teachings of his grandfather, Hillel, whose words often had a remarkable similarity to the Greatest Rabboni who would ever live. A few lines from the teaching of Hillel are: "Judge not thy neighbour until thou art in his place; . . . my abasement is my exaltation; he who wishes to make a name for himself loses his name; . . . what is unpleasant to thyself that do not to thy neighbour; this is the whole Law, all else is but its exposition."[3] Do those words sound familiar?

Gamaliel's teachings strongly reflected those of his grandfather. God, in His wonderful wisdom, made sure that the law was taught to Saul with a touch of rare grace.

God included a sample of Gamaliel's teachings in Acts 5:27–42. During the early days of the young church, the Jewish officials wanted to put the apostles to death, but Gamaliel advised them:

> Leave these men alone! Let them go! For if their purpose or activity is of human origin, it will fail. But if it is from God, you will not be able to stop these men; you will only find yourselves fighting against God. (Acts 5:38–39)

Obviously Saul sat at the feet of one of Judaism's most grace-filled teachers; however, he soon developed his own ways of thinking. Saul's brilliance moved him to the front of every class. He was a born leader. You can be sure Saul rejoiced in taking a primary role in the endless debates on the interpretation of the law. "A large part of the students' time was spent in hair-splitting definitions, and arguments every whit as complex, and even bizarre, as those that centuries later were to trouble the scholars and divines."[4]

Saul spent five of the most critical years of his life in Jerusalem. He experienced the Holy City during some of its most prosperous and thriving years. Here his childhood dreams came true. He became a teacher, a rabbi. The son of a Pharisee became a Pharisee. Decades later, when he wrote his first letter to the Corinthians, he may have

46

looked back over all the years of learning, the hundreds of debates, the trivial arguments, and stated a few words from the realm of personal experience. He wrote:

> We know that we all possess knowledge. Knowledge puffs up, but love builds up. The man who thinks he knows something does not yet know as he ought to know. But the man who loves God is known by God. (1 Cor. 8:1–3)

The knowledge that puffed Saul's head was not wasted, but it wasn't until years later that he discovered love. As students of God's Word, let's commit to receiving the full benefit of studying Scripture. Don't study just to increase knowledge. Let every study of the Word of God increase your love for the divine Author!

CHAPTER 4
STRANGLED BY THE
LAW

If anyone else thinks he has reasons to
put confidence in the flesh, I have more:
circumcised on the eighth day, of the
people of Israel, of the tribe of Benjamin,
a Hebrew of Hebrews; in regard to the
law, a Pharisee; . . . as for legalistic
righteousness, faultless.
(PHIL. 3:4–6)

"Arise, cry out in the night, / as the watches of the night begin; / pour out your heart like water / in the presence of the Lord. / Lift up your hands to him / for the lives of your children" (Lam. 2:19). I always planned to have at least ten children. Soon after we were married, my husband gave me the grave news: He only wanted a couple of children. I was devastated. I immediately retorted with the words, "But we agreed!" He smiled and responded, "No, Honey, you agreed." I have to snicker as I recall wondering if such a blatant omission from our premarital discussions was grounds for an annulment. Little did my husband or I know that I was already expecting child number one.

Finally holding Amanda in our arms had a strange effect on each of us. Keith decided he might just change his mind and want three or four. I, on the other hand, decided I might just stop with one. Nothing prepared me for the intense sense of vulnerability a seven-pound infant gave me. Someone suddenly had direct, unabashed access to my heart. I was terrified I would lose her. I prayed constantly for God to watch over her, then gripped the rail of her crib and stared at her while she slept, just in case He was too busy. Most of the time, I simply held her through her nap time so I could be assured she was OK and in good hands. Reluctantly, I'm sure, God entrusted me with another child, and I set out to drive her almost as crazy as I had my first.

No need for angels watching over my babies. They had me. Somewhere along the way, I decided they were not quite as fragile as I had assumed. After all, they had lived through my husband and me; they could probably live through anything.

Then they became teenagers. Although

I'm far less obsessive now, I find myself crying out in the night for them more than ever. I used to pray that God would surround them with people who were good influences. When my eyes began to open, I realized my prayers better adjust to greater reality. The truth is, godly influences are few. I pray for them to know what to do with bad influences and hope they become the good influences!

Young Saul left Tarsus with stars in his eyes. He headed for Jerusalem, the holy city of God. He did not leave home naive about the world. He grew up in a Greek city with every influence from the worship of idols to any conceivable sexual indulgence. But I don't believe he expected what he found in Jerusalem among those supposed to be the pious and the best. No, he was not naive about the heathen world. He was naive about the religious world. His father entrusted him to the finest rabbinic school, but he was not there alone. He was surrounded by good and bad influences. He saw people who were the real thing, and he saw people who were religious frauds.

We need look no further than the Word of God to see many of the influences Saul encountered among the Pharisees of Jerusalem. Saul was a contemporary of Jesus.

Soon after Saul finished his education in Jerusalem and presumably headed back to Tarsus, John the Baptist began to "prepare the way for the Lord" (Matt. 3:3). In no time at all, Jesus was on the scene, teaching in the same synagogue where Saul had recently stood. Saul found influences like the wise teacher, Gamaliel, but he also experienced influences like the ones Jesus so aptly described in the Gospels. In fact, many of the Pharisees and members of the Sanhedrin whom Christ encountered were Saul's instructors or classmates.

The term *Pharisee* was meant to represent genuine piety and deep devotion to God. Although exceptions certainly existed among the Pharisees, in the days of Jesus and Saul, the term had become synonymous with hypocrisy and cynicism.

Matthew 23 is an entire discourse addressed to the teachers of the law and Pharisees. I encourage you to get your Bible and read the chapter carefully. Notice all the specific ways Jesus described the same people Saul encountered in Jerusalem. When I did this, I made a list. For example, I didn't just note that they were hypocritical, but described the ways they were hypocritical.

My list looked something like this: they

made demands of others that they themselves did not keep (v. 4); they made their religious actions into show to impress others (v. 5); they loved to be the center of attention (v. 6); and they not only wouldn't enter the kingdom of God, they prevented others from entering (v. 13). What a horrible description.

Take a thorough look at those characteristics and the others in Matthew 23. Godly people are valiant people. They are people with the courage to ask God to spotlight areas of weakness, sin, and failure. Then God can strengthen, heal, and complete what is lacking.

As we look at the sins of the Pharisees, let's ask God to give each of us an honest, probing heart. Could any one of the phrases describe you? Allow the Holy Spirit time to speak to your heart. Would you be humble enough to recognize those the Holy Spirit indicates as possibly applying to your life? Will you agree to allow God full access to those areas of your life?

Before we feel like crawling in a hole because we share some of the same hypocrisies as the Pharisees, let's reconsider Matthew 23:37. What did Christ long to do in spite of the Pharisees' wrong actions or motives?

O Jerusalem, Jerusalem, you who kill the prophets and stone those sent to you, how often I have longed to gather your children together, as a hen gathers her chicks under her wings, but you were not willing. (Matt. 23:37)

Oh, the mercy of our God! The people Jesus confronted were considered the cream of the crop! Yet they were religious frauds and hypocrites; and Jesus loved them — even in the depth of their depravity "while we were still sinners" (Rom. 5:8). Will we ever be able "to grasp how wide and long and high and deep is the love of Christ" (Eph. 3:18)?

Saul knew many of the people to whom Christ was speaking in Matthew 23. Saul himself was a Pharisee and probably returned to Tarsus to serve as a teacher of the law. Imagine how his thinking was influenced by his contemporaries. I believe Saul set sail to Jerusalem as a young adolescent with a pure heart; but somewhere along the way the negative influences outweighed the positive, and his purity began to erode. The law became his god. That's what happens when you take the love out of obedience. The result is the law. Without love for God and His Word, we're just trying to be good.

Nothing will wear you out faster.

Have you been there? I have! Trying to obey God and serve Him before we've come to love Him can be exhausting.

Recently a friend shared a term that helps to explain what happened to the once-noble ranks of the Pharisees. The term is *identity boundaries.* You see, identity boundaries are the walls we put up to separate our group from other groups. Gangs wear certain colors to show who is in and who is out. Churches and denominations develop distinctive teachings to accomplish the same goal. The first-century Jews became so obsessed with identity boundaries that they forgot their purpose. They argued endlessly about washing hands or observing the Sabbath, but they forgot about loving God.

Saul epitomized such pharisaic obsession. He packed his diploma and headed for a place to serve. Whether he divided his time between teaching and his father's business is unknown. One thing you can count on: he was absolutely miserable. How do I know? In Philippians 3:6, he said his zeal was so great that he persecuted the church and his legalistic righteousness was "faultless."

We cannot begin to comprehend what Saul's life was like as he sought to live by the letter of the law because most of us do not have a Jewish background. Daily rituals determined the first words out of Saul's mouth in the morning, the way he took off his nightclothes and put on his day clothes, and how he sprinkled his hands before breakfast. He carefully avoided eating or drinking quickly and never ate while standing.

Saul pronounced numerous benedictions throughout the day. His entire day was filled with ritual, and at night he took off his shoes and garments in the prescribed order. He avoided certain sleeping positions and chose others. For the sake of his heart and liver, he probably attempted to begin the night on his left side and end the night on his right. He purposely kept his turning to a minimum. Tossing and turning through the night is misery to us, but to Saul it could have been sin!

These daily rituals paled in comparison to all the laws regarding the Sabbath. Restrictions existed for almost everything. For instance, prior to the Sabbath a Pharisee cut his fingernails and toenails not in consecutive order but alternately. He then burned the nails. He avoided spitting in a place where the wind could scatter the saliva so he would not break laws concerning sowing on the Sabbath.

Do you get the general idea of what Saul's life was like as he attempted to live by the law "faultlessly"? These examples are just a few of hundreds of man-made laws. I do not cite them in order to ridicule the Jewish people. I share a few of the written traditions with you to point out man's overwhelming tendency to tax God's instruction. The Sabbath observance could not have been further from God's intent by the time Christ was "made flesh to dwell among us." The day of rest was hardly recognizable to the One who ordained it.

Saul was strangled by the letter of the law. He tried desperately to keep all the outward acts of obedience while his heart slowly eroded. Saul gradually became the model for Isaiah 29:13: "These people come near to me with their mouth / and honor me with their lips, / but their hearts are far from me. / Their worship of me / is made up only of rules taught by men." Inevitably, Saul's faraway heart would turn to faraway actions.

Oh, God, forgive us when we act like modern-day Pharisees. Convict us at the very moment of our departure from the law of love You have written on our hearts. Give us hearts of devotion, not heads full of religion.

CHAPTER 5
MEANWHILE IN
JERUSALEM

The next day, . . . the chief priests and
the Pharisees went to Pilate. "Sir," they
said, "we remember that while he was still
alive that deceiver said, 'After three days
I will rise again.' So give the order for the
tomb to be made secure until the third
day."
(MATT. 27:62–64a)

I relived my teenage years all over again through my two daughters. I watch them dress in some of the same styles I wore in high school. They were ugly then. They're even uglier now. Solomon was right. "There is nothing new under the sun." Students of every generation wish away their school years. No doubt Saul also longed for an end to the hours of grueling study.

For Saul the end finally came, and he said his good-byes and headed back to Tarsus. I wonder how many days passed until he found himself wishing he could wake up back in Jerusalem. And of all the luck — he left just when things were about to get exciting.

In this study we encounter three groups within the Judaism of Paul's day. Herodians were influential Jews who supported the dynasty of Herod. Scholars think that Herodians were pro-Hellenistic and endorsed Herod's promotion of Greek thought and customs in Palestine. The Sadducees were a small group of very wealthy Jewish leaders. The Pharisees were the largest and most important of the Jewish groups. As the leaders of the synagogues, they exercised great control over the populace. They were religiously conservative, believing in angels and the Resurrection, unlike the Sadducees.

The years immediately following Saul's departure from the city of the Jews were the most significant in all of history. His fellow Pharisees found themselves in a situation that tied their tassels in knots. It all started when the guy with the weird diet and the camel hair started preaching.

John the Baptist didn't make many friends among the Pharisees. They didn't like him from the start; but they had no idea how much they would despise the One for whom John came to pave the way. John said of that

One, "After me will come one who is more powerful than I, whose sandals I am not fit to carry" (Matt. 3:11).

Sadly, not everyone listened either to John or to the Messiah for whom he prepared the way. Luke recorded the response of the Pharisees: "But the Pharisees and experts in the law rejected God's purpose for themselves, because they had not been baptized by John" (Luke 7:30).

How frightening to think we could reject God's awesome purposes for our lives out of hard-heartedness and pride! Christ loved the Pharisees. His bold approach was to tell them the truth so the truth could set them free, but they rejected it. In no time at all, He became the thorn in their flesh. They would not rest until they became the thorn in His.

Many of the Pharisees had ample reason to dislike Jesus. People who hide behind masks don't particularly like to be around those who peel them off. Jesus could look right through them. He exposed their self-righteous hearts by eating with sinners and healing on the Sabbath. Their attempts to corner Him in endless debates of Scripture left them looking foolish. Every confrontation seemed to fuel their hatred even more.

Not all of the Pharisees agreed with the

prevailing majority. Nicodemus was a Pharisee and a member of the Jewish ruling council. He came to Jesus obviously representing a number of Pharisees, because he used the words, "We know you are a teacher who has come from God" (John 3:2). He came in belief, yet he came in secret by night.

John 12:42 tells us that "many even among the leaders believed in him [Christ]. But because of the Pharisees they would not confess their faith for fear they would be put out of the synagogue." The next verse gives us a dark clue why these secret believers openly refused to own Jesus: "They loved praise from men more than praise from God." How utterly convicting. Have you ever failed to speak up for Christ for the same reason? I have, and it breaks my heart to know it.

At one time or another all of us have remained silent regarding our belief in Christ because we wanted the approval of others. Can you imagine the turmoil in the hearts of these leaders as they sat mutely and watched the biggest miscarriage of justice ever known to man? The silent believers were driven by fear while the vocal opposition was driven by jealousy and pride. This Nazarene was an intolerable threat.

They couldn't stop Him and, worse, they couldn't explain Him. Then one day, He finally went too far.

John 11 tells how the Sanhedrin, the chief judicial council of the Jews, finally concluded that Jesus must die. When Christ raised his friend Lazarus from the dead, "many of the Jews who had come to visit Mary, and had seen what Jesus did, put their faith in him" (John 11:45). Others who were there carried the story back to Jerusalem. The Sanhedrin began to fear.

John quotes the Jewish leaders' exact words: "If we let him [Jesus] go on like this, everyone will believe in him, and then the Romans will come and take away both our place and our nation" (John 11:48). What do you think, did they fear most the loss of their nation or of their "place"? Were they watching out for the people, or were they watching out for themselves?

God's sovereignty is a grand mystery. Part of that sovereignty shows when the enemies of God express the words of God or do the work of God. In this case, the high priest, Caiaphas, mouthed one of Scripture's clearest statements of why Christ came to earth. As the priest set in motion the plan to kill Jesus, he said it is better "that one man die for the people than that the whole nation perish" (John 11:50).

"From that day on" the chief priests and Pharisees set out to kill Jesus of Nazareth. John chapters 18 and 19 tell the story. They had Jesus arrested by night so as to avoid the crowds. They subjected him to a series of mock trials and then brought him to Pilate, the Roman governor, to be crucified. We get a glimpse of just how hypocritical these particular Pharisees had become. John tells us that "to avoid ceremonial uncleanness the Jews did not enter the palace; they wanted to be able to eat the Passover" (John 18:28).

These men were the teachers and classmates of Saul of Tarsus. What a telling glimpse of religion gone sour. They were so blinded by self-interest that they became willing to betray and murder Jesus, simply because He represented a threat to their power. As we seek to understand the heart of the Jewish Pharisee who would one day become the apostle to the Gentiles, we must not underestimate the evil that lived in his heart. Similarly, only to our peril do we overlook the evil in our own hearts.

One of the most viable tools Satan ever uses to work against God's purposes is self-interest. His manipulation through self-interest is as old as the Garden of Eden.

Satan used self-interest in the hearts of the chief priests and Pharisees. Christ was their enemy because He threatened their positions and feelings of piety.

How has the enemy tried to tempt you with self-interest so you would reject the purposes of God in your life? I believe I can say with authority that he will continue to tempt you in this area.

For a while, the chief priests and Pharisees may have believed they had won. Pilate relented just as they hoped, and the Lamb of God was nailed to a cross. Just hours later, "Jesus said, 'It is finished' " (John 19:30).

The Pharisees did everything they could do to make sure things stayed finished. They persuaded Pilate to place a guard on Jesus' tomb. Every loose end was tied. The tomb secured. The mouths stopped. It was finally over. Finally finished. Except for one thing.

On the first day of the week, very early in the morning, the women took the spices they had prepared and went to the tomb. They found the stone rolled away from the tomb, but when they entered, they did not find the body of the Lord Jesus. While they were wondering about this, suddenly two men in clothes that gleamed like lightning stood beside them. In their fright the women bowed down with their faces to the ground, but the men said to them, "Why do you look for the living among the dead? He is not here; he has risen!" (Luke 24:1–6)

A few very important things were finished, all right. But the Lord Jesus was not one of them. It's strange, isn't it? The very thing He finished we can't seem to leave alone; and the very thing He hasn't finished, we try to halt. The work of Calvary is finished. No more payment for sin is necessary. He did it all by Himself on the cross. We can't earn it. We can't add to it. It is finished. Yet we try to add our good works to His salvation.

However, the work He is doing on behalf of everyone who has accepted Christ as Savior is not finished. Salvation is finished. Sanctification is not. Completion is not. Philippians 1:6 promises that "He who began a good work in you will carry it on to completion until the day of Christ Jesus." Yet we wish He'd stop picking on us and let us be the boss. Like the Pharisees, we wish He'd stop interfering. Give this thought some consideration: sometimes more effort is required to keep rolling the stone back over the tomb than simply to cooperate with the work He seeks to finish in us.

As we conclude these early chapters of our study, think about a difficult question: Do we just want the cross without the resurrection? Are we trying to stuff the living, working Christ back into the tomb so He'll just save us and then leave us alone? Or do we want to know "the power of His resurrection and the fellowship of sharing in His sufferings"?

In the chapters to come, we will get to see Saul make the journey from enemy of the cross to servant of the Lord. We'll see God's power change a person from the inside out! His power can make someone entirely different — crucified with Christ and alive in the Spirit!

You can be sure the Jerusalem news finally hit the desk of a foreign Pharisee by the name of Saul. And we will find him more than willing to do his part to stop the madness.

■ ■ ■ ■

PART II
FINDING THE WAY

■ ■ ■ ■

God's Word doesn't tell us what we want to hear. God tells us what we need to hear. We need to know that the heroes of our faith were flesh and blood just like us. Only Christ is divine and perfect. Every other hero struggled with his or her own sin nature and had moments of faithlessness. God intends for us to admire heroes of the faith, not worship them. He gave us glimpses into many of their frailties and blatant sins not only to balance us but to give us hope. God inspired Paul to tell us "we are more than conquerors through him who loved us"

(Rom. 8:37). As we begin the study of his adult life we'll discover just how much needed conquering in the life of a religious zealot.

Only Jesus could turn such a self-proclaimed enemy of the gospel into one of the greatest lovers of the gospel who ever lived. If He could change Saul and mark eternity with his life, God can change us. Let's continue to offer Him a teachable heart, and let the transformation begin!

CHAPTER 6
NO INNOCENT
BYSTANDER

Acts 7:1–8:1

> *While they were stoning him, Stephen*
> *prayed, "Lord Jesus, receive my spirit."*
> *Then he fell on his knees and cried out,*
> *"Lord, do not hold this sin against them."*
> *When he had said this, he fell asleep.*
> *And Saul was there, giving approval to*
> *his death.*
> (ACTS 7:59–8:1)

No messenger could run quickly enough to satisfy Saul's curiosity about events in Jerusalem. I suspect he kept abreast of the growing menace facing his fellow Pharisees. Finally, the sightings ceased, but Jesus' followers circulated a preposterous account of His ascending into the heavens. The Pharisees really didn't care how He left. They were just glad He was gone. *If only we'd come up with that body,* they must have fretted. You can be sure students and teachers debated every conceivable theory.

A few no doubt wondered, *What if Jesus really did come back from the dead?* After all, they remembered that unfortunate Lazarus incident. How convenient it would have been for the Pharisees if the stir had simply died down. Instead, as the months passed, the number of Jesus' followers grew, as did their boldness.

Saul was probably disgusted over the way the Pharisees had mishandled the problem. If he wanted it done right, he'd obviously have to do it himself. So Saul packed his things and headed for Jerusalem, salivating for the chance to be the hero. Saul arrived in Jerusalem just in time to hear an infuriating speech from a man named Stephen.

Acts 6:8 says Stephen was a man full of God's grace and power who "did great wonders and miraculous signs among the people." When Saul arrived, his fellow Jews were trying to debate the follower of Christ, but Stephen's passionate love for Jesus was tying a group of empty, legalistic Pharisees in knots.

Many of us remember our own agony of emptiness. And right here on earth's miserable sod, Stephen was full — not just because he accepted Jesus as Savior, but because he surrendered his whole life to

Christ's will and purpose. The more Stephen poured out his life for Christ, the more Christ poured His life into Stephen.

Stephen was full of faith, full of God's grace and power. Only a person who is full of the Holy Spirit can possess the kind of power Stephen displayed and yet remain full of God's grace. You see, a person full of the Holy Spirit cannot be full of self. Pride never accompanies power in the fully yielded life.

Stephen showed biblical meekness — the power of God in a loving package — but his witness infuriated Saul's fellow Jews. So they cooked up some false charges against Stephen, much as they had against Jesus.

They brought Stephen before the Sanhedrin and confronted him with false witnesses. When those sitting in the Sanhedrin looked at Stephen, they got a shock. "His face was like the face of an angel" (Acts 6:15).

I wonder if they thought of Moses. Scripture says when he came down from Mt. Sinai, "his face was radiant because he had spoken with the LORD" (Exod. 34:29). Or did they recognize the marks of wisdom as indicated by King Solomon: "Wisdom brightens a man's face and changes its hard appearance"? (Eccles. 8:1).

Whatever the Jewish leaders thought, I doubt they expected what they got next. Stephen stood accused. His life literally hung in the balance. Instead of placating his accusers or defending himself, Stephen preached one of the most classic sermons in history. He rehearsed his and their Jewish history, showing at every point how God had prepared for and sent His Son. I encourage you to get your Bible and read Acts 7:1–53. Join Saul in the crowd as he listened to Stephen's speech before the Sanhedrin.

Obviously Stephen was not playing the part of a politician. He referred to his hearers as "stiff-necked," with "uncircumcised hearts" and "uncircumcised ears." Finally, they covered their ears, dragged him out of the city, and began to stone him.

The Bible mentions Saul for the first time in Acts 7:58. "Meanwhile, the witnesses laid their clothes at the feet of a young man named Saul." Remember him in the role of coat-watcher, because it's the last time you'll see it. Saul's zeal quickly took him on to active persecution of the followers of Jesus.

Before we leave Stephen, don't miss a final detail that may have planted the seed of the gospel even in a zealous young Pharisee's heart. While they were stoning him, Stephen cried out, "Lord, do not hold this sin against them" (Acts 7:60).

Do you have difficulty forgiving some offense committed against you or someone you love? Forgiving has many benefits. Only by forgiving can we free ourselves from the bitterness that haunts our lives, but forgiving does more than that. Forgiving provides a powerful witness for Christ. As we walk through the ministry of Paul the apostle, remember the forgiveness voiced by a dying believer. In a human sense, that one sentence may have borne more fruit than any from that day to this. Stephen's words of forgiveness were to have a permanent impact on Saul. The seed might take a while to germinate, but the rabbi from Tarsus would never escape the witness of Stephen.

When I think of my life, I think of all the Christians whose witness has shaped me. When I get to heaven, I know I want first to see my Savior, but when I've spent a few centuries at His feet, I wonder who else I'll want to see. I'd like to take a basin and a towel to wash the feet of those who have meant so much to me here. I think Stephen has a high place on Saul of Tarsus's "wash list."

Stephen. The first Christian martyr. What a shame, we may muse. Such a powerful life cut so short. What plans God must have had for him! What impact he would have had on the kingdom. Where were the angels of God? Where was his Shield? Where was the Protector? We are only privy to the chronicles of one day in the life of Stephen. Yet what a day it was. I believe it was the day he was born to live.

We tend to equate victory with survival, don't we? The only way to overcome peril is to live through it. How temporal our calculations! From glory's gaze, Stephen received the most awesome calling of all: he was counted worthy to die for Christ. Many of us may struggle to recount the names of all twelve apostles, but most of us can name the first Christian martyr without hesitation.

Worthy, indeed, was his calling. It brought the Son of God to His feet. He stood in Stephen's honor and watched from heaven while the frenzied crowds of His chosen people dragged Stephen from the city. Someone cast the first stone. Then came the second. Then hits came so quickly that one could not be separated from another. Don't underestimate Stephen by imagining his senses were dulled. I believe he felt each jagged blow. While Christ stood in Stephen's behalf, Stephen stood in His. As the fatal blows buckled his body, he sank to his death interceding for those who stoned him, " 'Lord, do not hold this sin against them' " (Acts 7:60). As his body lay in a heap, Stephen stood covered in blood — Jesus' blood.

Saul was there, giving approval to Stephen's death. The original Greek word for approval is *suneudokeo.* Are you ready for this? It means "to take pleasure with others." *Suneudokeo* is a word sometimes used of both parties in a marriage who are mutually pleased with something (see 1 Cor. 7:12–13). Applying the original meaning to Saul's actions, the scene becomes clearer. He was pleased with their actions, and they were pleased with his approval. A mutual admiration society. To provide further startling clarity, consider that the verb tense of the word describing Saul's action expresses continuous or repeated action. In other words, Saul was virtually cheering throughout the entire exhibit. He didn't just give his approval when Stephen breathed his last. He cheered on every blow, like points on a scoreboard.

As Jesus watched, He didn't miss a single nod of Saul's phylacteried head. Remember, Christ was up on His feet at the time. Can you imagine the alloy of emotions He must have experienced as He looked on the two key players in the kingdom that day? One for Him. One against Him. One covered in blood. The other covered by prayer shawls. One who could not save himself from men. The other who could not save himself from sin. One dead in body but alive in spirit. The other alive in body but dead in spirit. One loved by God. And the other loved by God. Grace, grace, God's grace.

Just a day in the life of a man named Stephen. A shooting star. He had one brief performance. One chance on stage. But it was absolutely unforgettable. As the curtain fell on his life, he received a standing ovation from the only One who really mattered. I have a feeling that seconds later the two of them hadn't changed positions much. Christ was still on His feet. Stephen was still crumpled to his knees. How sweet to imagine the first heavenly words he heard that day: "Welcome, Stephanos, My joy and My crown."

CHAPTER 7
A SUDDEN CHANGE
IN PLANS

Acts 9:1–10

As he neared Damascus on his journey, suddenly a light from heaven flashed around him. He fell to the ground and heard a voice say to him, "Saul, Saul, why do you persecute me?"
(ACTS 9:3–4)

If you asked me today what I question most at this point in my journey with Christ, my answer would not be, Why do bad things happen to good people? Nor would it be, Why have You allowed me this suffering? It would most definitely be, Why did You call me? With all my failures and frailties, why do I have the privilege of loving You, of knowing You the little that I do?

As the blinding light falls suddenly on a murderous persecutor, we may be left in the dark to understand why we each have been called; but our eyes will be opened to the One who called. And we will sigh and confess, "How very like Him."

Dr. Luke's account of Saul's conversion is recorded in Acts 9:1–19. You are probably familiar with the story. In my mind's eye I can just see young Saul strutting around Jerusalem, determined to make a name for himself. So our hotheaded rabbi sought authorization to arrest followers of Jesus in Damascus and return them to Jerusalem. He was on his journey when God intervened and knocked him off his donkey. Jesus spoke to Saul asking, "Why do you persecute me?" (Acts 9:4). The encounter left a blind and very chastened Saul being led into Damascus where he would hear about Jesus from a courageous believer named Ananias.

Would you agree that no example could much better illustrate the statement that a person can be sincere in his beliefs yet be sincerely wrong? Saul knew it all, and he knew nothing.

I remember some of my first experiences when this formerly dogmatic, closed-minded woman unwillingly discovered the shade of gray. I used to see everything in black and white. I've concluded that for those who only see gray, God often emphatically and lovingly paints portraits of black and white so they are forced to acknowledge the contrasts. For those who only see black and white, He introduces situations when answers aren't so easy, where lists "A to Z" cannot be found, and when points one, two, and three don't work. Gray.

At a very difficult time in our lives when we were constantly called for school conferences concerning our son Michael, Keith and I were amused after meeting one of his new counselors. He couldn't have been a day over twenty-five. He had a brand-new psychology degree and had our precious boy figured out. Everything he mentioned we had tried at least five years before — and at least five hundred times. We didn't say anything to spare his dignity, but when we got in the car we said, "Wasn't God merciful to give him Michael early in his practice?"

I was tempted to say to him, "Mr. Black and White, meet young Mr. Gray. He's going to add a brand-new color to your palette, and one day you'll be glad. Just like I was."

Life is full of grays, but today you and I get to enjoy a little black and white — the evil of a sinner's heart, the purity of a Savior's mercy.

After such noble beginnings, such strict following of God's laws, incomparable attainment of the knowledge of Scripture, and every external mark of righteousness — what happened? How did a brilliant young rabbi become a relentless persecutor of men and women? He certainly did not develop into a murderous zealot under the instruction of Gamaliel, his highly esteemed teacher.

Under similar circumstances, Gamaliel counseled his fellow leaders: "Leave these men alone! Let them go! For if their purpose or activity is of human origin, it will fail" (Acts 5:38).

Saul was not unlike Michael's bright young counselor. He thought he had all the answers. The obvious difference is that Saul's answers were lethal. Saul thought he was smarter than his teacher. No sense in waiting to see if the people of the Way would finally dissipate. He took matters into his own hands and tried to give them a much-needed shove. Acts 26:11 describes Saul's mental state perfectly: he had become obsessed.

> Many a time I went from one synagogue to another to have them punished, and I tried to force them to blaspheme. In my obsession against them, I even went to foreign cities to persecute them. (Acts 26:11)

I'm certainly no counselor, but I suspect that most obsessions rise from a futile attempt to fill a gaping hole somewhere deep in a life. Saul's external righteousness and achieved goals left behind an itch he could not scratch. Can you imagine how miserable he must have been? Religiously righteous to the bone, inside he had nothing but innately wicked marrow. All that work, and it hadn't worked. All his righteous passion turned into unrighteous zeal, and he became dangerous.

The Greek word for "obsessed" is *emmainomai.* The root word is *mainomai* which means "to act like a maniac." Our best attempts at homegrown righteousness are still but a moment from the unspeakable. Passions can turn a new direction with frightening speed. May none of us forget it. The prophet Isaiah said, "All our righteous acts are like filthy rags" (Isa. 64:6). If all the righteousness we have is our own, it's just an act. And acts don't last very long.

In this story we also get to see the purity of a Savior's mercy. Saul himself would later say, "God demonstrates his own love for us in this: While we were still sinners, Christ died for us" (Rom. 5:8). Christ met Saul on the path to his darkest, most devious sin. For that very moment, for the depths of

Saul's depravity, Christ had already died. Christ literally caught him in the act.

Toward the end of his life, Saul-who-became-Paul would sit in a jail cell and write: "Not that I have already obtained all this, or have already been made perfect, but I press on to take hold of that for which Christ Jesus took hold of me" (Phil. 3:12).

The Greek word translated "took hold" means "to lay hold of, seize, with eagerness, suddenness . . . the idea of eager and strenuous exertion, to grasp." Christ literally snatched Saul by the neck. Later, the persecutor turned apostle would write unforgettable words to Timothy, his son in the faith: "Here is a trustworthy saying that deserves full acceptance: Christ Jesus came into the world to save sinners — of whom I am the worst" (1 Tim. 1:15).

Jesus sent Saul to open the eyes of many and turn them from darkness to light so they could receive forgiveness of sins. No greater calling exists, as well as no room for pride. God's chosen servant was never more than a flashback from humility. No one can teach forgiveness like the forgiven. Thank goodness, Saul ultimately became a zealous proponent of forgiveness of sin. As our chapter draws to a conclusion, let's end with some important thoughts about zeal. In the conversion of Saul, we see demonstrated that

- we can wholeheartedly believe in something and be wholeheartedly wrong, and
- sincerity means nothing if it is misdirected.

Saul believed in his cause with all his heart, and it led him down the path to destruction. Saul was sincere. As he stated in Acts 26:9, " 'I too was convinced that I ought to do all that was possible to oppose the name of Jesus of Nazareth.' "

Christ not only snatched Saul from Satan that pivotal day, He snatched Saul from himself — from his own misguided zeal, from his own obsessions. He can snatch you from yours too. I'm living proof. I couldn't count the times during any given month that I thank God for saving me not only from Satan but from myself.

Having studied the life of Saul, how can we ever doubt that Christ can save? Is anyone too wicked? Anyone too murderous? Grace never draws a line with a willing soul. His arm is never too short to save (see Isa. 59:1). He can reach into the deepest pit or down the dustiest road to Damascus. Yes, some things are gray such as, Why did He choose us? But some things are still black-and-white — I once was lost, but now I'm found, was blind but now I see.

CHAPTER 8
FROM PERSECUTOR
TO PREACHER

Acts 9:11–43

Saul grew more and more powerful and baffled the Jews living in Damascus by proving that Jesus is the Christ.
(ACTS 9:22)

Few things are more precious than the expressions on a newborn's face as he or she is suddenly cast from the darkness of the womb into the bright lights of the delivery room. I vividly remember both laughing and crying at my daughters' faces screwing up indignantly as if to say, "Would the same wise guy who turned on that light mind turning it off?" Many years ago when a grown man was born again on a dusty road to Damascus, a light came on that no one was able to turn off. We will soon discover many who tried.

The Lord told Ananias he would find Saul at a certain house praying. The Bible doesn't

85

tell us the content of Saul's prayer, but it does tell us what happened next. Ananias came to Saul, and . . .

> Placing his hands on Saul, he said, "Brother Saul, the Lord — Jesus, who appeared to you on the road as you were coming here — has sent me so that you may see again and be filled with the Holy Spirit." Immediately, something like scales fell from Saul's eyes, and he could see again. He got up and was baptized, and after taking some food, he regained his strength. (Acts 9:17–19)

Paul's version of these events appears in Galatians 1:14–18. He was careful to tell the reader that he did not consult any man but went immediately into Arabia following his conversion. Apparently Saul thought he'd better get to know the One who obviously knew him so well. Unlike us, Saul's primary need was not discipleship. He learned more about Scripture in his young years than most learn in a lifetime! He needed to come to grips with the Author.

When his quiet exile with the Savior was over, he once again approached the ancient city of Damascus. What strange thoughts must have clouded his mind. He first came to Damascus to profane the name of Christ. Now he returned to preach the name of Christ. He first came to Damascus to take prisoner the followers of the Way. Now he would stay in their homes. He had to know he would be the talk of the town, yet the inevitable mockery did not slow him down.

We read that "Saul grew more and more powerful and baffled the Jews living in Damascus by proving that Jesus is the Christ" (Acts 9:22). The verse tells us two wonderful things about Saul:

1. *He grew more powerful.* The Greek word for "powerful" is *endunamoo,* also used in Hebrews 11:34 as a description of Samson. The supernatural power Samson possessed physically, God gave to Saul spiritually! Saul was probably a man of small physical stature. A writer in the second century described him as: "A man rather small in size, bald-headed, bow-legged, with meeting eyebrows, a large, red and somewhat hooked nose."[1] Little about his physical appearance was intimidating, but when the Spirit of God fell on him, he became the spiritual heavyweight champion of the world!

2. *He proved to the Jews that Jesus is the Christ.* The word *proved* means "to cause to come together, to bring together, . . . to join or knit together." Let's insert one of these

phrases in the Scripture so we can see the picture God is drawing for us. "Saul . . . [knit together] to the Jews . . . that Jesus is the Christ" (Acts 9:22). What did he knit together? The old with the new! He knit the teachings of the Old Testament Law and Prophets with their fulfillment in Jesus Christ. His speech to them was probably much like Christ's speech to the two travelers on the road to Emmaus.

Luke tells us that Christ appeared to the men on the road, but they did not recognize him. "And beginning with Moses and all the Prophets, he explained to them what was said in all the Scriptures concerning himself" (Luke 24:27). Both Christ and Saul proved He was the promised Messiah by knitting the promises of the Old Testament to their fulfillment in Jesus. The proof was there. All they needed to do was believe. Unlike the Gentiles, the Jews knew Scripture. They just hadn't recognized the One about whom the Scriptures were written!

Saul was hardly the kind of man to be ignored. Saul with the gospel was like my daughters with the radio. He kept turning up the volume. Inevitably, ironically, the Jews conspired to kill him, so Saul took the first basket out of town. According to his testimony in Galatians 1:18, Saul wanted to get acquainted with Peter anyway. From the look of things, this was a perfect time for a visit to Jerusalem.

Can you imagine how differently Saul must have approached the city this time? Every step he took had new significance. Damascus was northeast of Jerusalem, so Saul walked past the Mount of Olives and the Garden of Gethsemane. He walked through the Kidron Valley, dodging the hardened ground over ancient graves. He walked through the city gates where his face was recognized instantly. The chief priests expected him to return with prisoners. Instead, only one prisoner returned: a prisoner of Jesus Christ.

Talk about feeling alone! Perhaps one of the most pronounced characteristics of the Jewish people was a very strong sense of community. Being surrounded by Gentiles as Saul and his family had been in Tarsus probably only tightened the bonds of togetherness. He had always known the security of belonging. His conversion not only freed him from the bonds of sin; it also suddenly freed him from the bonds of human security.

God had issued Saul an undeniable apostolic calling. He probably assumed his place was with the other apostles. "When he came to Jerusalem, he tried to join the disciples, but they were all afraid of him, not believing that he really was a disciple" (Acts 9:26). As despicable as he had been, our hearts sting for him a little, don't they? Perhaps each of us can relate to the unique stab of loneliness.

Two wonderful words begin the next verse: "But Barnabas." We will meet many people through our study. Some will be honorable. Others will not. A few will be heroes. Without a doubt Barnabas was a hero. Acts 9:27 tells us Barnabas took Saul and "brought him to the apostles." Few things touch my heart more than Christian men who risk vulnerability in obedience to Christ. Barnabas reached out a helping hand to a discouraged man. Saul took that hand. Two lives bonded in that moment.

Barnabas offers us an example we don't want to miss. His name had been Joseph, but the disciples renamed him "son of encouragement." God used Barnabas over and over to give others the courage to be the people He called them to be. When Barnabas brought Saul before the other apostles, they may have remembered how each of them had been the focus of his encouragement at one time or another. Now he encouraged them to accept a new brother. Many probably criticized Barnabas for being gullible concerning Saul. Barnabas was willing to give people a chance even when others weren't.

Barnabas persuaded the apostles to accept the new convert, and the most powerful preacher in all Christendom was set loose in Jerusalem. Consequently, Saul did such a fine job of debating the Grecian Jews, he nearly got himself killed. We see an end to this chapter of Saul's experience in Acts 9:30. The brothers pushed Saul on a boat to Tarsus to keep him from losing his head. I can't help but chuckle at the words that follow Saul's departure: "Then the church throughout Judea, Galilee and Samaria enjoyed a time of peace" (Acts 9:31a). Saul had a way of stirring things up. No doubt, Tarsus had enjoyed her last breath of peace for a while. Saul was on his way.

Meanwhile, "The church throughout Judea, Galilee and Samaria . . . was strengthened; and encouraged by the Holy Spirit, it grew in numbers" (Acts 9:31a). Sounds like Barnabas still hung around awhile, doesn't it? Let's look for ways to be a Barnabas in another's life. Take every opportunity to encourage fellow believers.

CHAPTER 9
A PRIED-OPEN MIND

Acts 10

*For God, who was at work in the ministry
of Peter as an apostle to the Jews, was
also at work in my ministry as an apostle
to the Gentiles.*
(GAL. 2:8)

We have considered the events of Saul's
post-conversion life based on Acts 9 and
Galatians 1. Now let's explore an important
historical marker in those events. In Galatians 1:18, Paul told us he stayed with Peter
for fifteen days after he arrived in Jerusalem.

Fifteen days is a long time to have company — if not for Peter, for his wife! (Yes,
Peter was married! See Matt. 8:14–15.) At
that point, she was still keeping a strictly
kosher kitchen. She had no idea how differently she and her husband would soon be
looking at the food on their table.

Imagine the discussions between Peter and Paul — two giants of our faith. Scripture tells us Saul went to Jerusalem to get acquainted with Peter. The Greek term suggests far more than simple acquaintance. The term *historeo* means "to ascertain by inquiry and personal examination; to know or to visit, so as to consider and observe attentively and gain knowledge." *Historeo* is the word from which we derive the English word *history.* Remember, Saul was a student at heart! Surely all great teachers are! Saul didn't go to Jerusalem just to make a new friend. He went straight to Christianity's foremost professor for a history lesson! The tables turned as an uneducated fisherman became the scholar, and a highly educated rabbi became the student. Saul had so much to learn and, perhaps, unlearn. Peter also had volumes to learn from Saul whether he realized it or not. At least one lesson he would learn soon.

Not long after Saul's informative visit with Peter, Saul's new brothers in Christ urged him to go back to Tarsus (Acts 9:30). Saul was not mentioned again in the Book of Acts until late in the eleventh chapter. However, something happened in Peter's life in the interim that I believe flowed from his encounter with Saul. After Saul departed for Tarsus, Peter traveled to various places and was a vessel of God's powerful Spirit. No doubt he kept thinking about Saul. True to human nature, their differences probably crowded his mind more than their similarities.

One of their foremost differences was the contrast in their callings. Peter was entrusted with the Jews. Saul was entrusted with the Gentiles (Gal. 2:7).

Before we assume the two men simply shook hands and went their separate ways, let's try to crawl into the mind of the apostle Peter. Scripture pictures him as unduly interested in what Jesus called others to do. When he received his personal commission from Christ, John 21:21 tells us Peter looked at John and asked, " 'Lord, what about him?' " The scene makes me laugh every time. Peter seemed to always say aloud what others said to themselves. As I often say about one of my beloved children with the same habit, his brain stem was his tongue. He never seemed to have a thought that didn't come out of his mouth!

Follow my line of thinking. I suspect that in the months following Saul's visit, Peter often thought of Saul's calling and was relieved it wasn't his! Imagine how many times he must have thought about Saul's being called to minister to the Gentiles and thought, *Better him than me!* From a deeply rooted Jewish point of view, the difference in their ministries was mammoth! Saul might as well have been called to lepers. Peter may have even wondered if Saul's punishment for persecuting the church was to get the leftovers. In no time at all, God taught Peter a very important lesson through a vision.

Acts 10 tells the story of Peter and Cornelius. An angel told Cornelius to send for Peter. Meanwhile Peter went up on the roof to pray. It was about noon, and he was hungry. There God showed him a vision that was to change Christendom. The vision was of a large sheet containing all sorts of unclean animals. A voice told him, "Get up, Peter. Kill and eat." When Peter objected, the voice told him, "Do not call anything impure that God has made clean" (Acts 10:13–15).

The messengers from Cornelius arrived, and with the combination of the vision and the prompting of the Holy Spirit, Peter got the message. At Cornelius's home, the most opinionated and stubborn of the twelve came to say: "I now realize how true it is that God does not show favoritism but accepts men from every nation who fear him and do what is right" (Acts 10:34–35).

You see, God always dishonors prejudice. Peter probably not only saw himself as different from the Gentiles, but better. His attitude is nothing new. Like most of us, his prejudices were handed down through the generations. Many otherwise strong, God-serving, Bible-believing Christians are steeped in prejudice. Peter was one of those. Yet his willingness to have his closed mind pried open was testimony to his godly sincerity. Peter soon discovered that his new attitudes were very controversial. Acts 11 unfolds with the reaction of the other apostles who heard about Peter's encounter with Cornelius. They were appalled! Yet Peter's lesson became one from which they all learned.

My hero on the subject of prejudice is my daughter Melissa. She was born color-blind. If she has any prejudice at all, it's toward prejudiced people. In the eighth grade she fell "in like" with a hispanic boy at her school. She asked me if having a boyfriend outside her race was against Scripture. I explained that the words "unequally yoked" spoke of Christian beliefs rather than race.

This young man was the son of a very fine preacher. The boy was a committed Christian who was involved in his youth group.

He was also a fine athlete, which gave the two of them many things in common. I listened carefully, drew a deep breath, and said, "Melissa, I'm afraid you are just about to discover how cruel the world is. You are not doing anything wrong, but many people will probably talk about you as if you are. I will stand with you if you are determined to make a stand."

I was right. Rumors were all over our neighborhood by the time she walked down the hall with him the first time. Interestingly, the other teenagers didn't seem to notice. The parents were the ones who uproared! Most of my friends disapproved. Most of his parents' friends disapproved. The prejudice ran both ways. I was asked several times how I could let Melissa have a boyfriend outside her race. My answer was always the same. "Melissa is watching me carefully for biblical integrity. I must stand on the Word to raise my children. I must have no other standard." We took a fair amount of criticism, but our precious Melissa stood tall and ultimately emerged with more integrity than her accusers. Melissa and I formed a very strong bond through her encounter with prejudice. I ended up with her respect. She ended up as one of my heroes.

Having our minds pried open is rarely easy, but vision is rarely given to those who refuse. We are challenged to overcome prejudice on many levels, certainly not just race. Economics divide. Denominations divide. Ministries divide. Differences will always exist, but division doesn't always have to result. Although God chose Peter and Saul to minister to different groups of people, He intended for each of them to see the importance of the other in the overall vision. Saul later wrote, "For God, who was at work in the ministry of Peter as an apostle to the Jews, was also at work in my ministry as an apostle to the Gentiles" (Gal. 2:8). God had driven the point home to Peter through a series of visions in which He commanded, "Do not call anything impure that God has made clean" (Acts 10:15). Praise God that all who are in Christ have been made clean.

We must be careful to avoid spiritual elitism. Everything we are and anything we possess as believers in Christ is a gift of grace. Pure hearts before God must be cleansed from any hint of spiritual pride. We must aggressively fight the enemy when he seeks to nullify our growth and good works by making them invitations for pride and prejudice.

CHAPTER 10
NEW CHURCH, NEW NAME

Acts 11

For a whole year Barnabas and Saul met with the church and taught great numbers of people. The disciples were called Christians first at Antioch.
(ACTS 11:26)

Chapter 11 reintroduces Saul to the Acts account. It tells of a great turning point in his ministry. After the Grecian Jews tried to kill him in Jerusalem, Saul boarded a boat for Tarsus, his homeland (see Acts 9:29–30). Through Paul's own testimony in Galatians 1:21, we know that he went to Syria and Cilicia. Five years passed between his departure to Tarsus and his next appearance in Scripture. Many scholars refer to these as the "missing years." Although we have no details of Saul's life during this time, we can be sure the inhabitants of the cities he visited didn't describe him as missing! Probably the reason the events of those five years are missing from the Book of Acts is because Luke, the writer, was not an eyewitness.

Consider a few things that might have happened during the interim years. In Acts 9:16, the Lord told Ananias that He would show Saul how much he must suffer for His name. I believe God began fulfilling this prophecy almost immediately. Figuratively speaking, he was thrown into many fires during his ministry, yet few would have been any hotter than those in Tarsus. He was the local hero among the Jewish community in his hometown. Most people probably knew that Saul had left Tarsus years before for the express purpose of dealing with the followers of the Way. Now he returned as one of them. I doubt anyone threw him a homecoming party. We have no reason to assume his father had died, yet we see no reference to his reaction to Saul's conversion. His father may have acted as if his son had never been born.

Even today when a Jew from an orthodox family turns from Judaism, parents sometimes consider the defector to be dead. Some observe an event akin to a funeral. Others prefer to blot them from their lives and consider them never born. Many families do not react so harshly and permanently, yet remember — Saul's father was a Pharisee! His son's defection was a fate worse than death.

We have no idea how long Saul stayed in Tarsus. I certainly could not blame him for later traveling to other parts of Syria and Cilicia! Scripture suggests a concrete reason to believe these interim years were quite difficult. Read the apostle's testimony of his sufferings.

I have worked much harder, been in prison more frequently, been flogged more severely, and been exposed to death again and again. Five times I received from the Jews the forty lashes minus one. Three times I was beaten with rods, once I was stoned, three times I was shipwrecked, I spent a night and a day in the open sea, I have been constantly on the move. I have been in danger from rivers, in danger from bandits, in danger from my own countrymen, in danger from Gentiles; in danger in the city, in danger in the country, in danger at sea; and in danger from false brothers. I have labored and toiled and have often gone without sleep; I have known hunger and thirst and have often gone without food; I have been cold and naked. (2 Cor. 11:23–27)

God wasn't kidding when He said Saul would suffer for His name, was He? Yet, many of the perils mentioned are not recorded in the Book of Acts. The most likely time these sufferings took place was during the interim period that was not detailed in Acts. As Saul reentered the picture, we should assume his life had been anything but uneventful!

Persecution scattered the early Christians as far as Phoenicia, Cyprus, and Antioch. Some gutsy believers who had traveled to Antioch broke the mold. They began to share with Gentiles also. As a result of their testimony in Antioch, "a great number of people believed and turned to the Lord" (Acts 11:21).

When God desires to do "a new thing" (Isa. 43:19), He purposely seeks out a few righteous renegades who don't have a problem breaking the mold! Mold-breakers are usually people who don't care much about popularity or tradition.

I have a good friend at church who is a mold-breaker. He has been used of God to help make our church a viable presence in the new millennium. I don't mind telling you, he has had as many enemies as friends. These men from Cyprus and Cyrene were mold-breakers. The soil across the street from the synagogue looked awfully fertile to them — so they scattered and spoke!

I have to smile as I read the words in Acts 11:22, "News of this reached the ears of the church at Jerusalem." Antioch was about three hundred miles north of Jerusalem, but juicy news travels faster than a speeding bullet! Barnabas was dispensed to Antioch immediately. When he arrived in Antioch, he "saw the evidence of the grace of God" (Acts 11:23). Reality superseded rumor, and he was glad!

According to verse 23, Barnabas "encouraged them all to remain true to the Lord with all their hearts." He encouraged them to plan in advance to remain faithful to the Lord! I cannot overemphasize the importance of this exhortation. This principle is one I've diligently sought to teach my children. I've tried to make them understand that the point of temptation or the pinnacle of pain is not the ideal time to decide whether to stick with Christ. The most effective time to resolve to obey Christ is in advance of difficulty. Planning to stay faithful can greatly enhance victory.

I wish I could say I always resolved in

advance to "remain true to the Lord." Certainly, there were times I didn't. But I finally learned the wisdom of Barnabas's good advice and have been so thankful for the fruit of safety it bears. Barnabas had seen the cost of believing in Christ firsthand. He was teaching these new believers the kind of resolve that would hold up even against the threat of death. Under his faithful tutelage, a great number of people were brought to the Lord.

Although Barnabas was overjoyed at the great harvest the scattered seeds had ultimately produced, these missionaries were obviously in a situation over their heads. They needed a specialist, an expert discipler. They needed Saul. And right about then, he probably needed them. Barnabas headed for Tarsus, looking for Saul. So for a whole year Barnabas and Saul met with the church and taught great numbers of people. What a team they must have made — Saul the teacher, Barnabas the encourager. One taught the principles of a godly life. The other assured them they could do it with God's help.

The next phrase in Acts 11:26 conjures up many emotions in me: "The disciples were called Christians first at Antioch." *Christian,*

- an emotional word causing one man joy and another man fury — one man peace and another man turmoil.
- a dividing word unceasingly drawing a line. Either a man is or he is not, either he is for or he is against.
- a uniting word, drawing together un-likely pairs in workplaces and neigh-borhoods over one single bond.
- a defining word for which countless people have lived and countless people have died.

The Greek word the believers were called was *Christianos*. The name given was first adopted at Antioch. You may be interested to know that it does not occur in the New Testament as a name commonly used by Christians themselves. Christian was a label coined by unbelievers as a form of ridicule. Once again, how beautifully God stole the victory from Satan. The very word used as a mockery became the greatest privilege a man could boast.

Peter gave a different twist to this insult directed at believers. He said, "If you suffer as a Christian, do not be ashamed, but praise God that you bear that name" (1 Pet. 4:16).

Christians have been beaten, whipped,

starved, humiliated, mutilated, tortured, hung, burned at the stake, crucified, and fed to lions; yet two thousand years after a man called Jesus of Nazareth walked the streets of Jerusalem, 1,734 million people alive on this earth today call themselves by the ever-dividing, ever-uniting word: *Christian.* God is still scattering the seeds a few righteous renegades planted in a city called Antioch. Had they only known what they were starting.

■ ■ ■ ■

PART III
MILES AND MISSIONS

■ ■ ■ ■

Next we pack our bags and join Paul on his first missionary journey! You'll soon see that the apostle's life was anything but boring. His many experiences will prove that living and moving in the center of God's will does not mean we avoid opposition. To the contrary, we often meet challenges because of our choice to follow God! Being a sold-out servant of Jesus Christ requires courage; but, praise His name, He who requires it also supplies it. Throughout our study we have the privilege to learn from the example of a man who knew opposition intimately.

His key to victory was knowing the One in charge far more intimately.

God will use the apostle Paul to help us clear up a few popular misconceptions in many Christian circles today. All the enemy has to do to spread a lie is to twist the truth. Stay alert and open-minded. His Word is alive! (see Heb. 4:12).

CHAPTER 11
ONE BLIND
SORCERER

Acts 12:1–13:12

*While they were worshiping the Lord and
fasting, the Holy Spirit said, "Set apart for
me Barnabas and Saul for the work to
which I have called them."*
(ACTS 13:2)

Acts 11 concluded with trouble in Jerusalem. The church in Antioch gave generously
to the believers in Judea as they faced
impending famine. Barnabas and Saul
packed their bags and headed for Jerusalem
as ambassadors of famine relief.

We are going to proceed to Acts 13, but I
want you to be aware of several important
events that took place between the time Saul
and Barnabas left Antioch and their return.
A family of kings, all named Herod, ruled
Palestine. The Herod at this particular time
was Agrippa I, grandson of Herod the
Great. Herod the Great ruled Palestine at

the time of Jesus' birth and built the temple that stood in Paul's day. Part Jewish himself, he enjoyed great popularity with the Jewish leaders of Judea — courting their favor at any cost. This favor cost him dearly. He tried to cut the apostolic head off the church by having James beheaded. He then imprisoned Peter with hopes for a similar end.

Herod imprisoned Peter. The church prayed. God pulled a jailbreak, and in a bit of humorous detail, Peter stood at the door while a servant girl named Rhoda shouted, "Peter is at the door!"

Herod probably realized he was out of his league when Peter disappeared from prison. Left with no explanation, Herod had the guards executed and took a quick trip to Caesarea. There he did the inexcusable. He allowed himself to be worshiped as God. The tender side of me would prefer to think he died and then was eaten by worms; however, Scripture reverses the order. I'm glad I wasn't in on that scene! Acts 12:24 gives quick relief! "The word of God continued to increase and spread."

Having finished their mission, Barnabas and Saul returned to Antioch, bringing a special attendant with them — a young man named John Mark.

The first church in Antioch remains such an example to us. We've already seen willing evangelists, willing recipients, and effective discipleship revealed in the willingness of the infant church to give. Acts 13 unfolds with another mark of an effective church body: strong leadership.

Barnabas, Simeon, Lucius, Manaen, and Saul were prophets and teachers in the church. Notice that Saul was listed last of the five at this point of his ministry. These five prophets and teachers didn't just hold important positions; they each had a personal passion for God. While they were worshiping and fasting, "The Holy Spirit said, 'Set apart for me Barnabas and Saul for the work to which I have called them' " (Acts 13:2). The leaders of the church in Antioch were constantly ready to hear from God; therefore, when He spoke, they were listening!

Again and again in Scripture we see God's perfect timing. In Galatians 1:15, the apostle explains that he was set apart from birth (about A.D. 10). He did not receive salvation until around A.D. 36. He was not set apart for his signature ministry until around A.D. 46. Not one minute was wasted. God was training Saul during those formative years. Meanwhile, Barnabas the Encourager was proving his effectiveness among both Jews and Gentiles. When God's time came, both men were ready for the Holy Spirit to send them out. "So after they had fasted and prayed, they placed their hands on them and sent them off" (Acts 13:3).

I grew up in a denomination that prioritized missions and spurred a love and appreciation in my heart for missionaries. This moment is precious to me. Meet the first international missionaries: Saul and Barnabas! Set apart to be sent off — just like so many other faithful ones who have followed in their footsteps, forsaking the securities of home and family to follow Christ anywhere. As of this writing, nearly eighty thousand evangelical missionaries presently serve overseas.[1] I have no greater admiration for any group of people.

The Holy Spirit not only sends; He also equips. God gave more than wisdom and experience to aid Barnabas and Saul in their journeys. He also gave them a helper. We will call him John Mark to minimize any confusion with other characters named John. Saul's helper would later write the second Gospel, the Book of Mark.

Any study of the apostle Paul would be lacking in clarity without a map to trace his travels. You will find a map on page xv. I encourage you to follow Paul's three missionary journeys as well as his final trip to Rome. Our starting point is Antioch in Syria. From there they sailed to Cyprus and on to Salamis and Paphos. Tracing Paul's travels will help you keep information organized and increase your understanding and appreciation of his ministry. When the Bible mentions a village or region in one of his journeys, locate the spot on the map.

Saul met some interesting characters in his travels! He got no farther than his second stop when he met a man I'm sure he never forgot. His name was Bar-Jesus (or Elymas). He was the attendant to Sergius Paulus, the proconsul or governor of Cyprus.

Bar-Jesus committed a serious offense against both his supervisor and the kingdom of God. "The proconsul . . . sent for Barnabas and Saul because he wanted to hear the word of God" (Acts 13:7). Bar-Jesus did everything he could to oppose them and keep the proconsul from believing. The apostle rebuked the sorcerer, and God struck him blind.

Here we read that Saul was also called Paul! What a relief! I have tried to refer to him by the name used in whatever Scriptures we were studying. But we are least familiar with his Hebrew name, Saul, and most familiar with his Roman name, Paul. The Scriptures call him Paul from this point on, and so will we.

Paul called Bar-Jesus "a child of the devil" (Acts 13:10). He was actually using a play on words because the name *Bar-Jesus* in Aramaic means "Son of Jesus." In effect, Paul was saying, "You're no son of Jesus. You're a son of the devil!" He not only meant the term to be taken figuratively, he meant it literally as I hope you will see. The three descriptions given in Scripture support Paul's accusation against him. Consider how the following phrases Paul used apply to Elymas as well as to Satan:

- *Full of deceit.* The Greek word means "bait, metaphorically and generally fraud, guile, deceit." Remember, Bar-Jesus or Elymas was a sorcerer, which meant he was a *magus,* or presumed wise man, who "specialized in the study of astrology and enchantment."
- *Full of trickery.* The word is often used for theft achieved through "wicked schemes or plots."
- *Perverted the right ways of the Lord.* The word means "to turn or twist throughout; to distort, pervert, seduce,

mislead; to turn away."

So Paul's accusation that Bar-Jesus was "a child of the devil" was quite appropriate. You can imagine Paul came up against the schemes of the evil one many times as he sought to do the will of God. As we study his life, we can learn to identify the works of darkness and be equipped to stand against them.

Acts 13:11 records the first miracle we see God perform through the apostle Paul. He struck Bar-Jesus blind. Satan is powerful, but he is no match for the Son of God. The proconsul "believed, for he was amazed at the teaching about the Lord" (Acts 13:12). This Greek definition is a favorite. The word *amazed* is the Greek word *ekplesso,* which means "amazed" only in the sense of knocking one out of his senses. I can't count the times God has knocked me out of my senses through something He has taught me about Himself.

God wants to amaze us with the wisdom of His Word. He wants to blow our minds and widen our vision! He wants to show us how relevant He is. How can we do our part so He can do His? Serguis Paulus, the proconsul, revealed to us a marvelous link. Ultimately, he was "amazed at the teaching about the Lord" (v. 12), "because he wanted to hear the word of God" (v. 7). He was ready to receive, and God honored the desire of his heart! Let's learn to pray like the psalmist who said, "Open my eyes that I may see / wonderful things in your law" (Ps. 119:18). He may just blow our minds.

Think of times you picked up your Bible and were interrupted, distracted. How often when you attend a worship service are you distracted while preparing to go, on the way, or at the service? Does your annoyance become anger directed at a child, spouse, or friend? Our anger needs to be directed at the source. When you desire to study God's Word, Satan will do everything to distract. Ask the Holy Spirit to empower you to recognize the source of your distractions and to channel your anger where it belongs — toward the evil one.

CHAPTER 12
A LIGHT FOR THE
GENTILES

Acts 13:13–52

*"Therefore, my brothers, I want you to
know that through Jesus the forgiveness
of sins is proclaimed to you. Through him
everyone who believes is justified from
everything you could not be justified from
by the law of Moses."*
(ACTS 13:38–39)

Next we join Paul and Barnabas as they
continue their first missionary journey,
departing Cyprus and entering the large Roman province of Galatia. On the map you
will see the distances they were willing to
travel to preach the gospel. We don't do missionaries justice when we romanticize their
ministries. Missionary work is extremely difficult. The travels are taxing and often
frightening, as Paul and Barnabas discovered. Not everyone can take it, as the next
section of Scripture proves!

If you have your copy of the Scripture, I encourage you to read Acts 13:13–43. Our missionaries sailed from Paphos to Perga, on the coast of Asia Minor. There John Mark left the party and returned home to Jerusalem. We will save our discussions of John Mark's departure for later when the subject is raised again with greater detail in the Book of Acts.

Barnabas and Paul traveled on to Pisidian Antioch (not the Antioch in Syria where believers were first called Christians). On the Sabbath they attended the synagogue worship and received a wonderful invitation. Sometimes we yearn for God to crack open a receptive door to share our faith with a friend, neighbor, or coworker. We scramble to grab an opportunity that never seems to come. Other times God swings open a door so quickly, we're too stunned to walk through it! God swung the door open so quickly in Pisidian Antioch that He almost blew the beard off the rabbi! Practically by the time Paul and Barnabas found a chair, they were asked to share a message of encouragement.

Paul was not about to miss a golden opportunity. Like any good orator, he shaped his style and material to fit his audience. As he stood in the synagogue, he addressed

Jews and those who believed in the God of Israel. He presented the gospel by rehearsing for them their history.

I am convinced that Paul had a very specific purpose as he introduced Christ to the Jews through their own history. Remember when Paul went to Arabia after his conversion and spent some solitary time trying to sort things out? You may recall that he then returned to Damascus and "baffled the Jews . . . proving that Jesus is the Christ" (Acts 9:22). As we saw earlier, the word *proving* means "knitting together." In Arabia Paul had been knitting together the old and the new and found the two strands of yarn to be a perfect match. Paul's intention was to give the Jews in Pisidian Antioch a knitting lesson! He urged them to see how perfectly Christ knit the past with the present. They did not have to forsake their history. They just needed to accept the rest of the story!

Paul was such a prodigy of grace, he could not preach a sermon without it. He charged the Jews with having executed their own Messiah with "no proper ground" (13:28), yet he extended the invitation to any "brothers" (v. 38) or fellow Jews, to receive forgiveness through Christ. What glorious news! If a person who had shared the responsibility for Christ's death could be forgiven, can any person be beyond forgiveness?

Verse 43 shows that Paul and Barnabas's first experience in Galatia was positive. "Many of the Jews and devout converts to Judaism" met with them after the message and received their encouragement. Note the exhortation: the missionaries "talked with them and urged them to continue in the grace of God." Let these words be pressed into the soft concrete of your mind so they will be set in your memory when we consider the letter Paul will later write to the Galatians.

The initial reception was so positive, but when God works can Satan be far behind? The Jewish leaders "were filled with jealousy and talked abusively against what Paul was saying" (v. 45).

I wonder if the jealous leaders were prepared for what they got. Paul and Barnabas answered them boldly: "We had to speak the word of God to you first. Since you reject it and do not consider yourselves worthy of eternal life, we now turn to the Gentiles" (13:46).

Luke continues with a passage that may trouble you. Acts 13:48 tells us: "All who were appointed for eternal life believed." Some read into Paul's words that God appoints certain people to receive eternal life and preselects others to eternal condemnation. I can't think of many issues more important than this. Scripture clarifies Scripture. What do the following Scriptures tell you about God's desires for salvation?

- "The Lord is not slow in keeping his promise, as some understand slowness. He is patient with you, not wanting anyone to perish, but everyone to come to repentance" (2 Pet. 3:9).
- "God so loved the world that he gave his one and only Son, that whoever believes in him shall not perish but have eternal life" (John 3:16). Whoever in the entire world is a universal invitation if I've ever seen one!
- "He is the atoning sacrifice for our sins, and not only for ours but also for the sins of the whole world" (1 John 2:2).

John left no room for the idea that Christ died only for certain people. When Acts 13:48 tells us "all who were appointed for eternal life believed," Luke was employing a Greek military term somewhat foreign to us. *Tatto,* the original word for "appointed," is used figuratively in the New Testament and means "to set in a certain order." The word was used originally to describe the order in which soldiers were arranged. Paul wrote that the gospel "is the power of God for the salvation of everyone who believes: first for the Jew, then for the Gentile" (Rom. 1:16). This verse describes the order or arrangement perfectly. Notice, salvation is for everyone who believes, but the order or arrangement is "first for the Jew, then for the Gentile." Perhaps a paraphrase of Acts 13:48 based on the original definition of the word *appointed* would help: "When the Gentiles heard this, they were glad and honored the word of the Lord; and all who were appointed [next in order] for eternal life believed." In other words, the Jews in Pisidian Antioch had been given their opportunity; and now it was the Gentiles' turn.

That group of ancient Jews was privileged to receive the ministry of the apostle Paul himself, but in a flash they went from being subjects of ministry to being sources of opposition. We read in verse 50 that "the Jews incited the God-fearing women of high standing and the leading men of the city" against Paul and Barnabas. Ultimately, the enemy of salvation used the Jews just as they used the leading women and men of the city. All were puppets on his strings. Little has changed. Satan still takes advantage of women and men, seizing their powers of influence for his own purposes.

I want to ask the Holy Spirit to help us with a final assignment in this chapter: Meditate on your last seven days for several moments. Picture yourself in your usual roles as well as specific encounters. Think of ways you exerted the power of influence, whether rightly or wrongly. I will get you started with a few questions I am asking myself: Did you influence your spouse in a decision at work? Did you influence a friend who was upset with someone? Did you influence a class or a group of people in a meeting? Did you influence your boss or employees? Did you influence your children in situations they were in? Consider every point of influence you can remember, and add to your list as the Holy Spirit reminds you of others.

You're probably more influential than you thought. If you had lunch with friends this week, you probably influenced someone in some way. If a friend shared a problem with you, you influenced him or her somehow with your response. If you gave your opinion on a matter recently, you very likely affected someone else's. We are constantly exerting influence. Influence is a gift, a trust. We must be careful how we use it. Take heed. Satan can affect masses of followers through a few leaders.

Acts 13 concludes with Paul and Barnabas being thrown from the city, but not before "the word of the Lord spread through the whole region" (v. 49). They had done what God sent them to do in Pisidian Antioch. The truth had been told. Seeds had been planted. The results were up to Him. They shook the dust from their feet, laced their sandals, and headed for Iconium.

Perhaps you know how it feels to be obedient to God yet not see the results you wanted or expected. You may have met rejection, yet you're still fighting for the results you hoped for — trying to force a good ending. Is God pulling you forward while you dig your toes into the dirt, refusing to give up? Paul and Barnabas may have departed the city believing they had started well but finished poorly. They may have felt their efforts were in vain. Meanwhile, God looked from heaven and saw His Word spread like a blanket over the region. Don't try to judge your own effectiveness. Another opportunity for ministry awaits you. Shake the dust off those feet and move on. Joy lies ahead.

CHAPTER 13
A PRUDENT PAIR

Acts 14:1–20

Some Jews came from Antioch and Iconium and won the crowd over. They stoned Paul and dragged him outside the city, thinking he was dead. But after the disciples had gathered around him, he got up and went back into the city. The next day he and Barnabas left for Derbe.
(ACTS 14:19–20)

After leaving Pisidian Antioch in a cloud of dust, Paul and Barnabas traveled south in the province of Galatia to the city of Iconium. As you see on the map, they traveled quite a distance to their next destination. Few flat lands greeted them. The road literally rose up to meet them as numerous hills and mountains interrupted the landscape.

Paul was approaching forty years of age by this time. No sooner than his head hit his mat, his calves surely cramped and seared from the journey. The brilliant stars finally soothed him to sleep. He and Barnabas probably settled into the kind of relationship necessary for people paired for days on end. Rich talks fit between long intervals of silence. Small talk momentarily eased their awesome responsibility. Between Paul's tenacity and Barnabas's encouragement, neither lacked motivation. By the time they could see Iconium in the distance, they were spilling over with the kind of joyful anticipation that can only come from the filling of the Holy Spirit. A new challenge awaited them. Perhaps more of a challenge than they expected!

I want you to see two major characteristics Paul and Barnabas shared. When they got to Iconium, the missionary pair again began at the synagogue. They "spoke so effectively that a great number of Jews and Gentiles believed" (Acts 14:1). But like Pisidian Antioch before, the Jewish leaders' jealousy led them to poison the minds of the people against Paul and Barnabas.

Interestingly enough, just as the Pharisees and the Herodians overcame their mutual dislike of each other to oppose Jesus, some of the Jews and Gentiles temporarily overcame their aversion to one another for a common cause. They joined in opposing the gospel message and messengers.

In spite of the opposition, "Paul and Barnabas spent considerable time there, speaking boldly for the Lord, who confirmed the message of his grace by enabling them to do miraculous signs and wonders" (Acts 14:3).

Then things took a dark turn for our heroes. They learned of a plot to stone them. So naturally our miracle-working pair confronted their accusers, right? *Wrong.* They ran for their lives!

You may be surprised to hear that they fled in the face of the plans set against them. Shouldn't they have stayed and trusted God to guard them from attack since they were doing His will and preaching His message? Couldn't the same power used to perform signs and miracles be used to stifle their enemies?

I believe their actions offer us the first of two fitting descriptions of the dynamic duo: They were smart! I don't believe they were reacting out of pure fear. They were responding out of pure wisdom, and quickly! Proverbs 22:3 says that "a prudent man sees danger and takes refuge, but the simple keep going and suffer for it."

Christ often chose prudence. "Jesus went around in Galilee, purposely staying away from Judea because the Jews there were waiting to take his life" (John 7:1). On another occasion Christ's enemies picked up stones to stone him, "but Jesus hid himself, slipping away from the temple grounds" (John 8:59).

No reasonable person could mistake Christ's prudence for cowardice. Look at the words of Matthew 26:1–2: "When Jesus had finished saying all these things, he said to his disciples, 'As you know, the Passover is two days away — and the Son of Man will be handed over to be crucified.'"

Why didn't Christ slip out of their hands this time? John's Gospel gives us the answer on an earlier occasion when they tried to seize Jesus: "No one laid a hand on him, because his time had not yet come" (John 7:30). Christ did not resist His accusers when they came to arrest Him. The time had come for Him to give His life as a sacrifice for sin.

Paul and Barnabas responded to impending danger the way Christ did on several occasions. Supernatural power could have changed things. Christ could have opened the earth and commanded it to swallow His pursuers in Palestine or the pursuers of His beloved ambassadors in Iconium. Yet He chose to use another method. Christ did deliver Paul and Barnabas from an evil attack. He used their heads and feet to do it! I see two general principles at work regarding miraculous intervention in the New Testament:

1. Miracles were used more often for authenticity than intervention.
2. Miracles were used most often when natural means were either not available or not conceivable.

Jesus ordinarily used natural means of provision. When He and His disciples were hungry, they usually found something to eat. When they were thirsty, they went to a well and drew water to drink. He could have supplied anything they wanted supernaturally, but He chose natural means when available. He responded the same way to impending danger. He used His feet or sometimes a boat, and He departed.

Whether God uses natural means or supernatural means to deliver us from danger, both are divine provisions. God supplied the healthy legs that Paul and Barnabas used to flee. God provides the car we drive to the nearest public place when we're being followed. The person who walks on the scene out of nowhere and frightens off an attacker is an ambassador of God! This may be very difficult for you if you have been attacked or injured and wonder why you weren't delivered. I hope you will find comfort in the next part of the story because Paul has been in your shoes.

The pair proceeded to the city of Lystra and began to preach the good news. There they encountered and healed a man who had been crippled from birth.

Do you ever wonder why God doesn't more often perform miraculous works? Have you thought, *Just one good miracle would turn this place upside down?* If so, consider what happened here. Because of the miracle, the crowd began to declare: "The gods have come down to us in human form!" (Acts 14:11). Not exactly the result Paul and Barnabas desired.

The crowd brought bulls and wreaths to the city gates of Lystra to offer sacrifices to Barnabas and Paul as gods. Because of an old Greek myth, the people of Lystra were afraid not to honor Paul and Barnabas.

For generations a story about two Greek gods who visited earth had circulated among the people of Lystra. The two gods were met with scorn except for one poverty-stricken couple who showed them hospitality. According to the myth, the gods cursed the people but gave the couple an opulent palace. The people of Lystra were taking no chances in case these gods had returned.

We have already seen a vital fact about Paul and Barnabas: they were smart! Now we witness a second description of both men at critical moments: they were sincere. They rushed into the crowd, tearing their clothes, and declaring themselves mere men.

The sincerity of Paul and Barnabas is refreshingly obvious. They not only tore their clothes in grief because the people had made such a preposterous assumption, they wasted no time in setting the record straight. They did not capitalize on a moment's glory. They did not use their attentions to get a good home-cooked meal. They rushed out to the crowd, shouting, "Men, why are you doing this? We too are only men, human like you" (v. 15).

We all know that human beings are indescribably fickle. One minute we are laying palm branches in the road and crying, "Hosanna in the highest." The next minute we are crying, "Crucify Him," or, "I never knew Him." So it was with the adoring crowd at Lystra. One minute they were preparing to worship Paul and Barnabas. "Then some Jews came from Antioch and Iconium and won the crowd over. They stoned Paul and dragged him outside the city, thinking he was dead" (Acts 14:19).

That didn't take long, did it? Think about this carefully: Barnabas and Paul could have used the crowd's wrong impression that they were gods, but they maintained their integrity. A flashy miracle at just the right time and not one stone would have been thrown. The crowd would have bowed at their feet. Paul and Barnabas could have slipped out of town without a scratch; instead, Paul was stoned so severely that they dragged him outside the city thinking he was dead.

Can you imagine the pictures flashing in Paul's mind with every blow of a stone? I'm sure his memory replayed Stephen's radiant face. Paul probably could not bear to think of himself worthy to die for the name of Christ in the same way. He probably fell unconscious thinking he was about to breathe his last, but this was not Paul's time.

Paul and Barnabas had arrived in Iconium with joyful anticipation, only to have to depart quickly under threat of stoning. They had escaped one of the most painful forms of punishment ever devised. They wiped their brows, gave a sigh of relief, and headed into Lystra. Before they knew what had happened, the stones were flying; they had no place to run, nowhere to hide.

Many years later Paul still remembered the events in Iconium and Lystra and shared a peculiar testimony. He said, "You, however, know all about . . . what kinds of things happened to me in Antioch, Iconium and Lystra, the persecutions I endured. Yet the Lord rescued me from all of them" (2 Tim. 3:10–11).

Any person in his or her right mind would prefer to be rescued before the first stone is thrown, not after the last! Yet Paul described both his experience in Iconium (where he departed prior to suffering) and his experience in Lystra (where he departed after suffering) as the Lord's divine rescue. Perhaps his inspired choice of words will intensify your appreciation of his exquisite testimony. The original word for "rescue" in 2 Timothy 3:11 is *rhuomai,* which is derived from a word meaning "to drag along the ground." *Rhuomai* means "to draw or snatch from danger, rescue, deliver." Please read the remainder of the definition with great care and meditation: "This is more with the meaning of drawing to oneself than merely rescuing from someone or something."

You see, God wasn't only interested in drawing Paul out of difficulty or danger. He wanted to draw Paul closer to Himself.

133

Every time God delivers us, the point is ultimately to draw us closer to Himself. Whether we get to avoid pain and suffering or we must persevere in the midst of it, our deliverance comes when we're dragged from the enemy of our souls to the heart of God.

CHAPTER 14
HARDSHIPS ON THE KINGDOM ROAD

Acts 14:21–28

They returned to Lystra, Iconium and Antioch, strengthening the disciples and encouraging them to remain true to the faith. "We must go through many hardships to enter the kingdom of God," they said.
(ACTS 14:21b–22)

Paul and Barnabas departed from Lystra after Paul was stoned so severely his body was dragged from the city as dead. "But after the disciples had gathered around him, he got up and went back into the city" (Acts 14:20). We are safe to assume the disciples did not just gather around him and gawk. They surely prayed for him. Whether the answer to their prayer was immediate healing or simply rescue from death, he was certainly rescued by his faithful God. While his persecutors dragged the apostle outside

135

the city, His Savior dragged him further into His heart.

Our next portion of Scripture unfolds in Derbe. In just a few verses in Acts 14, we see Paul and Barnabas backtrack through a number of cities on their way to Syrian Antioch where they had been commissioned. "They preached the good news in that city [Derbe] and won a large number of disciples. Then they returned to Lystra, Iconium, and Antioch, strengthening the disciples and encouraging them to remain true to the faith. 'We must go through many hardships to enter the kingdom of God,' they said" (Acts 14:21–22).

On the map you can see they chose the long route. Why didn't they simply head to (Syrian) Antioch, their mission home base, straight from Derbe? Why in the world would they backtrack through Lystra (where Paul was stoned and left for dead), Iconium (where they narrowly escaped being stoned), and Pisidian Antioch (where they were persecuted and expelled)?

Acts 14:22 tells us exactly why they walked back into potential peril. They went to strengthen the disciples and encourage them to remain true to the faith. They faced risk to tell the new believers, "We must go through many hardships to enter the kingdom of God."

Paul and Barnabas didn't mean a person must go through trials to become a Christian. Remember, they were speaking to disciples in the faith. Their hearers' salvation was already secured. The key to their exhortation is found in the meaning of the word *must*. The Greek word *dei* means "is inevitable in the nature of things." Hardship is inevitable in the nature of things.

Hardship has a place in the believer's life because "our light and momentary troubles are achieving for us an eternal glory that far outweighs them all" (2 Cor. 4:17). When we're going through difficulties, they never seem light or momentary, but remember that Paul is comparing them to "an eternal glory that far outweighs them all." The apostle also reminds us that "our struggle is not against flesh and blood, but against the rulers, against the authorities, against the powers of this dark world and against the spiritual forces of evil in the heavenly realms" (Eph. 6:12).

When we receive Christ as our Savior, we ignite the ire of His enemy Satan; however, 1 John 4:4 reminds us, "You, dear children, are from God and have overcome them, because the one who is in you is greater than the one who is in the world." Praise God!

As you see, hardships are inevitable for us because

- God wants to give us eternal victory by working His glory in and through them.
- Satan wants to bring us defeat by causing us to struggle and fall.

Hardships are inevitable because of the glorious nature of God and the heinous nature of Satan.

Paul and Barnabas considered this message of inevitable hardships such a priority that they risked everything to go back to those three cities and tell it. Their message of encouragement through warning of hardship may seem to be a paradox to us. At first consideration, we may not find a message about unavoidable troubles very strengthening! Certainly, we don't find it encouraging! But let's dig a little deeper and see if we can discover some strength or encouragement from their message.

First, recognizing the inevitable nature of hardships can motivate us to redirect our energies. Fear of trials sometimes depletes more energy than facing trials! Once we accept the inevitability of hardship, we can redirect our focus from fear of trials to faithfulness. In the face of tribulations, we often sense a heavenly strength filling our souls right on time.

I know what it's like to let fear deplete your energy. I was so afraid I would lose my first child to crib death that I could hardly rest. Every few hours I jumped out of bed to see if she was breathing. Losing a child wasn't my only fear. From the time my mother officially became a senior adult, I often cried on the way home from her house because I feared something might happen to her before I saw her next.

Even if either tragedy happened, all my sleepless nights or buckets of tears would not have helped me a bit. God finally taught me to redirect my energies toward getting to know Him and love Him through His Word so I can be equipped for anything.

The last year has been one of the most difficult seasons of my entire life. One crisis seemed to roll in behind another. I faced losses I thought I could not bear. My heart is very sore, but it's still beating. I am not glad my hurts happened. I'm not rejoicing over the loss. But I am alive, and life is still strangely abundant. Had God not taught me His Word and made Himself the uncontested love of my life, I think I might have wanted to quit. If you are like me and you tend to fear having your heart broken, ask Him to help you redirect your energies toward faithfulness instead.

Realizing the inevitability of hardship does another thing for us. It encourages us in the faith rather than discourages us. After this past year, I would be pretty discouraged if I thought hardships in the lives of surrendered Christians were unusual and signs of disobedience.

A dangerous prosperity gospel fills our Christian airwaves today. Many believe that if you have enough faith, you'll be both healthy and wealthy! Preachers and teachers are telling anyone who will listen that hardship is never the will of God. They proclaim that every difficulty is from the kingdom of hell; and if we stand in unwavering faith, we will be happy and physically prosperous.

My relatives had a name for that kind of teaching — hogwash. We will never become so spiritual that we will cease experiencing hardship.

First Peter 1:7 tells us one reason why difficulties will come throughout our lives. It says of trials, "These have come so that your faith — of greater worth than gold, which perishes even though refined by fire — may be proved genuine and may result in praise, glory and honor when Jesus Christ is revealed."

Hardship sometimes comes as a direct result of sin and disobedience. We usually are aware when consequences of sin have caused us deep suffering, but many other times trials have nothing to do with disobedience. Believing a heretical prosperity gospel can leave us terribly discouraged, wondering what we've done wrong. We wonder why we can't seem to muster enough faith to be healthy, problem free, and prosperous.

Recently I grieved while I watched a friend claim and reclaim his wife's healing while she was dying of cancer. He was a member of a church that teaches that you can "name it and claim it." He sent out letters asking many of us to pray certain healing Scriptures in her behalf and not waver in belief. My heart was so broken for him. I prayed every one of those Scriptures for her and claimed them on her behalf. Several days later I learned God had taken her home before I had even received the letter asking for prayers. I was unknowingly praying for someone who was completed and perfected before the very throne of grace.

She wouldn't have come back if she could have. She had been healed but not the way we had prayed. I continue to pray for the family she left behind because their grief may be intensified by disappointment in God and in their own faith.

Please be encouraged to know that difficulty is not a sign of immaturity or faithlessness. The Holy Spirit will do His job and let you know if you are suffering because of sin. Otherwise, remember — we must go through many hardships to enter the kingdom of God. Incidentally, unbelievers also suffer many hardships. The difference is this: ours are never in vain.

I hope we have shared some of the strength and encouragement Paul and Barnabas gave to the believers in Lystra, Iconium, and Pisidian Antioch. Those new converts saw living examples of perseverance through suffering. Paul and Barnabas departed from each city under difficult circumstances. They went out of their way to return so they could say, "We're OK! We've survived! And we're still believing and serving!" In seeing the joy and commitment of God's suffering servants, they knew they could survive too.

The time came for Paul and Barnabas to leave, but they did something to ensure an ongoing strengthening and encouraging of their new disciples.

Acts 14:23 tells us they appointed elders in each church. The Greek word is *presbuteros,* which means "older, a senior." The *Holman Bible Dictionary* tells us the "elders in the Pauline churches were probably spiritual leaders and ministers, not simply a governing council."[1] Not coincidentally, Paul and Barnabas wanted to leave the new believers with ongoing strength and encouragement, so they carefully appointed elders who were not only spiritually mature but, if I may say so gently, *old!* However, the older men were not the only ones charged with responsibility.

In Titus 2:3–6, Paul also charged older women, younger women, and younger men to faithful service. Sounds to me like God values the wisdom and life experience of older men and women. It also sounds to me like He chooses to use people of every age whose hearts are turned to Him.

Life is difficult. The converts in Lystra, Iconium, and Pisidian Antioch were surely strengthened and encouraged as they saw living examples of people who were surviving hardships with victory and joy. Listening to Paul and Barnabas testify must have greatly impacted their ability to endure. We don't have Paul and Barnabas, but we have hosts of older people who are more than happy to tell us about the faithfulness of God — if we'll just stop, ask them, and listen.

Chapter 15
Harder Than It Has to Be

Acts 15:1–35

"It is my judgment, therefore, that we should not make it difficult for the Gentiles who are turning to God."
(ACTS 15:19)

I love to travel. I especially love meeting brothers and sisters in Christ. As much as I relish the new faces and places, there's no place like home. I heave a sigh of relief when I set my bags down inside my door and put my arms around my husband. I feel at home with my family. I experience the same feeling when I kneel to pray with my Sunday school class. I feel at home. They know me better than any group on earth. They have seen my ups and downs, yet I am bathed with love and acceptance every time I walk in the door.

Paul and Barnabas felt the same way about the church in Antioch. This was the first church they "birthed" together. Antioch was home base. The believers there welcomed them like family and savored their testimonies. The last verse of Acts 14 wraps the tumultuous chapter like an old terry-cloth robe wraps a tired body after a terrible day: "They stayed there a long time with the disciples." A welcomed respite.

Have you ever noticed that just when things seem to calm down a bit, something or someone comes along to throw a kink in it? Paul and Barnabas had worked hard in Antioch. The people were responsive and anxious to learn. A strong, viable Gentile church had emerged, but the church was young and very impressionable. Now we need to consider the poor impression a few outsiders had made on the church at Antioch. Paul and Barnabas returned to Jerusalem to settle a doctrinal question. This trek does not constitute a missionary journey nor the final road to Rome, so it does not appear on your map. Let's dive into Acts 15.

One thing you can say for legalists: They are single-minded. Verse 1 tells us that during Paul and Barnabas's stay at Antioch: "Some men came down from Judea to Antioch and were teaching the brothers: 'Unless you are circumcised, according to the custom taught by Moses, you cannot be saved.' "

The next verse says, "This brought Paul and Barnabas into sharp dispute and debate with them." Somehow I can just see it. Paul wasn't about to let such teaching go unchallenged. So the two missionaries of grace traveled to Jerusalem to seek a resolution with the church leaders.

As they traveled, they told what God had done among the Gentiles, and this made the believers glad. Mark it down. How people respond to the activity of God marks the dividing line between legalists and alive believers. Legalists split hairs while believers rejoice that children have come into Christ's family.

Legalism — more than any other, that one little word is probably responsible for causing more churches to die, more servants to quit, and more denominations to split. Like a leech, legalism saps the lifeblood out of its victim. It enters the door in the name of righteousness to vacuum out all the dirt and ends up vacuuming out all the spirit. Don't confuse legalism with recognition and pursuit of godly standards.

When our pair reached Jerusalem, one of the most important meetings in history ensued. "Some of the believers who belonged to the party of the Pharisees stood up and said, 'The Gentiles must be circumcised and required to obey the law of Moses' " (Acts 15:5). Two sets of legalists emerge in this portion of Scripture:

1. The Judean visitors to Antioch who told Gentile Christians they must be circumcised to be saved.
2. The believers in Jerusalem from the party of the Pharisees who told them they must also obey the law of Moses.

The statement of the Pharisees became the basis of the "Jerusalem Council." Peter argued for acceptance of the Gentile believers on an equal basis with their Jewish counterparts.

Eventually James, the brother of Jesus, stood and delivered the verdict. He said, "It is my judgment, therefore, that we should not make it difficult for the Gentiles who are turning to God" (Acts 15:19). The Jerusalem Council drafted a letter to the church in Antioch and appointed two leaders, Judas and Silas, to accompany Paul and Barnabas in their return. The council asked the believers to avoid four practices that were particularly offensive to their Jewish brothers. Naturally, the believers in Antioch were glad to receive the encouraging message.

Let's offer the legalists more grace than they offered Gentile believers. I'll assume they made a mistake rather than acting out of pure meanness. In giving them the benefit of the doubt, I see at least three mistakes they made in behalf of the new Gentile converts.

1. *They drew a universal standard from their personal experience.* Since they had been circumcised prior to salvation, they decided everyone else should be as well. Through the ages people have struggled with the same wrong assumption based on their own personal experience. If God worked one way in their lives, any other way must be invalid. Let me illustrate with the story of two men.

The first man lives a godless, depraved life. The Spirit of God convicts him. He falls on his face, surrenders to Christ as Lord of his life. He serves faithfully and never falls back into the old patterns of sin. He becomes a preacher and boldly proclaims the message that people are not saved unless they instantly surrender their entire lives to the lordship of Christ. If they have ever fallen back, they were never saved at all.

The second man received Christ at a very

early age, and then fell away in rebellion for years. He returns to Christ as the penitent prodigal, slips into his old ways several times, and finally reaches freedom in Christ. In his opinion, a person's state of salvation cannot in any way be judged by his actions. He believes a man can live like the devil for a season of his life and still be saved.

Both men are born again, but both men are mistakenly applying their experience to every other believer. Each of these men could find some degree of scriptural support, so who is right? God is. He is right and justified in saving whomever He pleases. There is only one way to be saved: by grace through faith in the Lord Jesus Christ (see Eph. 2:8–9). God uses many methods to draw people to Himself. He is far more creative than we want to think. Only He can judge the heart.

2. *They tried to make salvation harder than it is.* James delivered a strong exhortation to the Jerusalem Council in Acts 15:19: "We should not make it difficult for the Gentiles who are turning to God." What a frightening thought! We must ask ourselves a very serious question: Do we make it difficult for people around us to turn to God? Do we have a list of rules and requirements that turns people away?

Part of the exquisite beauty of salvation is its simplicity. Any man, woman, or child can come to Christ with absolutely nothing to offer Him but simple faith — just as they are. Salvation requires nothing more than childlike faith — believing that Jesus Christ died for my sins and accepting His gift of salvation. The heart and the life sometimes turn instantaneously like the first example. Other times the heart turns instantaneously but the life adjusts a little more slowly like the second example. Let's not make salvation more difficult than it has to be.

3. *They expected of others what they could not deliver themselves.* In Acts 15:10, Peter said, "Now then, why do you try to test God by putting on the necks of the disciples a yoke that neither we nor our fathers have been able to bear?" In essence Peter was asking, Why are you expecting of someone else what you can't deliver yourself? The question is one every believer should occasionally ask him or herself. Do we have almost impossible expectations of other people? Do we expect things of our mates we wouldn't want to have to deliver? Do we expect perfection in our children and tireless commitment from our coworkers? Are we yoke brokers just looking for an unsuspecting neck?

Yoke brokers are miserable people because they are never satisfied with less than perfection. Their obsession with everyone else's lack of perfection helps them keep their minds off their own. Yoke brokers are selling a yoke no one wants to buy — their own. If anyone has ever expected of you something you knew he or she couldn't do, then you have an idea how it feels to be the hapless victim of a yoke.

Let's return to the simplicity of salvation. Not adding to. Not taking away. When we paint the picture of our salvation for others to see, we may use different colors, textures, and shapes on the edges of the parchment. But in the center can only be a cross. Anything else cheapens grace and cheats the believer. Paul wasn't about to let that happen to his beloved flock.

James reminded the Jewish believers in Acts 15:18 that salvation coming to the Gentiles had been known for ages. They were seeing the fruition of an old plan in which God would do a new thing. He gave His Son on the cross to set the captives free, not to imprison them under the impossible laws of men. As Ezekiel so well put it long ago: "They will know that I am the LORD, when I break the bars of their yoke and rescue them from the hands of those who enslaved them" (Ezek. 34:27b).

God can break any yoke, even those we don't realize we're wearing. Thank goodness, the message of freedom prevailed at the Jerusalem Council. Paul and Barnabas departed with a letter personalized for the Gentile believers in Antioch. At first glance the letter seems somewhat contradictory. Gentile believers didn't have to be circumcised to be saved, but they were urged to abstain from several practices forbidden under Jewish law. Were they free from the law or not? Yes and no. They were free from the law of Moses but not free from the life-giving laws of God.

The freedom God gives is to come out and be separate from the practices of the former worldly life. The letter to the believers in Antioch was a declaration of liberty; the four areas of abstinence would help them remain free.

Let's pinpoint one of the four areas that offers us an important learning opportunity: The believers in Antioch were told to abstain from food sacrificed to idols. Gentile believers might have reasoned that although they would not dream of sacrificing to idols anymore, what harm could be done by simply buying the leftover food at a good price after it was offered?

Satan sometimes tempts us the same way. We don't desire to go back to our old life-styles, but certain parts of it seem so harmless — some of the old friends, the old hangouts, and the old refreshments. The elders warned that nothing is harmless about the practices of the old life. Eating foods sacrificed to idols could weaken them to former practices or cause someone else to stumble.

The Gentile believers would not forfeit their gift of grace by eating foods sacrificed to idols, but they would risk their freedom and compromise their separateness. They were wise to avoid anything that would place them close enough to the vacuum to be sucked back in. Safety and freedom are found in staying so far away that you can't even hear the vacuum cleaner running.

Paul and Barnabas were back home. Back with their beloved flock. They returned to tell them they were free and to tell them a few ways to stay free.

■ ■ ■ ■

PART IV
UNEXPECTED
SOJOURNERS AND
WIDER PATHS

■ ■ ■ ■

Now we are about to embark on our second
missionary journey with the apostle Paul.
The more we continue our journey, the
more we will discover the importance of
coworkers in the gospel. Paul rarely worked
alone. Studying his life affords us the
marvelous privilege of peeking into many
other lives as well. Inevitably, however,
where you find people, you find problems!
We may see Paul at his worst and at his best.

The same man who had the propensity to be irritable and unreasonable could be spiritual and tender moments later. Sound familiar? We have a lot to learn as we continue to study the apostle to the Gentiles.

This portion of Scripture may tug a little tighter on your heartstrings. Don't pull back from God. Get emotionally as well as spiritually involved in your journey. Imagine how you would feel in Paul's sandals. Think about ways you might have reacted differently. Let God penetrate your heart and mind with His Word. Don't push Him to the comfortable perimeters. He wants to do something wonderful in your life!

CHAPTER 16
DIVIDE AND
MULTIPLY

Acts 15:36–41

They had such a sharp disagreement that they parted company. Barnabas took Mark and sailed for Cyprus, but Paul chose Silas and left, commended by the brothers to the grace of the Lord.
(ACTS 15:39–40)

Sailors speak of the call of the sea, but something stronger than the sea called Paul. He relished his days in Antioch. How beautifully the garden had grown from a few seeds scattered six years earlier! He enjoyed the privilege of returning to the same quarters every night and laughing over a meal with good friends. He busied himself with the work of a pastor. He loved these people and his partner, Barnabas. But filled with the Spirit of God, Paul felt compelled to go where the Spirit led.

We may plan to stay forever and commit

with noble intentions to do one thing for the rest of our lives. But when the Spirit of God moves within us, we must move with Him or be miserable. Paul knew God had called him to Antioch only to send him out again. He had learned to obey both the abiding and the moving of the Holy Spirit. He had been allowed by God to abide in the comforts of Antioch for a season. Now the Spirit of God compelled him to move again.

I love being drawn into the story line and relationships of Scripture, but involvement also increases the disappointment when our heroes show their humanity. We are about to see how God uses flawed people like you and me.

Acts 15:36–41 tells us how Paul and Barnabas prepared to revisit the churches from their missionary journey. Remember John Mark, who bailed out on the first journey? Barnabas was one of those men willing to take a risk on a hotheaded young Pharisee who had come to Christ or a young missionary who had failed on his first attempt. Paul, on the other hand, was hard and tough. Barnabas said John goes. Paul said John stays. John went. With Barnabas. Paul took Silas as Barnabas's replacement.

I think Paul and Barnabas were just that

different, but Colossians 4:10 gives us a bit more insight into their disagreement. John Mark was more than a fellow believer to Barnabas. They were also cousins. Barnabas was the first to accept Paul and welcome him among the brothers in Jerusalem. Together they faced the kind of peril and persecution that bonds two people for a lifetime! They were a team. When the Holy Spirit compelled Paul to return to the towns where they had preached, he wanted his dear friend and partner to go with him. Imagine how difficult this severance must have been for them.

Dr. Luke shows the magnitude of difficulty in the description in Acts 15:39: "They had such a sharp disagreement that they parted company." Strong emotions spawn sharp disagreements. They each had strong emotions about John Mark and toward each other. Obviously, both Paul and Barnabas were upset by their differing opinions.

Somehow, disagreements between people have a strange way of inviting observers to pick sides. I've caught myself trying to decide who was right and who was wrong. I feel a strange need to make up my mind and get in one camp or the other. Romans 14:1 gives us an invaluable guide at such moments: "Accept him whose faith is weak, without passing judgment on disputable matters."

Let's start becoming aware of our tendency to get involved, at least emotionally, as judge and jury when people disagree. Next time we're in a similar situation, perhaps we should ask ourselves, Does someone always have to be right and another wrong?

Paul and Barnabas both were Spirit-filled servants of God, yet they differed vehemently on whether John Mark should join them. We might assume either Paul or Barnabas was not under the leadership of the Holy Spirit; because the Spirit could not possess two opinions. Or could He? I believe both men could have been under the direct influence of the Holy Spirit and yet still have differed. How? The Holy Spirit might have been saying yes to Barnabas and no to Paul. He might have wanted Barnabas, but not Paul, to take John Mark. Why? So God could divide and multiply. Paul had matured so effectively under Barnabas's help and encouragement, they had grown equally strong. Though they might have preferred to serve together the rest of their lives, God had a more practical plan. He had other young preachers He wanted each man to train. As a result of their differing convictions, two preachers became four, and soon we'll see another. Paul and Barnabas went their separate ways — two mentors, each with a new apprentice. The empty place in Paul's ministry left an appropriate space for a man named Silas to fill.

Scripture tells us most divisions are not of God, but Acts 15 suggests that sometimes God wants to divide and multiply. Can you imagine how much simpler church life could be if we accepted that God could place two people under different convictions to multiply ministry? I've seen this phenomenon occur at my own church. Two very strong leaders in our church differed over whether we should have traditional worship or contemporary worship. Who was right? Both of them. God divided one worship service into two, and we now reach more people.

Often differences erupt due to less noble motivations — two opinionated people unwilling to budge. Unless we invite God to come to the rescue, the results can be disastrous. Ministries and partnerships often divide and dwindle rather than divide and multiply. On the other hand, when God leads two people who have walked together to a fork in the road, He can do something wonderful *if* they and their constituents are mature enough to deal with it!

Unfortunately, sometimes we may be the ones involved in a dispute. We may find ourselves strongly differing with someone about matters related to church or ministry. Differing convictions don't have to become razor-sharp contentions. Let's end this chapter by exploring a few ways we can avoid turning convictions into contentions. If you like checklists, here is a four-step plan for dealing with conflicts between believers.

1. *Identify the real source of the argument.* Job 16:3 asks a relevant question: " 'What ails you that you keep on arguing?' " Ask the Holy Spirit to shed light on the true source. Sometimes we believe that conviction is the motivation for our differing views until we allow God to reveal our selfishness or unwillingness to change. Part of spiritual maturity is risking our position in favor of the will and glory of God. Let's be willing to allow Him to shed light on any selfish or worldly motive.

2. *Submit the issue to God.* James 4:7 exhorts, "Submit yourselves, then,

to God. Resist the devil, and he will flee from you." An important part of giving anything to God is taking everything from Satan. Ephesians 4:26–27 tells us not to sin in our anger and thereby give the devil a foothold. Satan has a field day with our arguments and quarrels. When we ask God to remove all selfish, worldly motives and influence of the enemy, issues often either disappear or downsize to a workable level.

3. *Resist the temptation to sin in your anger.* Anger in and of itself is not sin. It is an emotion, and sometimes a very appropriate emotion. Unfortunately, anger heightens the risk of wrong actions or words. Each of us regrets something we've said or done in anger. Let's ask God's help when we are angry at another believer so that our feelings do not turn into wrong actions.

4. *Pray* for *the other person involved and, if possible,* with *that person.* Prayer changes things and people! Philippians 4:6 invites us to pray about everything. Can you imagine how defeated the enemy would be

if two divided church leaders or laymen got down on their knees together and prayed for God's glory? We don't have to be together on every issue, but we can be together in prayer!

None of these steps are easy for us, but God can keep differing convictions from becoming contentions if we let Him. Sometimes the fear of being wrong or having to relent will keep us from inviting God into the middle of a dispute. I hope our study of this passage has helped us to become more open to the possibility that both people can be on the right track, even when they are feeling led in different directions. We've seen an occasion when differences ultimately brought gains rather than losses. If God could use a sharp disagreement between two of His faithful servants, then Luke 1:37 has been tried and proved under some of the most difficult human conditions: Nothing is impossible with God!

CHAPTER 17
THE BIRTH OF A
SPIRITUAL SON

Acts 16:1–3

He came to Derbe and then to Lystra,
where a disciple named Timothy lived,
whose mother was a Jewess and a
believer, but whose father was a Greek.
(ACTS 16:1)

Acts chapter 16 unfolds as Paul returns to
Derbe and Lystra to check the temperature
of the churches. Though he begins his
second missionary journey in cities previously visited, God will soon adjust Paul's
eyes to a wider vision.

At Lystra Paul encountered a young
believer who was to play a major role in the
apostle's future ministry. The young man's
name was Timothy, and Scripture tells us
his mother was a Jewish believer and his
father was a Greek. Paul wanted to take
Timothy along on the journey, "so he
circumcised him because of the Jews who

lived in that area, for they all knew that his father was a Greek" (Acts 16:3).

Before assuming Paul violated his own teachings, understand why he had Timothy circumcised. Jews recognized Timothy's Jewish heritage. His mother was a Jewess. They would have been terribly offended and refused to allow him into the synagogues to preach. Paul wanted Timothy to minister to both Jews and Gentiles. He had him circumcised so the Jews would not be offended and close their minds to his testimony.

I hope we can capture some insight into Paul's heart by observing how he loved and related to people. He must have been very endearing to many people. He had many close friends and associates. We rarely see him working alone. More than anyone recorded in all of Scripture, Paul taught believers to work together. He was both a preacher and a teacher, yet he was never a one-man show. He clearly enjoyed working with other servants and was quick to acknowledge their valuable contributions.

One of my favorite parts of this study is exploring some of Paul's friendships; yet as many as he had, one would differ from all the rest. Many years later I'm sure his heart was washed with emotion as he recalled his return to Lystra and the risk he took on a young man named Timothy. From the very beginning, Timothy was special. Allow Scripture to shed some light on his distinctives.

In 1 Timothy 4:12 Paul counseled Timothy not to let anyone look down on him because of his youth, yet the advice came fifteen years after Timothy joined Paul. Timothy was a unique choice because of his youthfulness. Paul's words in 2 Timothy 3:15 demonstrate that in spite of his youth, Timothy was fertile soil from which ministry grew: "From infancy you have known the holy Scriptures, which are able to make you wise for salvation through faith in Christ Jesus."

I believe Paul saw Timothy's tremendous potential for fruit bearing. The opportunity to train Timothy while he was still young and teachable was probably a benefit to Paul's ministry, not a hindrance.

Recently a fellow believer told me the wonderful news of his twelve-year-old son's surrendering to the ministry. These parents knew his heart and were overcome with joy and humility over their son's serious decision. The response of others was somewhat perplexing, however. People said things like "God is obviously going to use him someday" and "I hope he still feels this way when he is old enough for God to use him." A person doesn't have to turn twenty for the Lord to use him in ministry.

Anyone with the maturity to surrender entirely to God is mature enough for God to use. What could be more important than a ministry by students for students on a junior high school campus? To this student and others like him, I extend the words of the apostle Paul: "Don't let anyone look down on you because you are young, but set an example for the believers in speech, in life, in love, in faith and in purity" (1 Tim. 4:12).

Do you know any young people who are trying to be genuine servants of God? If so, they may be discouraged because no one is taking them seriously. Why not make a point of encouraging a young servant through a note, a call, or a pat on the back?

Timothy was special for another reason. He had a unique upbringing. He came from a family with a Jewish mother and a Greek father. You may have greater insight into Timothy's childhood because of differences in your own parents' belief systems. Growing up in a home with one believing and one unbelieving parent is very difficult. In those days, having a Jewish mother who had accepted Christ and a Greek father who didn't believe would have been both different and difficult.

I have two daughters in college. I am very concerned about a seemingly harmless belief system that society has been shaping in children's minds. My generation was the first to be raised on movies and fairy tales in living color. Movies like *Cinderella, Snow White and the Seven Dwarfs,* and *Beauty and the Beast* redefine romance as two people from totally different worlds falling deeply in love. Typically, their only problem is their unyielding family. Ultimately, love overcomes and they live happily ever after.

We need to teach our children the truth about real romance and love that lasts. The sparks that fly from two different worlds converging in one couple usually end up burning someone!

Paul delivered a strong exhortation in 2 Corinthians 6:14: "Do not be yoked together with unbelievers." The Greek word for "yoked" is *zugos,* which means "a yoke serving to couple any two things together and a coupling, a beam of a balance which unites two scales, hence a balance." In the next verse Paul asked a question to make his point: "What harmony is there?" When two completely different belief systems are joined together, the result often is a lack of balance and harmony. You may have grown up in this kind of home, so you know how rocky this life can be. Perhaps you may presently be in a home where spiritual beliefs differ drastically. If so, I hope you receive some encouragement from Timothy's experience. God can prevail and bear wonderful fruit from an unequally yoked couple as we will see, but their lives often are more complicated than they had to be.

Keith and I have miraculously made it for twenty years, but we've had to work very hard to overcome many differences in our belief systems. We are both hoping our daughters find romance with young men who were reared with spiritual beliefs close to their own.

What could be more exciting than two people coming together and entrusting their uncertain futures to God's purposes, bound by a common love for His Son? Now, I call that real romance.

Timothy was unique for a third reason. He had a unique perspective. Timothy had been intimately exposed to three practices he and Paul would encounter in ministry:

1. Agnosticism because of his father's unbelief,
2. Judaism because of his mother's

heritage, and

3. Christianity because of his mother's acceptance of Christ as Messiah and Savior.

Even though he did not have the security of two believing parents, he gained an insight that would prove valuable in ministry. God wasted nothing in either Paul's or Timothy's background. He won't waste anything in your background either, if you will allow Him to use you.

We can see a fourth aspect of Timothy in that he had a unique maturity. In our society we've almost become convinced that bad influences are stronger than good. Timothy certainly is evidence to the contrary. We have a wonderful biblical precedent proving that godly influence can carry a much heavier weight than ungodly influence.

The words of 2 Timothy 1:5 offer strong encouragements to anyone married to an unbeliever. Paul wrote: "I have been reminded of your sincere faith, which first lived in your grandmother Lois and in your mother Eunice and, I am persuaded, now lives in you also." You can rear godly children in spite of imperfect circumstances. The word *sincere* provides one key to winning a child to faith. Timothy's grandmother and mother both possessed a sincere faith. The word is *anupokritos,* which means "without hypocrisy or pretense." Originally the word meant "inexperienced in the art of acting." What a wonderful way to be inexperienced!

Lois and Eunice lived their faith. Timothy saw genuine examples of faithfulness. Their lives were devoted to God even when the company left. They were genuine — not perfect, but real. Their sincerity won Timothy to the truth.

I once thought Exodus 20:5, which refers to the sins of the fathers being visited upon the children, was one of the scariest verses in the Bible. Then I looked up the word *visit* (KJV) and realized what it meant. The word is used for taking a census or a head count. Allow me to paraphrase this way: When a parent practices sin and rebellion against God, adversely affected children, grand-children, and great-grandchildren share some of the same tendencies. God can take a census in that family and find those continuing results. But sin and rebellion are not the only heritage passed down to future generations! Faithfulness has an even greater influence!

Contrast God's promise in Deuteronomy

7:9. It promises that God keeps His covenant of love "to a thousand generations of those who love him and keep his commands." Hang in there, parent! Let your children see the sincerity of your faith. Let them see you praying and trusting. Nothing carries the weight of sincere faith!

For Christ Paul sacrificed many things dear to the Jew: marriage, children, strong extended family. God honored Paul's sacrifice by giving him other priceless gifts. Timothy was one of those gifts. He filled a void in Paul's life that no one else ever matched. Years later Paul described Timothy as "my dear son." Perhaps God thought a crusty old preacher needed a young whippersnapper as much as Timothy needed him.

What about you? What constitutes your heritage of faith? You may have a heritage of faith from one side of your family. Or you may be the first believer in several generations. Paul considered Timothy to be his son in the faith even though he was not his biological father. You've probably received a heritage of faith from a spiritual if not a natural mother or father. Find out who gave your spiritual parent his or her heritage of faith.

Meditate on your spiritual family tree. Thank God for your heritage. As you conclude this chapter, pray for the generations that will follow you. Just think, if Christ tarries, your faithfulness could affect a thousand generations. Isn't God wonderful?

CHAPTER 18
THE LEADERSHIP OF
CHRIST'S SPIRIT

Acts 16:4–15

When they came to the border of Mysia,
they tried to enter Bithynia, but the Spirit
of Jesus would not allow them to. So they
passed by Mysia and went down to
Troas.
(ACTS 16:7–8)

Our next passage takes us into new territory, both logistically on our map and
spiritually in our understanding of a difficult concept. As they ventured farther
from home, new challenges awaited Paul,
Timothy, and Silas. These new challenges
were not only in their relationships with
people and places but also in their relationship to Christ.

No matter how God has prepared us in
advance, when we surrender our lives to
serve God, we are not fully grown. In fact,
the greatest challenges to learn and grow

are ahead!

We probably did not see a light and hear a voice from heaven as did Paul, but we met Christ somewhere on the road to our chosen destinations. Our lives took a turn at that point, and we've been sojourning ever since on the roads He's placed before us. Life is not only about receiving Jesus and one day seeing Him. Life also is about walking with Christ and learning from Him on the winding road.

Acts 16:6 seems a strange verse: "Paul and his companions traveled throughout the region of Phrygia and Galatia, having been kept by the Holy Spirit from preaching the word in the province of Asia." The passage reminds me of myself when I have misplaced something. I search through this drawer and that cabinet. Paul and company seem to have searched in similar fashion for God's purposes. One thing is obvious, one less so: Obviously, God did not allow them to preach in Asia. Less obviously, we have an addition to the missionary band.

An important change in the references to Paul and his men appears in verse 10. Suddenly, instead of *they*, which is used as recently as verse 7, the expression becomes *we*. Somewhere on this significant journey,

Luke joined the growing band of missionaries.

Early church fathers identified Luke as being from Antioch.[1] In Colossians 4:14, Paul referred to him as a dear friend and a doctor.

A number of scholars believe Paul's thorn in the flesh might have been a physical illness. Perhaps Luke offered himself both spiritually and professionally to the service of Christ; then he traveled with Paul and his associates as a physician and record keeper. Whatever his original motivation for joining them, we are forever indebted to his obedience in providing vivid accounts of the life of Christ in his Gospel and the lives of the apostles in the Book of Acts.

Assuming Luke caught up with Paul, Silas, and Timothy on their journey, he was fortunate to find them at all after their sudden change in plans! The redirection God gave the disciples as they attempted to enter the province of Asia offers us several timely learning opportunities. We learn that even the most noble plans of God's anointed servants sometimes differ from the plans of God.

Paul wanted to take the gospel to the province of Asia. He could not have imagined God having any reason to object, yet "they tried to enter Bithynia, but the Spirit of Jesus would not allow them to" (Acts 16:7). Why would God object to the preaching of the gospel in the province of Asia? One reason may have been timing. Later God opened "a great door for effective work" for Paul and his associates in Ephesus, in the province of Asia (1 Cor. 16:9). A second reason may have been His plan to use Peter rather than Paul in Bithynia. The inclusion of Bithynia in 1 Peter 1:1 indicates that God gave Peter some level of access to the area. Whether the problem is the wrong place, the wrong time, or the wrong person, God exercises His right to redirect His children.

These Scriptures remind us that God can sometimes say no or wait, even when godly people have unanimously voted yes! Spiritual maturity does not mean that we will never make the wrong plans. In fact, spiritual maturity often means having the courage to admit we've made the wrong plans.

How can we know when God is redirecting us? Let's see if we can discover how Paul probably recognized the closed door to Asia. Did God use opposition? Apparently not, because when Paul spoke of the door opening later in Ephesus, he said "a great door for effective work has opened to me, and there are many who oppose me" (1 Cor. 16:9). Opposition didn't seem to slow Paul down much. Did God use a supernatural means like the vision He gave him regarding Macedonia? I don't think so, because if He had, the vision probably would have been recorded just like the one several verses later.

I believe God hindered Paul in the same way He often hinders us when we are heading the wrong direction: through the inner working of His Spirit.

Before we consider what the leadership of the Spirit is, let's determine what it is not. Jude 8–19 tells us that scoffers who follow their own ungodly desires, "follow mere natural instincts and do not have the Spirit." We can't rely only on our feelings as we try to do God's will. The leadership of the Spirit is far more than "mere natural instincts."

Romans 8:9 tells us God has placed His Spirit within each person who has received Christ. One reason His Spirit takes up residence inside us is to tell us things only believers can understand, leading us in areas of obedience to Christ. The Holy Spirit always leads believers in Christ, but we don't always recognize His leadership. A few basic practices can help us follow the leadership of the Holy Spirit.

1. *Study God's Word.* God will never lead us any direction contrary to His Word.
2. *Yield to the Holy Spirit's control.* Being yielded to God's authority keeps us pliable and open-minded to a possible change of plans.
3. *Pray for clear leadership in specific directions God wants you to take.* You might consider adopting David's approach to prayer in Psalm 27:11. He asked God to teach him His ways and to lead him in a straight path.
4. *Pray for wisdom and discernment to recognize specific directions.* In Ephesians 1:17 Paul asked God to give believers "the Spirit of wisdom and revelation" to know Him better. That request is a good guideline for us too. Start asking God to give you the Spirit of wisdom and revelation!
5. *Make plans, but hold on to them loosely!* I don't believe God intended for Paul, Silas, and Timothy to travel haphazardly through the countryside. Paul was a very intelligent man. He probably formulated

an itinerary just like most of us would, but he kept his plans open just in case God had different ideas!

6. *Learn to recognize peace as one of God's prompters.* Peace is one of the most obvious earmarks of the authority of Christ. A sense of peace will virtually always accompany His will and direction — even when the direction might not have been our personal preference. On the other hand, a lack of peace will often accompany a mistaken path — even when the direction is definitely our personal preference. As we grow in Christ, we will learn how to appreciate peace over personal preferences. Remember, Christ is the Prince of Peace. His peace will accompany His authority.

Paul and his fellow servants were yielded to the leadership of the Holy Spirit. Therefore, they were pliable when God prompted them not to enter the province of Asia by removing their sense of peace and approval. Thankfully, they were willing to allow God to change their plans. More than any other disciple, God used Paul to teach about the activity of the Holy Spirit. Paul could not teach what he had never learned. He learned to follow the leadership of the Holy Spirit one day at a time, one city at a time — on-the-job training. Let's learn from his example and be willing to change our course when we sense God has different plans.

Paul and his small band of missionaries did not have to wait long for redirection. God used a vision to lead them into uncharted territory. Paul had a vision of a man of Macedonia begging him, "Come over to Macedonia and help us" (Acts 16:9). As a result the missionary band traveled to Philippi where Paul found no synagogue, so he preached at a gathering place outside the city.

There by the river he encountered a woman named Lydia. We've seen Paul have more thrilling encounters. Verse 14 simply says, "The Lord opened her heart to respond to Paul's message." Nothing outwardly dramatic happened. Almost seemed ho-hum, didn't it? But take a good look at your map one more time. After temporarily closing a door in the province of Asia, God strained their eyes to see a much wider vision. The gospel of Jesus Christ went to Europe! Within a couple of hundred years, Christians numbered in the tens of thousands in Europe. And it all started with a businesswoman named Lydia.

No one would ever suspect some of the feelings of spiritual inferiority professional Christian businesswomen harbor at times. For everyone who ever wondered if God could use a professional businesswoman, meet Lydia. She was a city girl, a salesperson. A home owner with enough room to house a host of people. Yet her professional life was balanced by the priorities of her spiritual life. She worshiped God. She didn't see the Sabbath as an opportunity to catch up on some sleep and straighten up the house. She gathered with other believers. She found a place of prayer (v. 13). She opened her home. She made herself available to God. Because she did, "the Lord opened her heart to respond" (v. 14). And God gave birth to the gospel in Europe. I'd say that businesswoman had a pretty important ministry, wouldn't you?

In Acts 16 we see seasoned believers and new believers learn to respond to the leadership of the Holy Spirit. Because they were completely surrendered to God's will, Paul, Silas, and Timothy did not fret when the Spirit of Christ hindered them from following through with their plans. They simply awaited new marching orders. We often hear people say, "When God closes a door, He opens a window." Sometimes we might just be underestimating Him. We just saw Him close a door and open a continent.

CHAPTER 19
THE MIDNIGHT SONG

Acts 16:16–40

About midnight Paul and Silas were praying and singing hymns to God, and the other prisoners were listening to them.
(ACTS 16:25)

Life presents us with extremes. As we look back over our personal histories, the years seem to fall into ups and downs, valleys and mountaintops. We sometimes feel we've lived only in the ups or only in the downs. Paul and his small band of missionaries spent a short time in Philippi. In that time, they were "guests" in two places: a mansion and a dungeon. Let's meet Paul in the extremes.

As Paul, Silas, Timothy, and Luke were going to the place of prayer one morning, they encountered a demon-possessed slave girl. This girl was able to predict the future, and her owners were exploiting her for a great deal of money. When she saw the missionary band, she began to follow them shouting, "These men are servants of the Most High God, who are telling you the way to be saved" (Acts 16:17). For days she continued to follow them until Paul lost his patience. Tired of the unwanted demonic testimony, he commanded the demon to leave the girl.

Few of us have ever encountered a demon-possessed slave girl. But all of us have felt exactly like Paul when he finally had enough! I'm not sure patience was Paul's natural strong suit, so I find myself amused at his best attempts to control himself. As he and the others tried to preach, teach, and meet for prayer, this young, disturbed woman followed them and shouted incessantly. Obviously the apostle had tried not to react, but after many days he became troubled. I can't help but grin as I share the original definition of *troubled* with you. None of us will have difficulty relating to it. The word *diaponeo* means "to be tired . . . become wearied . . . at the continuance of anything."

When was the last time someone continued an annoying habit until you wanted to scream? I recall a bumper sticker that read,

"I have one good nerve left, and you're on it."

The apostle had the power to do something about his frayed nerves, and he commanded the spirit to come out of the girl. As a result, her exploiters lost a source of income. They were more than troubled. They were incensed. Paul and Silas ended up being dragged into the marketplace to face the authorities, not because of the charges made against them, but because they had ruined a good scheme. The magistrates had them stripped and beaten. "After they had been severely flogged, they were thrown into prison, and the jailer was commanded to guard them carefully. Upon receiving such orders, he put them in the inner cell and fastened their feet in the stocks" (Acts 16:23–24).

You may be wondering why four men preached the gospel in Philippi but only two of them were punished. Where were Luke and Timothy when the sparks started flying? The Roman world had recently experienced a fresh surge of anti-Semitism, and Emperor Claudius had expelled all Jews from Rome. Because few things are more contagious than prejudice, Philippi (a Roman colony) quickly caught the virus. Timothy and Luke may have been considered

Gentiles by the Roman authorities. Since the governors of Philippi knew virtually nothing about Christianity, Paul and Silas were dragged before a strongly anti-Semitic magistrate and persecuted because of their Jewish heritage. Imagine how the foursome felt: divided over their backgrounds, two were freed, and two were carried away maliciously. I'm not at all sure which two had the easier sentence.

The Book of Hebrews acknowledges the kinds of roles both pairs played in Philippi that day: "Remember those earlier days after you had received the light, when you stood your ground in a great contest in the face of suffering. Sometimes you were publicly exposed to insult and persecution; at other times you stood side by side with those who were so treated" (Heb. 10:32–33).

Do you see Scripture acknowledging the authentic pain a person experiences when a friend or loved one suffers? God is very aware that standing close to someone who is hurting hurts! He does it every day. Whether we are the ones suffering or we're alongside another, His grace is sufficient for our need. Aren't you refreshed to see God validate in Scripture the experience of the deeply concerned bystander? You can cry out for help when you're hurting for someone else. He'll hear you and acknowledge your need!

Luke and Timothy deeply needed God's comfort as they watched the severe flogging of their partners. First, Paul and Silas were stripped — an incomprehensible humiliation to anyone with a Jewish background. Then they were mercilessly beaten with rods.

Paul probably suffered from both sides of the great contest we considered in Hebrews 10:32–33. He suffered his own blows, but he also stood by Silas as he was stripped and severely whipped. What a frightful initiation into ministry this must have been for Silas. Can you imagine how Paul ached for his new assistant? Did he wonder if Silas could take it? If so, he found that no one needed to underestimate Silas. Luke and Timothy strained for a last look at their partners as the authorities dragged them to prison. They probably wondered if they would ever see them again. Luke and Timothy's night may have been longer than Silas and Paul's. And much less eventful!

The two bloodied servants of God were taken to a dungeon and placed in stocks, unable to move, pain wracking their bodies. Though they were bound in iron chains, they found freedom to sing. We cheat the faithful servants from showing us God's glory if we believe God anesthetized their pain. Death would have been a relief. The challenge of their moment was living until the pain became bearable.

Pain is never more vivid than in the midnight hour. The night lacks the kindness of the day when demands and activities distract. Bound in stocks, each time their hearts beat every nerve ending throbbed with pain. In spite of their anguish, their prayers ascended before the throne and God gave them "songs in the night" (Job 35:10).

Prayers come naturally when we are distressed — but songs? Finding notes is difficult when your body is gripped with pain. Nonetheless, a few notes found their way into a melody, and their melodies turned into hymns. Every stanza issued a fresh strength, and their voices were unchained — penetrating walls and bars.

The most difficult part of my service as a Sunday school teacher has been watching my members bury loved ones. Several years ago one of my members lost her fifteen-year-old son in an automobile accident. I will never forget accompanying our friend to the funeral home and helping her choose a casket. All four of us walked to the car and drove away without saying a word.

Within a couple of blocks, one of us began to cry, and then the rest joined her without saying a word. After several minutes of silence, another began to sing with broken notes, "I love you, Lord . . . and I lift my voice . . . to worship You . . . O, my soul rejoice." I could hardly believe the nerve of my fellow member to sing at a time like that. Before I could look at her with proper horror, the mother's best friend joined in, "Take joy, my King, in what You hear . . . may it be a sweet, sweet sound in Your ear."

The words fell from their lips a second time and to my shock, the brokenhearted mother began to sing. If she could sing, I knew I could not remain silent. We sang the rest of the way home that day. Not one of us had a solo voice, and yet I wonder if I will ever hear a sound so beautiful again. I knew that day what God meant when He told us to lift up the sacrifice of praise. When praise is the last thing that comes naturally to us and we choose to worship Him anyway, we've had the privilege of offering a genuine sacrifice of praise.

When we sing a midnight song or speak praises in the darkest hours, the chains of hopelessness not only drop from our ankles but sometimes from the ankles of those who listen. We can preach the gospel in many ways, but the message is never more clear than when God's people refuse to cease their praises during intense suffering.

In their bondage, Paul and Silas were free to sing. They were also free to stay. Finally their songs were eclipsed by the rumblings of an earthquake. The foundations of the prison trembled before an awesome God. The prison doors flew open, every chain was loosed, and the jailer drew his sword to kill himself. Paul's words penetrate my heart: "Don't harm yourself!" (Acts 16:28). How many people have sought to harm themselves over hopelessness? The jailer knew he would be held responsible for their escape. "Don't harm yourself! We are all here!" shouted Paul.

Sometimes God frees us from chains so we can turn our backs on our slavery and walk away like Peter in Acts 12. He was free to leave. As a result, the church that was praying for his release was edified. Other times God frees us from chains so we can remain where we are to share the message of freedom with other captives. Paul was free to stay. Because he did, a man asked, " 'What must I do to be saved?' " (16:30). And an entire household found sweet liberty.

I met a young man who had experienced

freedom from the bondage of homosexuality. Although he was a dedicated servant, God had never appointed him to share that part of his testimony nor minister to those still chained in that lifestyle. Like Peter, he had been freed to leave.

After God delivered me from the bondage of my childhood victimization, He called me to share my basic testimony and reach out to other survivors of abuse. I had been freed to stay. Both my friend and I experienced the glorious freedom of Christ. One was free to leave and one was free to stay, but we each trust God with His perfect plan for our lives.

God reserves the right to use His servants and their experiences in different ways. Let's try to resist copying a blueprint from another person's ministry. God is very creative, and He always has purpose in the specific ways He chooses to use us. Be willing to allow Him to put some things to public use and other things to private use. Today, we've seen a slice of Paul's life in the extremes: a welcomed guest and a prisoner. Either extreme could have been a test. Paul passed. As life draws us to extremes, may we pass our tests as well.

CHAPTER 20
THE NOBLE EXAMPLE
OF THE BEREAN
BELIEVERS

Acts 17:1–15

Now the Bereans were of more noble character than the Thessalonians, for they received the message with great eagerness and examined the Scriptures every day to see if what Paul said was true.
(ACTS 17:11)

Our next passage takes us to two stops on Paul's second missionary journey. We know Luke accompanied the missionaries to Philippi, but his terminology suggests that their paths parted for awhile, presumably for the sake of the gospel. Luke's references to "we" rather than "they" will pick up again several chapters later in the Book of Acts. For now we see Paul and Silas in Thessalonica.

Before we proceed, let's highlight a few points from Acts 17:1–9. Paul and Silas had traveled one hundred miles from Philippi to

Thessalonica without the benefit of a motorized vehicle. They seemed to know exactly where they wanted to go and certainly did not lack the stamina to get there! You may be wondering what criteria made one city more a priority than another. Obviously, the first criteria was the leadership of the Holy Spirit. If He did not lead, they did not go.

Paul cited another criteria in Romans 15:20. He said, "It has always been my ambition to preach the gospel where Christ was not known, so that I would not be building on someone else's foundation."

God used the leadership of the Holy Spirit and Paul's desire to go into territories untouched by the gospel. In each new venue, not only did he customarily preach in the synagogues first; he employed the same method each time. He sought to prove that Jesus was the Christ with the Old Testament Scripture. I believe he used this method with them because God had used it so effectively on him in the desert of Arabia. He knew this technique could work on the hardest of hearts because it had worked on his.

As a result of the message and the method, some Jews and many Greeks believed. Wherever there is an awakening, you can expect opposition. Soon the seed of jealousy was planted in other Jews, and they formed a plan to incite a riot.

The Christians in Thessalonica got Paul out of jail and sent him off to Berea. Having narrowly escaped in the night, the tenacious missionaries traveled approximately fifty miles to Berea. Miles away from their destination, they saw a most imposing landmark: Mount Olympus rising high into the sky from the foothills of Berea. Only twenty miles from the sea, Berea had everything to offer: warm coastal breezes tempered by snowcapped mountains. What could be more inviting than a city set between the mountains and the ocean? Exceeding the noble sight, however, was the nobility of the people. The Bereans possessed characteristics that provide an excellent standard for believers today:

1. *They were willing to receive.* Acts 17:11 tells us the Bereans received the message. The Greek word is *dechomai,* which means "to accept an offer deliberately and readily." The Bereans accepted the offer to come and hear what Paul had to say.

Many churches work overtime to offer opportunities for Christian growth and encouragement through conferences, retreats, Bible studies, discipleship training, and other methods. Often, a relative few attend.

Sometimes the ones who don't are the very ones who criticize the church for not doing enough. Many times we don't lack opportunities, we lack willingness. The Bereans accepted the offer to hear Paul teach and preach, and the fruit was bountiful.

2. *They were ready to receive.* The Bereans not only accepted the offer to hear Paul, they were eager to receive what he said. The original word for "eagerness" is *prothumia,* which indicates a predisposition for learning *(Strong's).* Our experiences in Bible study, worship services, and other discipleship opportunities are greatly enhanced when we approach each one with a predisposition for learning. We need to prepare ourselves with everything we can to have a receptive disposition before we arrive.

3. *They cross-examined the message with the Scriptures.* Paul must have been a very effective communicator, yet the Bereans did not take his word for everything. They measured the accuracy of his message against Scripture through their own personal examination of the Word. The original word for "examined" in Acts 17:11 is *anakrino,* which means "to ask, question, discern, examine, judge, search" *(Strong's).*

We all need to learn to study the Scriptures for ourselves. All believers have the right to ask questions and examine the Scriptures to check the accuracy of the teaching they hear. Congregations can be easily misled if they do not feel or exercise the freedom to double-check teaching and preaching against the Word of God. A savvy communicator can use the Scriptures taken out of context to teach almost anything! Any portion of Scripture must be compared with Scripture as a whole.

Some years ago, a national forest had to close off a portion of the park to tourists. A number of bears starved to death during the time the park was closed. They had grown so accustomed to being fed by the tourists, they had ceased feeding themselves. We can likewise grow so accustomed to being spoon-fed the Word of God that we forget how to examine the Scriptures for ourselves.

We can also cease checking the nutritional value of what we're being taught! My most earnest prayer would be that this Bible study, and others like it, be a help in teaching you how to examine Scripture for yourself. Yet I plead with you not to accept my instruction without question. Always check my teaching against a thorough examination of the Word. I would never knowingly mislead you, but I am subject to human error just like every other teacher. I ask you to examine the Scriptures every day to see if what I'm saying is true.

The Bereans not only performed the right practices; I believe they possessed the right heart. They didn't examine the Scriptures to see if they could find error in how Paul had dotted an "i" or crossed a "t." Their motive was not to argue. Some people double-check their pastors and teachers on every issue just to find an error so they can feel superior. The Bereans had no such motive. They were eager to believe, but they were wise to check Paul's teaching against the only standard of truth — the Scriptures. After careful study, they found his teaching sound and placed their faith in the Savior he preached. A wonderful and sometimes rare combination occurred in Berea: the best kind of preacher met the best kind of audience. And a great awakening of faith resulted.

As we conclude this section of our study, we can reap one last benefit from the Bereans' approach to teaching. Soon the Jews in Thessalonica found out Paul was preaching in Berea. They were vindictive enough to travel fifty miles to agitate and stir up the people! As long as congregations exist, there will always be someone ready and willing to stir up the people. The original word for "stir up" has an interesting meaning. The word *saleuo* means "to rock, topple, shake, stir up" *(Strong's)*. The enemy of our souls will use every means and every human agent he can to topple us and shake us up. If all we have going for us are the opinions of men through sermons or lessons, when life shakes us up, little will be left. When we've learned to examine the Scriptures for ourselves, we have a few things nailed down when life starts to rock. I cannot express to you how studying God's Word has helped me when the earth around me seemed to quake. At times when everything seemed to fall apart in my life, the Word abiding in me kept me from falling apart with them.

As you continue to study the Word of God, one nailed-down, personally discovered truth will turn into many, and you will be better equipped to face anything that comes your way. Nothing will profit you more than learning to examine the Scriptures for yourself. Let every preacher and teacher be a catalyst to your own personal journey through the Word. Spend time exploring. Invest in an exhaustive Bible concordance, a good Bible dictionary, and a sound set of commentaries. Accept opportunities to get into in-depth Bible studies and really get to know the Word. Be ready and willing to receive from the many opportunities available — but with the ability to discern truth from error through deep personal examinations of the Scripture. Imitating the noble practices of the Bereans will be your safety as teachers come and go — and your sanity when life rocks and rolls.

■ ■ ■ ■

Part V
An Unfamiliar Road

■ ■ ■ ■

In this portion of our study, we will reach the midpoint of our journey with the apostle Paul. I feel like we just got started, don't you? Exciting adventures await us over the chapters to come! I'm not giving away a single clue. You'll have to stay aboard and discover them for yourself! We will conclude our study of Paul's second missionary journey in this section. We will share a rare look at the apostle Paul. Believe it or not, he could be insecure and intimidated.

God is so awesome. He chooses to do extraordinary works through ordinary men

— and women! Through our study, let's learn how we can develop a passion and perseverance that will enable us to be part of something extraordinary!

CHAPTER 21
THE IDOLS OF
ATHENS

Acts 17:16–34

"For as I walked around and looked carefully at your objects of worship, I even found an altar with this inscription: TO AN UNKNOWN GOD. Now what you worship as something unknown I am going to proclaim to you."
(ACTS 17:23)

Come along as we see a lesson in contrasts. The next audience Paul encountered differed drastically from the noble Bereans. Meet the ancient Athenians. They will make you wonder how people who knew so much could understand so little.

Paul had a fruitful ministry at Berea until troublemakers came from Thessalonica. Then at the urging of the believers, once again, Paul found himself moving on. This time the destination was Athens. Some of the believers escorted Paul there and left him — where he awaited the arrival of Silas and Timothy.

According to Acts 17:16, Paul reacted strongly to the sight of a city full of idols. Imagine going on a mission trip to a city like Varanasi, India — a Hindu holy city filled with temples and images depicting hundreds of gods.

Paul set about his usual task of preaching the gospel, but in Athens the audience was different. The philosophers lived to hear some new idea and invited Paul to their meeting of the Areopagus on Mars Hill. There he preached an unusual sermon. He reached across the gulf of culture and beliefs that separated his hearers from Christ. He found an object lesson from their culture that he used to share the gospel with them. He found that they had an altar "with this inscription: TO AN UNKNOWN GOD" (Acts 17:23). Beginning from that point, Paul shared the gospel with the philosophers. He said in effect, "Let me tell you about this God you don't know."

Paul's hearers listened until he got to the all-important issue of the Resurrection. Their philosophy was the predecessor to modern New Age thinking. They believed the ultimate goal of existence was to escape the bonds of physical life, so when they heard Paul speak of resurrection, some of them scoffed.

This stop on Paul's second missionary journey was unlike all the others. I observed four distinct facts about his visit. First, the city itself was so different. The preceding cities Paul visited were much smaller and less sophisticated. Although Athens was at least one hundred years past her days of glory, she was still a sight to behold. Athens had maintained her reputation as the center of higher learning with one of the most sought-after universities in ancient history. She was full of philosophers and freethinkers.

Second, Paul encountered the imposing city all by himself. Presumably escorts left him at the gates, and Timothy and Silas never had a chance to join him before his departure. We have a tender opportunity to see the sincerity of Paul's heart. Acts 17:17 tells us, "He reasoned in the synagogue with the Jews and the God-fearing Greeks, as well as in the marketplace day by day." He had no emotional or spiritual support and probably little physical support. None of the others would have known if he had simply been too intimidated to preach. No one would have blamed him anyway. Yet day by day he tried to reason with any Athenian who would listen, because he was so concerned that they needed Jesus Christ.

A third consideration making this trip peculiar was Paul's speech. I believe Acts 17 contains one of the best sermons he ever preached. He used the perfect illustration (the unknown God) and drew his audience to the perfect invitation.

Yet my fourth observation about the uniqueness of this trip is the lack of response to the gospel. Acts 17:34 tells us that only a few people became believers in Athens. Paul never mentions a church resulting from his work. He never made contact with them again as far as we know. Based on the information in Scripture, the few believers never multiplied into more. Paul's experience in Athens proves that the best of sermons will never change an unwilling person's heart. On the other hand, the weakest message can have a profound effect on a person willing to listen and be changed.

As we conclude, look at one final difference between this trip and many others in Paul's ministry. He was not persecuted, nor was he forced to leave the city. Acts 18:1 tells us he simply left. Glance back over the previous chapters of the Book of Acts. Count the times he ran into very little opposition or persecution. You will search in vain to find another experience exactly like the one he had in Athens.

Why didn't they lift a hand to persecute him? Because they were too cold to care. Paul's experience in Athens is a perfect example of a situation in which people were open-minded to a fault. Their motto was "anything goes." Everyone was welcome to his own philosophy. Live and let live! If it works for you, go for it! Athens was the birthplace of the tolerance movement.

Often persecution is not nearly the enemy that indifference is. The Athenians did not care if Paul stayed or left. They believed virtually everyone was entitled to his god. A few sneered. Others were polite enough to say they would be willing to listen to his strange teachings again. But most never realized Paul was escorted into town by the one true God. And most never cared.

Acts 17 has changed the way I pray about the nations. I cannot count the times I've asked God to crumble the spirit of opposition and persecution in many nations where Christians are a small fighting force. I will still continue to ask God to strengthen and protect those facing opposition and persecution. However, I now find my heart drawn across the map to places where a quieter dragon of perhaps equal force has made his den — the spirit of indifference. Christianity can grow and flourish under some of the most difficult opposition, but it will prosper very little where people refuse to be changed by it.

CHAPTER 22
WITH FEAR AND TREMBLING

Acts 18:1

I came to you in weakness and fear, and with much trembling.
(1 COR. 2:3)

We are now about to see a side of the apostle Paul that may surprise you. He was a human being with insecurities like ours. I find encouragement in the normal emotions and human reactions of some of God's best. How could we ever have the courage to minister if we thought those who preceded us were superhuman? God used average men and women. Paul was not superman. He had the same feelings, fears, and insecurities we share. We gain a new insight into the mind of the apostle as we journey with him to the next stop on his second missionary journey. All aboard for Acts chapter 18 and the city of Corinth. Let's look at Paul's state of mind after his departure from

Athens and fifty-mile hike to Corinth.

Paul described how he approached Corinth in 1 Corinthians 2:1–5. He said he "did not come with eloquence or superior wisdom" (v. 1), "resolved to know nothing while I was with you except Jesus Christ and him crucified" (v. 2), and that he came "in weakness and fear, and with much trembling" (v. 3).

I find it interesting that in Acts 18:9–10 Christ spoke to Paul in a vision and said, "Do not be afraid; keep on speaking, do not be silent. For I am with you, and no one is going to attack and harm you, because I have many people in this city." Paul had been in danger many times before, yet to our knowledge God never before used a vision to encourage him not to fear.

Let me share what I believe about Paul. Admittedly, I am speculating based on the hints in the accounts. I suspect that Paul's visit to Athens affected him far more than we realize. Few people believed and received Christ. Paul was overwhelmed by the polytheistic beliefs of the residents. They wanted to argue philosophies rather than consider the truth. The Athenians did not throw Paul out of the city or persecute him in any obvious way. The few converts appear to have produced little fruit. Apparently no church was established. Paul spent most of his days in Athens alone. Although 1 Thessalonians 3:1 indicates Timothy and Silas might have come as he asked, they were quickly sent elsewhere. After a brief stay in Athens, he simply moved on in frustration.

Paul had plenty of time to think on his way to Corinth. He spent several grueling days alone. During those long hours, I believe he convinced himself that every effort in Athens had failed. As we often do, I suspect he became so focused on the negative that he lost sight of the positive.

Have you ever noticed how lengthy times of solitude affect us differently depending on our state of mind? Aloneness exaggerates our emotions and sensitivities. For example, we can sometimes sense the presence of God and hear His voice far more clearly when we have several days alone. Solitude, on the other hand, can exaggerate negative feelings. We find ourselves almost thinking too much! We look back on a situation and decide nothing good came from it at all. Insecurity turns into immobilization, and intimidation turns into terror! If you have ever had a lengthy time alone in which your mind "ran away with you" with negative thoughts, then you probably understand something of what Paul was feeling.

I believe the more Paul thought about his experiences in Athens, the worse he felt. First Corinthians 2:1 may suggest that Paul felt intimidated by the Athenians, and those feelings accompanied him to Corinth. Athens attracted intellectuals who could debate eloquently and were eager to flaunt their knowledge. As he tried to preach to them, the Epicurean and Stoic philosophers disputed with him. Some sneered, "What is this babbler trying to say?" (Acts 17:18).

Paul was the pride of his graduating class — the child prodigy! You can imagine the beating his ego took in Athens. I think Paul felt like a failure. First Corinthians 2:2 says by the time he reached Corinth he "resolved to know nothing . . . except Jesus Christ and him crucified." Thank goodness, he knew the only thing he really had to know! He determined to base his life and ministry on Christ — his one certainty!

In 1 Corinthians we see an insight Paul eventually gained from his experience. Are these words evidence that he may have been thinking back on the Athenians? "For the message of the cross is foolishness to those who are perishing, but to us who are being saved it is the power of God. For it is written: 'I will destroy the wisdom of the wise; / the intelligence of the intelligent I will frustrate' " (1 Cor. 1:18–19).

God used the entire experience to show Paul an important lesson. In 1 Corinthians 2:14 he wrote, "The man without the Spirit does not accept the things that come from the Spirit of God, for they are foolishness to him, and he cannot understand them, because they are spiritually discerned."

Paul ultimately gained the insights he wrote in 1 Corinthians; but as he traveled to Corinth he was still in turmoil. On the miles between Athens and Corinth, Paul probably hashed and rehashed his experiences. He wished he had said this or that. Sometimes we can't explain exactly what we believe. Other times, we think of just the right answer when it's too late. We end up feeling foolish because we weren't persuasive.

Obviously, Paul's experience had a great impact on his next opportunity. He entered Corinth "in weakness and fear, and with much trembling" (1 Cor. 2:3). The word *weakness* comes from an original word used for a sickness. The word suggests that Paul was so scared he was physically ill. The word for "trembling" indicates something we've all experienced: hands shaking from nervousness. The opposite word is *confidence.* By the time Paul reached Corinth, he had lost his confidence. Possibly he wondered if the fruit he had seen in other cities had come from God's blessings on Barnabas or Silas.

Does seeing Paul's experience in this light help you to relate to him as a fellow struggler on the road to serve Christ? When was the last time you lost your confidence? Or when did you last have to do something that made you so nervous your hands shook and you were physically ill? You probably didn't know the apostle Paul shared the same feelings. Neither did I. I hope you can find encouragement in his experience.

The enemy would have enjoyed preventing Paul from ministering in Corinth because of feelings of inadequacy, but Satan was unsuccessful. God used Paul's feelings to give a great "demonstration of the Spirit's power" (1 Cor. 2:4). The word for "demonstration" in this passage is *apodeixis,* which means "proof." What a wonderful term! Do you see what Paul meant? He was so intimidated by the time he reached Corinth; the abundant fruit ultimately produced through his preaching was proof of the Holy Spirit's power!

God often proves Himself when we feel we have the least to offer. In 1 Corinthians 1:26–31, Paul explained why God sometimes uses this method. He said not many of the Corinthian believers were wise or influential by human standards. He said that "God chose the foolish things of the world to shame the wise; God chose the weak things of the world to shame the strong" (v. 27). God chose this methodology so we would be clear that the power came from Him and not from us. He concluded, "Let him who boasts boast in the Lord." Perhaps Paul's words will mean more to you now that you know how he felt when he left Athens. God sometimes uses us most powerfully when we feel the least adequate.

God has proved Himself faithful so many times when I felt inadequate or like a failure. Just before the taping of my first video series, God allowed me to go through a very difficult time. My confidence took a severe beating. I was so emotionally exhausted that I did not know how I would get through the taping. I sat before the Lord very early the morning we were to begin taping, and I told Him I did not think I was going to make it. I had worked so hard in preparation; yet as the time arrived, I had nothing to offer. I was too tired even to sob! The tears simply ran down my cheeks.

I wearily said to the Lord, "You're on Your own here. I have nothing to give." The skies did not open that very second with a divine outpouring of strength. I walked on the set three hours later completely in faith. Thousands of dollars worth of equipment had been shipped to Houston. An amazing number of personnel had worked to prepare. Six cameras had been set in place. An audience had gathered. Everything and everyone was ready — but me. I walked out on that set with only enough strength to get on my knees in front of them and pray.

When I got up off my knees to teach, a stream of strength seemed to pour from heaven. Not in buckets. It was more like an intravenous drip. Just enough for me to know He was sustaining me minute by minute. I never felt a rush of adrenaline. I never felt a sudden gust of mighty wind. All I know is that many demanding hours of work took place over the days of that taping, and never did I lack the strength necessary to complete the task. Never in my adult life have I had less confidence, yet He gave me enough of His to keep my knees from buckling.

You may wonder why God allowed me to go through such a difficult season of inadequacy just before that task. I wondered myself until I received the first letter from a viewer of the video series. I wept as I read her words of thanks, and I whispered back, "It was God. Not me." With the second taping came another set of circumstances through which God proved Himself. I laughed with my assistant when I was asked to do a third series, and we both said, "I wonder what's going to happen this time!"

Perhaps God has opened a door for you, but you have no confidence. Is insecurity holding you back from the ministry God has for you? Each of us struggles with insecurities and the loss of confidence. No one has ever been used more mightily than the apostle Paul, yet he was so scared at times he made himself sick!

Are you familiar with some of the wonderful promises in Scripture directed specifically for times of weakness? Proverbs 3:26 says, "The LORD will be your confidence / and will keep your foot from being snared." In Deuteronomy 33:25, we are promised that "Your strength will equal your days." And Paul reminds of this promise again in 2 Corinthians 12:9–10: "My grace is sufficient for you, for my power is made perfect in weakness. . . . For when I am weak, then I am strong."

Oh, beloved, God is faithful. Even when the enemy tries to batter us and make us lose confidence, God can take the victory with a demonstration of the Spirit's power. In those times God sometimes produces a harvest of fruit unlike any other. Those who have been touched are encouraged in a faith that does "not rest on men's wisdom, but on God's power" (1 Cor. 2:5). They end up seeing God instead of us. Hallelujah.

CHAPTER 23
THE TENTMAKERS

Acts 18:2–24

*Because he was a tentmaker as they
were, he stayed and worked with them.*
(ACTS 18:3)

Dr. Luke seems to have included a sentence
of pure trivia in Acts 18; yet in it we may
discover a hidden treasure. At first glance,
Acts 18:18 seems strange. When Paul left
Corinth, "he had his hair cut off at Cenchrea because of a vow he had taken."
Luke's writing is so tight, so succinct, his
inclusion of Paul's quick stop by the barber-
shop is almost comical. Why in the world
would we need to know Paul got a haircut?
Actually, this verse holds a primary key to
understanding Paul's visit to Corinth. The
point is not the haircut. The point is the
reason for Paul's haircut.

Paul's haircut resulted from a vow he had
made. Remember, Paul was a Jewish Chris-

tian. His Jewish heritage was deeply rooted. He understood that Christ did not save him to make him forget but to complete that heritage. At times he still applied some of the former practices of the Jew, not as legalities but as wise choices. Virtually without a doubt, the vow to which Luke was referring was the Nazirite vow.

Numbers 6:1–8 tells us about the Nazirite vow. The second verse perfectly explains the nature and purpose of this vow: "If a man or woman wants to make a special vow, a vow of separation to the LORD."

The word *wants* identifies the first crucial element of the Nazirite vow — it was voluntary. The word *special* points to the second element. The Nazirite vow was special because of its voluntary nature and because it was offered to men and women alike (v. 2) — unusual in ancient Judaism. Third, notice that the purpose of the vow is *separation.* The Hebrew word is *pala,* indicating something consecrated to God, distinguished from others, and something marvelous and even miraculous often coming from something difficult *(Strong's).*

Now let's see if we can put that definition into understandable terms. If an Israelite man or woman was going through a time when he or she felt the necessity to be extraordinarily consecrated to God, the person would voluntarily take this vow. Usually they would choose to take the vow when experiencing difficult circumstances or temptations. To be victorious or obedient, they needed extra help and concentration on God.

Paul's recent experiences in Athens were not the only problems he faced in coming to Corinth. He had to confront incredible depravity in this cosmopolitan city. Even by today's standards, Corinth was extremely sexually explicit. The most significant pagan practice was the cult of Aphrodite. Aphrodite represented lust and every kind of sexual perversion. Her followers literally worshiped her through acts of immorality — often in plain sight. Paul had never seen anything remotely like the perversion he would encounter in Corinth.

The haircut in verse 18 is not the beginning of the vow. The haircut signaled the end. Before he entered Corinth's gates, Paul wisely committed himself to the vow of the Nazirite so he could maintain consecration to and concentration on Christ, the only One who could lead him to victory (see 2 Cor. 2:14).

Paul's actions teach us an important lesson. We need to avoid temptation, but when we must face it, we can prepare ourselves.

Numbers 6:3 commands anyone taking the Nazirite vow to abstain from wine or strong drink. I have chosen to abstain from alcohol not because I believe alcohol is forbidden, but because I believe it could become a distraction to me. No one told me to abstain from alcohol. I voluntarily made the decision after an honest self-evaluation. I do not believe I could deal with both alcohol and the serious devotion God has asked of me. I can think of too many ways Satan could use it to trap me.

Another practice of the Nazirite is our clue to understanding Acts 18:18. Those who took the Nazirite vow were to allow their hair to grow long as a physical sign of special devotion to God. If they temporarily forgot their vow, the quickest glance in a mirror would remind them. Others would also ask why they let their hair grow so long, and they would have an opportunity to testify about their devotion to God. Once Paul's need for extraordinary consecration to God was over, he went to Cenchrea and got a haircut!

I am impressed with Paul at this point. How about you? His weaknesses, insecurities, and temptations were the same as ours; but he was wise in dealing with them.

Matthew 10:16 is one of my favorite verses. Jesus told his followers to be as "shrewd as snakes and as innocent as doves." Innocence does not mean naïveté. In fact, had Paul approached Corinth naively, he could have gotten into serious trouble. The kind of innocence Christ described was righteousness in spite of reality!

Paul intended to keep his head on straight while in Corinth. He did not want to be enticed into any kind of trouble. He applied another bit of wisdom, which offered him further protection while he was there. He purposely did not take money from the Corinthians. He was careful to avoid the temptations that sometimes accompany money and ministry. A Macedonian church sent him some money so he would be free to preach, but he supported himself by a far more typical method — he got a job!

In Acts 18:2–3, we meet Priscilla and Aquila. They were a couple who became good friends and coworkers with the apostle Paul. Those names sound good together, don't they? (Like Beth and Keith, you might say.) Paul stayed with this godly couple because he was a tentmaker as they were.

What wonderful opportunities we've had to see the human side of Paul! The more we view him as a person not so different from us, the more we will see ourselves with the potential for his kind of godly passion. Paul's deep spirituality did not keep him from getting hungry at supper time or needing a new pair of sandals after a fifty-mile hike!

CHAPTER 24
ONE STICK OF
DYNAMITE

Acts 18:24–28

Meanwhile a Jew named Apollos, a native of Alexandria, came to Ephesus. He was a learned man, with a thorough knowledge of the Scriptures. He had been instructed in the way of the Lord, and he spoke with great fervor and taught about Jesus accurately, though he knew only the baptism of John.
(ACTS 18:24–25)

When Paul completed his long stay in Corinth, he sailed for Syria, accompanied by Priscilla and Aquila. Once again the apostle to the Gentiles made a beeline to the synagogue to reason with the Jews, but in Ephesus he found a different reception. The Jews at the synagogue asked him to spend more time with them. This time, however, Paul declined. He went on with his journey to Antioch, leaving Priscilla and

Aquila behind.

Do you find Paul's return to the synagogue interesting? Recall his last experience with the Jews in the synagogue of Corinth. He became so frustrated with them, "he shook out his clothes in protest and said to them, 'Your blood be on your own heads! I am clear of my responsibility. From now on I will go to the Gentiles' " (Acts 18:6). I thought he had finished preaching to the Jews altogether. But in Ephesus he went right back to the synagogue and reasoned with them again. Paul's ministry was far more productive among the Gentiles, so why did he continue to return to the Jews in virtually every city he visited?

In Romans 9:2–5, Paul answered that question. He so desperately wanted his fellow Jews to know Christ that, if possible, he would have died for them. He could hardly bear for the Jews to miss Christ. He must have been ecstatic over the favorable response of the Jews at the synagogue in Ephesus, but again we see why Paul was such an effective minister and servant. He had surrendered his life to the leadership of the Holy Spirit. He was not driven by his own desires and rationalizations. In his position, I might have convinced myself I was supposed to remain in Ephesus, at least for a while, based on my own desires to see God do a work among a people I loved and an apparent open door. They were begging for more! Yet Acts 18:20 tells us he declined. Paul firmly and lovingly said no.

I have a difficult time saying no. Do you? Paul probably had a difficult time, too, but he was careful to remain focused on God's priorities for him. Paul's example teaches us a timely lesson. The fact that a need exists does not mean God has called me to meet that need.

Recently I saw a sticker that said, "There is a God and you're not Him." A good reminder, isn't it? We are wise to trust Him when He seems to be leading us contrary to those things we want to do or those things that seem to be so rational and fitting.

We now get to discover one reason God did not lead Paul to remain in Ephesus. A Jew named Apollos came to Ephesus. He was a powerful, passionate preacher with a thorough knowledge of the Scripture. When Paul left, he may not have known it, but the void left an opening for a dazzling preacher. When we can't say no even when God does not give His approval, two unfortunate repercussions often result: we don't do a good job and we don't leave an opening for God's chosen person to fill.

If you are like me, when someone asks for a volunteer, you may feel you must raise your hand if fifteen seconds pass. We think, *If no one raises her hand, I guess it has to be me!* God may be wanting to raise up some of those timid people who have never said a word. They may have to go home and let God work on them for a few days before they have the courage to volunteer; but if someone jumps forward just to fill the gap they will remain uninvolved.

The account of Apollos gives us one more lesson before we move on. He traveled to Achaia to preach. Corinth was the capital of Achaia, so he walked into exactly the same audiences the apostle Paul had. Initially Apollos only knew part of the gospel. "When Priscilla and Aquila heard him, they invited him to their home and explained to him the way of God more adequately" (Acts 18:26). With his newfound knowledge, Apollos preached the same kind of message but with his own style.

We get a good glimpse into human nature as Paul later addressed the believers in Corinth. They responded to those who came and preached to them by forming warring camps. The people then reacted much like we react today. We tend to compare Christian leaders and fall into camps behind our choices. We must make a concerted effort to avoid doing so. Each of us could cite an example, but one readily comes to my mind. Every branch of indepth Bible study has loyal supporters who swear by that particular method or teacher. Some would rather fight than switch. God is wooing people to His table for the meat of His Word like never before. He is joyfully using many different methods and styles to accomplish His goal of equipping His church to be effective and holy during difficult days.

God has raised many fine teachers and preachers for our day. Let's reap the benefit of as many as possible and value their contributions whether they are magnetic like Apollos, analytical like Luke, forthright like Paul, or warm like Priscilla and Aquila. Paul's style may have been one reason some of the Corinthians preferred Apollos: Paul didn't mince words. His answer to camping around certain speakers? Oh, grow up! (1 Cor. 3:3–4).

CHAPTER 25
A GREAT SHOW OF
GOD'S GLORY

Acts 19:1–23

God did extraordinary miracles through
Paul.
(ACTS 19:11)

My oldest daughter, Amanda, was very frightened of storms when she was little. Loud peals of thunder sent her into near panic, even when we were in the safety of our home. One day when the sky seemed to be falling, I held her in my arms and said, "Honey, the heavens are just displaying the glory of God (see Ps. 19:1). They are showing us how mighty He is." Her little forehead furrowed as if she were really thinking over what I had said. Some weeks later, she was upstairs playing when a storm hit. I heard her feet scurry like lightning down the stairs. Then she yelled at the top of her lungs, "Mommy! God's really showing off today!"

God seemed to work "overtime" on Paul's next stop as He revealed His power in extraordinary ways. God used special demonstrations of power to authenticate His ambassadors and persuade belief. As we accompany Paul on the next stage of his third missionary journey, we will witness some pretty exciting events. We might end up agreeing with Amanda: "God's really showing off today."

Acts 19 tells of the distinctive ministry in Ephesus. More than anywhere else in the apostolic era, it was a time when God chose to display His power. The accent of the chapter appears in verse 11: "God did extraordinary miracles through Paul."

The chapter begins with Paul's meeting an interesting group of believers. They did not know about the Holy Spirit, and they had received only the baptism of John. These people were in a strange situation — in limbo between the Old and New Testaments. Paul told them of Christ with the result that they received the Holy Spirit, spoke in tongues, and prophesied.

Verses 8–10 summarize the ministry in Ephesus. Paul preached in the synagogue for three months until opposition arose. Then he moved his ministry to a lecture hall where he concentrated on discipling believers, with the result that "all the Jews and Greeks who lived in the province of Asia heard the word of the Lord" (v. 10).

After Luke summarized the ministry in Ephesus, he focused the microscope on several specific events. He told that God worked with such power that pieces of cloth that had touched Paul were taken to the sick, and "their illnesses were cured and the evil spirits left them" (v. 12). Luke then told what I find to be a hilarious story of the seven sons of a Jewish priest named Sceva. These Jews were so impressed by the power of God that they used the name of Jesus to try to cast out demons. "The evil spirit answered them, 'Jesus I know, and I know about Paul, but who are you?' " (v. 15). What a slap in the face! People would rather be insulted than insignificant! Actually, the encounter turned into more than a verbal slap in the face. The last we saw of the seven sons of Sceva, they were flying through the door one by one, naked and bleeding. Their pride wasn't the only thing that took a beating. I can hardly read the story without laughing. I'm sure God has a great sense of humor. This account makes me wonder if the devil may even have one.

Jews and Gentiles alike responded in awe to the events happening around them and ultimately held the name of the Lord Jesus in high honor. "Many of those who believed now came and openly confessed their evil deeds. A number who had practiced sorcery brought their scrolls together and burned them publicly" (vv. 17–19). Virtually an entire city came to highly esteem the name of Christ and cleanse their homes of evil materials.

I told you God was showing off! He was showing off His Son! God works in countless ways we cannot see. He remains active in our lives even when we are unaware. Sometimes, however, He makes Himself entirely obvious so that what we see will strengthen our faith in what we cannot see. The early church was learning concepts completely new to most. God purposely showed His visible handprints so many would place their lives in His invisible hands. God made Himself or His work obvious in Ephesus in the following ways:

1. *God made His Holy Spirit obvious.* The original converts knew virtually nothing about the Spirit. Even their knowledge of the Old Testament didn't help much, because the Spirit's activity was so different after the coming of Christ. Remember, in the Old Testament, only about one hundred people were ever described as having the

Holy Spirit in or on them. Prior to Christ and the birth of the New Testament church, the Holy Spirit's purpose was not to mark salvation, but to empower certain individuals for designated tasks. Since the birth of the church, the Holy Spirit takes up residence in every believer in Christ (see Rom. 8:9). John's baptism was a sign of repentance in anticipation of the coming Christ. Christian baptism is a mark to demonstrate the salvation Christ has given and the receipt of the Holy Spirit.

God knew the concept of the Holy Spirit would be difficult for new believers to understand as He raised up His church. Therefore, He sometimes accompanied His Spirit with a sudden physical evidence such as speaking in tongues. Few topics have caused division like speaking in tongues. No matter what you believe about tongues, during his ministry Paul was clear on at least two points concerning the activity of the Holy Spirit:

1. All believers are baptized by the Holy Spirit. The Spirit resides in all believers equally (see 1 Cor. 12:13).
2. Not all believers spoke in tongues (see 1 Cor. 12:30).

Many believe God never uses the gift of tongues today. Many others believe God always gives the gift of tongues to every true believer. I believe we are wise to avoid words like *always* and *never.* He told us to love one another, not judge one another.

2. *God made obvious His blessing on true discipleship.* Interestingly, the same group who previously asked Paul to spend more time with them (see Acts 18:20) quickly got over him when he returned! "Some of them became obstinate," and Paul took a group of the followers aside and began discipling them daily (Acts 19:9). Can you imagine being part of that Bible study? Don't miss the bountiful fruit produced from Paul's discipleship group: within two years "all the Jews and Greeks who lived in the province of Asia heard the word of the Lord" (Acts 19:10). The churches of Laodicea, Colosse, and Hierapolis were all founded as a result of this great and supernatural movement of God.

Like Gideon's army (see Judg. 7), a few well-trained soldiers in the Lord's service can be more effective than hundreds who have never been discipled. God honors His Word and often overtly blesses discipleship with fruit far beyond human effort. Paul was an effective teacher, but God still produced fruit far beyond his efforts. When a few seeds produce a huge crop, God's up to something supernatural! Acknowledge it and praise Him!

3. *God made His ambassador obvious.* God clearly tells us through His Word that the method He used to mark authenticity in the apostle Paul was rare. God meant to draw attention to the apostle Paul because He knew the apostle could be trusted to bring attention to Him. In one way, Paul was no different than the cloths that carried healing power. God used the ordinary to do the extraordinary.

4. *God made His power over the occult obvious.* One reason God showed His marvelous power to such a degree in this particular city was because Ephesus was a renowned center for magical incantations. In his book *Paul the Traveller,* Ernle Bradford wrote, "Ephesus was the centre of occult studies, indeed it has been called 'The Home of Magic.' "[1] He also tells us, "Ephesus was full of wizards, sorcerers, witches, astrologers, diviners of the entrails of animals and people who could read one's fortune by the palm of the hand or the fall of knuckle-bones."[2] Many of the Ephesians were neck deep in the occult, but virtually the entire population was extremely interested in

supernatural phenomena and the powers of the unseen world. This is one reason Paul was most outspoken to them about spiritual warfare in his letter to them, the Book of Ephesians. While Paul was in their midst, God intentionally got their attention by surpassing anything they had ever seen.

5. *God made true repentance obvious.* This activity of the Holy Spirit is perhaps my favorite of those that God performed in Ephesus. Some works of God are more subtle but not necessarily less supernatural. According to John 16:8, one of the most important activities of the Holy Spirit is to "convict the world of guilt in regard to sin and righteousness and judgment." Matthew 3:8 tells us to "produce fruit in keeping with repentance." When the new converts burned their sorcery books, they brought forth some impressive fruit.

God can reveal Himself through natural means or supernatural means. Both are at His complete disposal. Although God also worked in subtle ways, He apparently chose to reveal Himself through several phenomenal means while Paul was in Ephesus. Why did He make His activity so obvious among the Ephesians? Because Satan had made his work so obvious there. Satan is powerful, but he is no match for the Almighty God.

Sometimes I am completely perplexed by God's willingness to humor us. His mercy knows no bounds. When He wanted to lead the Magi to the Christ child, He did not lead them by a mark in the sand. He led them through a star because they were stargazers — then He went beyond anything they had ever seen. In the same way, when God wanted to lead the Ephesians to the Savior, He did not lead them through a cloudy pillar. He got their attention through supernatural phenomena, because that's where they were looking. God wants to be found. He does not will for any to miss Him, and He is so gracious to show up right where we are looking — so He can take us beyond anything we've ever seen.

God sometimes reveals Himself to a homeless man hiding under a bridge through a blanket brought to him by a caring minister. He sometimes reveals Himself to a drunk through a servant who cares for him and offers him Living Water. He sometimes reveals Himself to a prostitute through a godly police officer who tells her Christ can set her free.

If we're waiting for the needy to walk through our church doors, we may wait a long time. God doesn't wait for people to come to Him. He goes to them and desires to intervene right at the point of their need. He's looking for a few brave people, like the apostle Paul, who are willing to go rather than wait for them to come. He's not looking for show-offs. He's looking for people through whom He can show off His Son. May we be some of those people.

■ ■ ■ ■

PART VI
TRAVEL TIES AND
HARD GOOD-BYES

■ ■ ■ ■

The apostle Paul's experiences afford the observer golden opportunities to laugh and cry. The next few chapters deliver both. No one could charge the apostle Paul with aloofness and unavailability among those he served. He got completely involved. Our present journey will prove that Paul gave his heart and strength as he ministered to each flock. Even though he knew farewells were inevitable, he still formed deep relationships that would make departures painful. He chose to follow the will of God even when his coworkers begged him not to go.

How I pray that God is having His way in your life. May God enable you to hear Him speak directly to your heart and allow you to sense His tender touch as you study each lesson. He is worthy to be our first priority — our heart's desire.

CHAPTER 26
THE RIOT IN
EPHESUS

Acts 19:24–41

*"You see and hear how this fellow Paul
has convinced and led astray large
numbers of people here in Ephesus and
in practically the whole province of Asia.
He says that man-made gods are no
gods at all."*
(ACTS 19:26)

As we jump back into Acts 19, let's take
another look at several Scriptures I purposely did not emphasize before. Verses 21
and 22 tell us that Paul decided to go to
Jerusalem and then to Rome. He sent Timothy and Erastus to Macedonia, but he
stayed a while longer in Ephesus.

Paul surely knew the heights and depths
in Ephesus. Satan attacked the apostle
relentlessly, but he was no match for the
power of God. Righteousness prevailed,
repentance fell, and Paul had never been

more greatly used. About the time the word of the Lord spread widely and grew in power, Paul's missionary heart began to quicken and draw him elsewhere. For the first time, we see the apostle set his sights on a destination unparalleled in his ministry.

While Paul was in Ephesus, the Emperor Claudius was poisoned and the Roman Empire fell into the hands of a seventeen-year-old boy named Nero. Christians soon suspected he was the Antichrist. Rome would ultimately be an important part of Paul's life. Paul's wisdom told him to go to Rome. God did not want him to miss it, so He also placed a virtually irresistible compulsion in Paul. Just in case the motivations of wisdom and burden were not enough, we are about to see a third: trouble — lots of trouble.

In our study so far, Paul was opposed only twice by the Gentiles. The first case of opposition occurred in Philippi (Acts 16:16–19) when Paul cast the demon from the fortune-telling girl. In Acts 19 a silversmith named Demetrius stirred up opposition because the Christian revival was a threat to the income of those who sold idols. In both Philippi and Ephesus, it was profit that motivated Gentiles to oppose Paul.

Obviously, a person does not have to be

entirely genuine to be effective! Demetrius appealed to the people of Ephesus both financially with the claim that Paul was hurting trade and spiritually with the idea that he was robbing Artemis of her majesty. Demetrius apparently reasoned that one of those two needles would surely hit a vein in everyone. He may have lacked integrity, but he didn't lack intelligence. His approach worked better than he could have dreamed. The people began shouting, "Great is Artemis of the Ephesians!"

In Greek mythology, Artemis was believed to be the daughter of Zeus. The temple the Ephesians had built in her honor was so mammoth, it was later considered one of the Seven Wonders of the Ancient World. The Ephesians exceeded the size of the temple of Artemis, however, with their ability to make a buck in her name. The silver craftsmen were making a fortune off silver charms and statuettes of her likeness. You can be fairly certain most of the merchants cared very little about robbing Artemis of her majesty. You can also be certain the outspoken apostle had assured them she had none.

The scene must have been something to behold. The crowd shouted "Great is Artemis of the Ephesians" for hours. Paul wanted to go into the theater to speak to the crowd, but his friends persuaded him not to go. In the situation I find a number of fascinating clues into the person and personality of Paul.

Based on Paul's willingness to address the crowd (v. 30), we may assume that he sometimes had more courage than sense! He was going to speak out in behalf of Christianity no matter what! The theater in Ephesus held twenty-five thousand people! When God gives us good sense, He expects us to use it. I believe the only time we are to walk into a dangerous or very risky situation is when we have crystal-clear leadership from God.

Also based on verse 30, I believe Paul's disciples were not afraid to disagree with him. He was not a religious dictator who surrounded himself with yes-men. Times obviously existed when his colleagues said no. He was not only a preacher and teacher, he was a discussion leader (see Acts 19:9). Leaders who are afraid of others disagreeing with them usually don't leave much room for discussion.

I am fairly impressed by a third assumption we can make: Paul sometimes let the wisdom of others take precedence over his own desires. We read that Paul's friends would not let him go. If I know anything at all about the apostle, he had to let them not let him! Short of being physically tied down, I can't imagine how they could stop him from going unless he submitted to their wisdom. He could have rebuked them for not believing that speaking up was worth the risk of dying. Instead, he obviously listened to them and relented. I am refreshed by leaders who do not think they always have to be right.

One more assumption I would like to make is based on verse 31. Paul obviously had many good friends. When we began our journey together, I'm not sure any of us pictured Paul as friendly. Although he possessed a passion for Christ and a perseverance in servitude, I never really thought of him as being genuinely gracious. I assumed he was respected far more than he was liked. Paul obviously had good friends from every walk of life: Jews, Gentiles, rich, and poor. Aquila and Priscilla did not leave their home and travel with Paul because he was unpleasant! Obviously, he possessed a genuinely likable personality. Many people surrendered to serve Christ as a direct result of Paul's influence. Had he been an ogre, people would not have been so ready to follow his example.

Verse 31 describes another group of people who were extremely fond of Paul: officials of the province. They loved him enough to beg him not to venture into the theater. Let's learn something about judging others. We tend to describe people in brief phrases: he's always funny, she's always so bossy, he's such a controlling person, she never fails to be upbeat. God created human beings to be the most complex creatures alive. None of us can be wrapped up in a single phrase. Yes, Paul could be unyielding, but he could also be persuaded. He could be tough, and he could be very gracious. He was not so different than the rest of us, perhaps, on any given day!

Meanwhile the crowd of twenty-five thousand Ephesians was a madhouse. The Jews got a man named Alexander to try to make a defense, "But when they realized he was a Jew, they all shouted in unison for about two hours: 'Great is Artemis of the Ephesians!' " (Acts 19:34).

The Jews probably pushed Alexander to the front to provide a disclaimer for them. They wanted him to tell the crowds that Paul's teaching was separate from theirs, and they were not responsible for the financial harm done to the silver craftsmen.

The Jews knew without a doubt that the

silver craftsmen were profiting off the ignorance and sinful practices of pagans. They certainly had a stake in confronting idolatry. Exodus 20:3–4 unmistakably forbids idolatry. Because of their opposition to Paul, however, they violated their own consciences and belief system. Can you relate? Have you ever violated your own conscience or beliefs because you were angry or opposed to something?

Finally, consider the beliefs of the Ephesians. They believed the image of Artemis had fallen from heaven. Some scholars assume they were describing a meteor that hit Ephesus, and the people imagined it looked like a multibreasted woman. Therefore, they assumed it was the goddess Artemis and hailed her as the deity of childbirth. I am sometimes amazed at the things people believe.

About seven years ago I prepared to teach the Book of Genesis in Sunday school. In an attempt to be prepared for questions and rebuttals, I thought I'd study the theory of evolution. I was somewhat intimidated by the prospect, but I checked out a few books and started my research. I only had to flip a few pages before my chin dropped to the ground. At times I even laughed out loud. I couldn't believe the theory is taught as fact in many public schools. After a fairly in-depth comparison, I decided it took far more faith to believe in evolution than creation!

When Paul came to Ephesus, he brought the message of a Messiah sent from God who offers eternal life to every individual who believes. I'm no rocket scientist, but I find Paul's message far more believable than a goddess falling out of heaven in the form of a meteor. Yes, God requires faith — but not as much as a number of other belief systems falling out of the skies today. Go ahead and believe Him. He's very believable.

Chapter 27
A Long-Winded
Preacher

Acts 20:1–12

*Seated in a window was a young man
named Eutychus, who was sinking into a
deep sleep as Paul talked on and on.*
(ACTS 20:9)

I am so amused by our next text. God used
my desire to be like Paul to motivate me to
write this series. So far, I've noticed that
most of the characteristics I share with him
are those of his human rather than his
spiritual nature. A common colloquialism
states, "If the shoe fits, wear it." I don't
know what size shoe you wear; but I can tell
you in advance, this lesson is a size 7
medium. Just my size. Read on. It just may
come in your size too.

In two verses Luke tells us that, after leaving Ephesus, Paul traveled through Macedonia and into Greece where he stayed for
three months. The Jews again plotted against

him as he prepared to sail for Syria, so he took the land route back through Macedonia once more. Counting Luke, eight people accompanied Paul back through Macedonia.

The group spent a week in Troas, culminating in the event I find so humorous and convicting. Paul taught, and because they were going to leave the next day, he talked until midnight. Luke tells us that the upstairs room where they were meeting contained many lamps. A young man named Eutychus fell asleep, fell out the window, "and was picked up dead" (Acts 20:7–9).

You know you aren't having a good day when you fall asleep in church and are picked up dead. Unlike most of us, however, Eutychus stayed dead for only a short while.

Luke wrote meticulously without inclusion of unnecessary details. What bearing do you suppose the lamps had on the account of the midnight meeting? And while we are supposing, can you think of any reasons why God made certain Luke joined Paul in time for this strange set of circumstances?

We want to grasp as accurately as possible the kind of man Paul was. The love of Christ so compelled him that his energy seemed to have no bounds. We will do his memory no harm, however, by pointing out that sometimes his energy exceeded that of his audience. Like many other preachers and teachers, Paul preached longer than his audience was prepared to listen!

Figuratively speaking, at this point I am pulling the shoe out of the box and putting it on my guilty foot. A woman once said to me after one of my lectures, "I'm going home and taking a nap. You've worn me out." Sometimes those of us in teaching, preaching, and speaking positions talk too long. Mind you, we can have the best of intentions. I can entirely relate to the apostle for being so long-winded; this was his last chance, and he was determined to say everything he could before he departed.

In Paul's defense, I must explain one of the pitfalls accompanying the gift of teaching. Teachers often feel that whatever they learn, they must teach — every last word of it! I have forty-five minutes on Sunday mornings during which I often try to teach everything I learned in hours of preparation. Sometimes I've tried to teach all I knew and a lot of things I didn't! Paul obviously didn't always know when to wrap up a message either. Don't you get a kick out of Luke's words "Paul talked on and on"?

I believe God purposely gave us the opportunity to giggle over a fairly typical event: a preacher or teacher outlasting the audience. However, God provided a very effective eye-opener by doing something quite atypical. He gave Paul a chance to raise the dead!

Picture the scene with me a moment. A large group of people were gathered in one room, and the lamps provided just enough heat to make the atmosphere cozy and warm. Most of the listeners had awakened with the rising sun, and the time was now approaching midnight. Eutychus was sitting in the windowsill, trying to stay attentive. The young man's eyelids would drop; then he would force them open. He finally fell into a deep sleep, probably had a dream that caused him to jump, and out the window he flew. This story would not be humorous without the happy ending. Since you know God raised Eutychus from the dead, wouldn't you have loved to see Paul's face when the boy fell out of the window? He ran downstairs as fast as his legs could carry him. "Paul . . . threw himself on the young man and put his arms around him. 'Don't be alarmed,' he said, 'He's alive!' " (Acts 20:10). What a relief! A wonderfully rare phenomenon took place that day.

I find myself amused once again as the

scene ends. Paul went back to business as usual. He climbed three flights of stairs, broke bread with them, and talked until daylight. All in a day's work. I have a feeling no one fell asleep this time. In fact, they may have been wide awake for days! Here is my moral to the story: may God bring back to life whom man hath put to sleep.

For some strange reason, I feel led to be brief with this chapter. Just make me one promise as we conclude: never sit close to a window when working on one of my lessons. Meanwhile, I'll see if I can get this size 7 shoe off my foot and back in the box where it belongs.

CHAPTER 28
A TENDER HEART

Acts 20:13–38

They all wept as they embraced him and kissed him. What grieved them most was his statement that they would never see his face again. Then they accompanied him to the ship.
(ACTS 20:37–38)

Already I am being tested on our previous lesson! This text is so rich that I could keep talking until midnight. After his eventful night in Troas, Paul set sail on his journey toward Jerusalem. He purposely sailed past Ephesus, yet he summoned the elders to come to Miletus and meet with him.

Paul had little time; so he left the Ephesian elders the basic necessities. Like a father with moments left to share his heart with his children, Paul shared things that were priority to him. He reminded them of his attention to them. He shared his as-

258

sumptions, his ambition, his heartfelt admonition, and his deep affection. Let's look at each of these priorities. You'll notice first his attention to them. He said, "You know how I lived the whole time I was with you, . . . I served the Lord with great humility and with tears, . . . You know that I have not hesitated to preach anything that would be helpful to you" (Acts 20:18–20).

I believe Paul was personally attentive to the Ephesians because he became involved with them emotionally as well as spiritually. Remember, he remained among these people for several years. I believe he poured himself out among them as much or more than any other group to whom he ministered. They saw his *humility*. The word involves "the confession of his sin and a deep realization of his unworthiness to receive God's marvelous grace." He was open with them about his past sin and his feelings of unworthiness in the ministry God had given him. They not only saw his humility, they saw his heart. He did not hide from them his tears or the pain of his hardships.

The Ephesians knew Paul was genuine. He approached them withholding nothing. He did not hesitate to preach anything that would be helpful. He loved them enough to teach them anything and everything that would be of benefit, even if they didn't like it. He was willing to hurt their feelings momentarily, if it would help their hearts eternally.

Paul had given them everything he had while he was there. In verse 27, he restated: "For I have not hesitated to proclaim to you the whole will of God." He didn't just teach them the many wonderful things God wanted to do for them. He also taught them the truth about hardships that would inevitably come and the calling of the crucified life.

In his attentiveness, Paul withheld nothing from the Ephesians. Next he told them of his assumption for the future: "And now, compelled by the Spirit, I am going to Jerusalem, not knowing what will happen to me there. I only know that in every city the Holy Spirit warns me that prison and hardships are facing me" (Acts 20:22–23).

Paul assumed he was bound to have difficulties in Jerusalem because the Holy Spirit had warned him of hardships in every other city. He couldn't imagine Jerusalem being an exception. In fact, he probably assumed he would have more problems than ever as he returned to Jerusalem.

He also assumed he would never see the

Ephesians again. I have a feeling he might have feared he would be put to death in Jerusalem. Some scholars believe he did see the Ephesians once more. Others believe he did not. At this point he spoke to them as if he would never see them again.

Next Paul shared with them his chief ambition: "If only I may finish the race and complete the task the Lord Jesus has given me" (Acts 20:24). He was so determined to be faithful to the task God had assigned him, his certainty of suffering could not dissuade him.

Fear is a very powerful tool. Don't think for a moment Satan did not try to use fear to hinder the apostle from fulfilling God's purposes, and don't think Paul was not terrified at times. Of course he was. To think otherwise would minimize his faithfulness. Paul was afraid, but his love for Christ exceeded his fear of suffering and death. His primary ambition was finishing his task faithfully. Notice the phrase in verse 24: "the task the Lord Jesus has given me." Paul felt no responsibility to complete the task Christ had given Peter, or Barnabas, or Timothy. He believed and taught that God has specific plans for each believer. He expressed the concept clearly in Ephesians 2:10: "We are God's workmanship, created in Christ Jesus to do good works, which God prepared in advance for us to do."

God has a task for you — one He planned very long ago and suited for our present generation. Remember you are not responsible for completing anyone else's task, just yours. God desires for us to encourage one another in our tasks (see Heb. 10:24–25), but we are responsible only for completing our own.

Believing he would never see the Ephesians again, Paul not only shared with them his attentions, his assumptions, and his ambitions, he had an urgency to share with them an admonition. He warned the Ephesian elders about the vulnerability of the young church (Acts 20:25–31). He told them to expect savage wolves to try to devour the flock. Paul considered the warning so vital, he repeated it over and over during the three years he was among them.

Don't miss an important part of his admonition. In verse 28, Paul named two groups the elders were to keep watch over: themselves and the flock God had given them. What an important message Paul's words send to us! We can hardly keep watch over a group if we don't keep watch over ourselves! The Greek term for "keep watch" is *prosecho*. "As a nautical term, it means to hold a ship in a direction, to sail towards . . . to hold on one's course toward a place." Many leaders have seasons when their lives seem temporarily out of control. Most people who have served God for decades have had a season in which they got off course. Those who never depart from the course in many years of service deserve our highest commendations, but they are rare.

I do not believe a leader who temporarily veers away from the course should never be allowed to lead again. I can't find a biblical precedent for such thinking. On the other hand, we are wise leaders to step out of leadership when we are having a difficult time staying on the course. We simply cannot lead others to a place to which we are not steering our own lives. Yes, leaders must watch over their own lives very carefully; but Paul also told them they must act like shepherds keeping watch over their flocks.

We don't have to be church elders for these words and warnings to apply to us. If God has assigned you a flock, you have a serious responsibility to keep a close watch over your own life and to care deeply for theirs. A crucial part of keeping watch over our flocks is knowing the Word of God! Back in Acts 20:30, Paul warned that "men will arise and distort the truth." The word *distort* denotes an action of twisting or turning. Satan is a master at twisting and turning the Word of God. He's been honing his twisting skills since his first successful attempt in the Garden of Eden. He subtly twists the Word in hope that we won't realize we've been misled until after he wreaks havoc. Paul had very little time to address the Ephesian elders, yet the warning to watch over themselves and their flocks was an absolute priority.

Paul shared one last element with the Ephesians. He shared his sincere affection for them. The final picture painted at the end of Acts 20 touches my heart so much. Paul was a man of many words, but the primary message of his affection for the Ephesians came more in action than in words. Any man as beloved as Paul had most assuredly loved. He was the very one who taught others, "Love never fails" (1 Cor. 13:8). I wonder if at this moment he thought love also never fails to hurt. He committed them to God, said a few last words, then knelt with them and prayed.

Don't quickly pass by this moment. Let it take form in your mind. Imagine a group of men, replete with all the things that make them men — size, stature, strength, controlled emotions — on their knees praying together. Thankfully, this is not a picture I have trouble imagining. My pastor often asks the men of our church to join him at the altar down on their knees in prayer. As a woman in the church, nothing makes me feel more secure. To me, a man is his tallest when he is down on his knees in prayer.

Imagine the next scene between Paul and the elders. "They all wept as they embraced him and kissed him" (Acts 20:37). One by one each man hugged him and said good-bye. With every embrace I'm sure he remembered something special — a good laugh shared, a late night over a sick loved one, a baptism in a cold river, a heated argument resolved. He had been their shepherd. Now he would leave them to tend their flocks on their own. In the midst of painful good-byes, perhaps Paul thought what I have a time or two when my heart was hurting. Perhaps he thought, *I will never let myself get this involved again.* But, of course, he did. And so will we, if we continue to walk in the footsteps of our Savior. To extend hands of service without hearts of love is virtually meaningless.

The chapter concludes with Paul and his friends walking side by side down the path to the docks, beards still wet with tears. Had

I been Paul, I would have gotten on that ship as quickly as possible and dared not look back. That's not what happened. Luke opens the next chapter with the words, "After we had torn ourselves away from them, we put out to sea and sailed straight to Cos" (Acts 21:1). I think Luke, who was waiting at the boat (see Acts 20:13), literally had to go and tear the apostle away from them.

Obviously, the Ephesians had some idea how blessed they were to have the kind of leader Paul was to them. He was a leader who kept watch over himself and his followers. In nautical terms, the best kind of captain. One who kept the vessel on course even if his compass took him far from those he loved. He had given them all he had. The best kind of good-bye is the kind with no regrets.

CHAPTER 29
FROM THE MOUTHS
OF PROPHETS

Acts 21:1–16

Then Paul answered, "Why are you weeping and breaking my heart? I am ready not only to be bound, but also to die in Jerusalem for the name of the Lord Jesus."
(ACTS 21:13)

In Acts 21, we board so many ships with Paul, we could develop sea legs. Paul and his companions pursued and completed a grueling maritime journey back to Palestine. I think women can be a touch too practical. I find myself wondering how Paul and his associates washed their clothes. I wonder if Paul suffered in ways he deemed too ordinary to share with us. Did he experience seasickness? I would almost rather be beaten than be seasick. Our protagonist probably suffered in big and small ways more times than he could re-

267

count (see 2 Cor. 11:26).

Look at your map for a moment. We saw Paul with the Ephesian elders at Miletus where he set sail. Paul's immediate goal was Jerusalem. Ultimately he felt compelled to go on to Rome. As you can see, Miletus is quite a distance from Jerusalem. Based on Acts 21, the trip took several weeks. Like us, Paul probably wished he could skip the tiring travel and miraculously show up at his destination. As usual, God had far more important plans. He had meaningful encounters along the way. You see, to God, our journey is as important as our destination. As we seek to know His will and go where He sends us, God doesn't just wait for us at our next stop. He travels every mile right beside us.

Although Paul had the opportunity to stretch his legs at several ports on his way to Jerusalem, he disembarked twice for a number of days. His first lengthy stop was not by choice. Because the first boat made so many stops, the traveling preachers sought out a vessel going straight across to Phoenicia (Acts 21:2), hoping to save time. To their dismay the ship docked in Tyre for seven days to unload cargo. Have you ever noticed how often God has a blessing on the unscheduled stops along our way? God had a blessing waiting for Paul and the others on their unscheduled stop.

Acts 21:4 tells us that Paul sought out the Christian disciples in Tyre so that he and his men would have a place to stay. Acts 11:19 tells how Christians had been planted in Phoenicia, the region in which Tyre was located. They were scattered by the same wave of persecution in which Stephen was martyred.

Don't forget how deeply Paul, then known as Saul, had been involved in the persecution that caused these believers to scatter. Had they heard about the amazing convert, or did they believe he was still a terrible threat? Either way, they were surprised to lay eyes on the sea-weary travelers. I never cease to be amazed at the hospitality of believers in the New Testament church. Even in my grandmother's day, she and many others often opened their homes to total strangers who needed a place to rest for a night on their long travels. I am saddened by our loss of hospitality today. The disciples in Phoenicia opened their homes to Paul and his fellow travelers. Their hearts were so instantly bound with his, they begged him not to go to Jerusalem.

Paul had been "compelled by the Spirit" (Acts 20:22) to go on to Jerusalem. Yet Acts

21:4 says, "Through the Spirit they urged Paul not to go." Don't let this expression confuse you. I don't believe they were saying the Holy Spirit did not want Paul to travel to Jerusalem. I believe the Holy Spirit burdened their hearts with an awareness that trouble lay ahead. Therefore, they concluded the apostle should certainly avoid it. To Paul's credit, once he determined the will of God, no amount of flesh and blood could stop him. When the ship was ready to set sail, he was ready to board it.

This time, entire families of believers accompanied him to the harbor. Can you imagine what a sight this scene must have been for others to behold? Men, women, and children kneeling in the sand praying with one heart and mind for the apostle and his beloved associates. Just picture what the sand must have looked like after Paul boarded the ship and the crowd went back home. Footprints leading to and from the shore. Then nothing but kneeprints clustered together in the damp sand. A sight for God to behold. Long after the tide washed away every print, the power of those prayers was still at work.

We want to focus on Paul's second lengthy stop. Acts 21:8 tells us Paul and the others disembarked in Caesarea and stayed in the house of Philip. He was an evangelist and one of the seven. We can learn volumes about this mighty man of God from these two expressions. Philip is first mentioned in Acts 6:5 in the list of the seven. Not only was Philip a Spirit-filled Christian and a very wise man, he was also an extremely effective evangelist. We can compile something of a profile based on Acts 8:26–40. When we see his faithfulness, it is no wonder he had four daughters who prophesied. We considered the rich heritage Timothy received from his mother and grandmother. Philip's faithfulness obviously had a similar effect on his daughters.

Young people are far more likely to surrender their lives to serve God when they have seen genuine examples firsthand. Many are touched by the faithfulness of youth ministers, Sunday school teachers, and pastors, but nothing can match the lasting impact of a faithful parent. If my children don't think I'm genuine, no one else's opinion matters to me. On the front page of my Bible, I've written a reminder I'm forced to see every time I open it: "No amount of success in ministry will make up for failure at home."

You may be wondering if Paul had to be resuscitated when he met four women who prophesied. In his defense, I would like to say that Paul was the first to recognize women with the gift of prophecy (when he taught spiritual gifts in 1 Cor. 11). A study of the entire life and ministry of Paul reveals an interesting fact. He had a vastly different outlook and attitude toward women than many people suppose. Unfortunately many people have based their thinking about him on a couple of excerpts from his writings. If Paul had disapproved of Philip's four daughters, he would have been the first to tell him!

What exactly were Philip's daughters doing anyway? What does prophesying mean? The original word for "prophesying" is *propheteuo,* which means "to declare truths through the inspiration of God's Holy Spirit. . . . To tell forth God's message." A prophet is a "proclaimer, one who speaks out the counsel of God with the clearness, energy, and authority." In ancient days, prior to His completed revelation, God often used prophets or "proclaimers" to warn people about the future. Virtually all God wanted foretold, He ultimately inspired in His written Word, the Bible; so the gift of prophecy is most often used today as the proclamation of God's truth. Whether or not they foretold any part of the future, Philip's four daughters — in today's terms

— were Christian speakers!

Both the Old and New Testaments speak of prophetesses. Although the concept is not new, I believe with all my heart that God is using something old to do something new. Recently I've had the strangest feeling that God is up to something unique in the body of Christ. He seems to be raising up a strong remnant of well-equipped servants. We see great movements of God among both men and women, not only in this nation but around the world. Yes, many who are not serious are falling away. At the same time a wonderful remnant of godly people is hitting their knees in repentance, then standing up to fight the good fight around the globe.

In Acts 2:18, God said He would pour out His Spirit on both men and women. I believe the growing numbers of strong Christian men and women speakers are examples of God's fulfillment of His promise. I am convinced we are living in the midst of a significant work of God on His kingdom calendar.

Let's turn our attentions now to another prophet Paul encountered at the house of Philip. His name was Agabus. Like Ezekiel of old, Agabus delivered his message through an enacted parable. By tying his own hands and feet, Agabus predicted that imprisonment awaited Paul in Jerusalem.

Agabus must have been extremely convincing, because his actions had a far greater impact than the disciples' words in Tyre. On his last stop, although Luke and the others accompanied Paul to Tyre, only the Phoenician disciples urged him not to go to Jerusalem (see Acts 21:4).

In Caesarea, after Agabus's prophetic performance, Luke, the other missionaries, and the people all urged Paul not to go (Acts 21:12).

In turn, Paul also responded with strong emotion. Though he could hardly tear himself away from the Ephesian elders in Acts 20:37, he never wavered in his resolve. He also remained unmoved when the disciples in Tyre urged him not to go. Yet we see him respond with enormous emotion when his beloved associates — Luke, Timothy, and the others — wept and pleaded with him not to go. Let's try to capture an accurate picture. These men were not just crying. The original word for "weeping" is the strongest expression of grief in the Greek language. These men were sobbing. Paul responded tenderly, "Why are you weeping and breaking my heart?" (Acts 21:13).

Have you experienced a time when someone desperately wanted you to do something that you could not do? If so, then you have some idea of how Paul felt. Paul's beloved friends were so crushed over what awaited him, their strength dissolved, their noble sense of purpose disintegrated, and they begged him not to go. Had he not been so convinced of the Spirit's compelling him to go, he surely would have changed his mind. He voiced his determination to each of them: "I am ready not only to be bound, but also to die in Jerusalem for the name of the Lord Jesus" (v. 13b).

Have you begged and pleaded with God for something you are realizing you're not going to get? Do you sometimes feel you must give up and just let the Lord's will be done? We sometimes feel as if we're playing tug-of-war with God. In bitter tears we sometimes let go of the rope, tumble to the ground, and cry, "Have your way, God! You're going to do what You want anyway!"

God is not playing a game. He doesn't jerk on the rope just so He can win. In fact, He doesn't want us to let go of the rope at all. Rather than see us drop the rope and give up, He wants us to hang on and let Him pull us over to His side. God's will is always best even when we cannot imagine how. Surrendering to His will does not mean you lose. Ultimately, it means you win. Keep hanging on to that rope and let Him pull you over to His side. One day you'll understand. And you'll see His glory.

CHAPTER 30
A PROPHECY
FULFILLED

Acts 21:17–36

The whole city was aroused, and the people came running from all directions. Seizing Paul, they dragged him from the temple, and immediately the gates were shut.
(ACTS 21:30)

Over the objections of the other believers, Paul set his face to go to Jerusalem. He insisted, "I am ready not only to be bound, but also to die in Jerusalem for the name of the Lord Jesus" (Acts 21:13b). Luke notes that, "When he would not be dissuaded, we gave up and said, 'The Lord's will be done.' " So they accompanied Paul on the journey.

Had Paul's arrival in Jerusalem been a performance, he certainly would have received mixed reviews. The apostle encountered three distinct responses to his coming:

acceptance, apprehension, and accusation.

1. *Paul met acceptance.* What blessed words: "When we arrived at Jerusalem, the brothers received us warmly" (v. 17). Don't miss Luke's terminology, "When we arrived." After being unsuccessful in their attempt to plead with Paul to avoid Jerusalem, one would not be surprised if Paul's companions had said, "You go ahead if you want. The rest of us refuse to be so foolish."

Nearly thirty years earlier, Christ's disciples also tried to talk Him out of going back to Judea when they knew trouble awaited Him. When He could not be dissuaded, Thomas said, " 'Let us also go, that we may die with him' " (John 11:16). Neither group was called to give their lives in association with their leader at this point, but surely God acknowledged their willingness.

What a sigh of relief must have come when Paul and his associates were greeted with warmth and approval by the believers in Jerusalem. Only one verse attests to Paul's testimony to James, the elders, and the others (Acts 21:19), but you can assume he talked for some time. "Paul reported in detail what God had done among the Gentiles." The hearts of James and the others are evident in their reception of his testimony: "they praised God" (v. 20). Notice, they did not praise Paul. Unfortunately, acceptance was not the only response Paul met.

2. *Paul met apprehension.* After hearing Paul's wonderful news, James and the elders had good news of their own, and a little bad news. They gave Paul the good news first: "Many thousands of Jews have believed" (v. 20). What glorious words! What could Paul have wanted more? According to Romans 9:3, absolutely nothing! He would have agreed to be cursed forever if the Jews would accept Christ. I wonder if Paul immediately began shouting hallelujah and dancing and praising God; regardless, they jumped quickly to the bad news. They almost seemed to be sparing his dignity. Yes, many had believed in Christ, but James and the elders observed, "All of them are zealous for the law. . . . But they have been informed that you . . . [tell] them not to live according to our customs" (vv. 20–21). In other words, they're saved — but they're mad. Talk about throwing a bucket of ice water on a warm reception.

This dilemma draws compassion from my heart for both James and Paul. I feel compassion for James. We have all been in his position. He was caught in the middle of anger and disagreement between people he cared about. Just imagine the gnawing in James's stomach as Paul was giving a detailed account of all God was doing among the Gentiles. James knew he would have to tell Paul about the Jews.

When was the last time you were stuck in the middle of a situation involving Christians on both sides? Like James, you may have felt responsible for the resolution of the entire issue. He was the leader of the Jerusalem church. He understood how both sides felt.

I also feel compassion for Paul. He expected opposition from unbelievers, but to be hit immediately in Jerusalem by the disapproval of fellow believers must have drained his energy and excitement. Furthermore, much of what they were saying about him wasn't even accurate. He never told Jewish Christians not to circumcise their children. He told them not to insist that Gentile Christians circumcise theirs! He was trying to make the point that circumcision had nothing whatsoever to do with salvation.

Perhaps you know how Paul felt when he met disapproval among his own and found he had been misunderstood. Have you ever thought, *I expected this kind of thing from unbelievers, but I wasn't expecting this from my own fellow believers?* If so, you are a part of a large fraternity, with Paul as a charter member.

James and the elders immediately suggested that Paul join four men in their purification rites, so that all would see he still respected the customs. Paul submitted to their authority and did as they asked. His point regarding the ancient Hebrew customs was to practice them when wise or observe them as a reminder but not to live under them as a burden and a means of salvation.

Several times in Paul's ministry he was placed in a similar position with both Jews and Gentiles. He explained his actions in 1 Corinthians 9:19–23. He said that though he was free in Christ, he made himself a slave to everyone, to win as many as possible. He said he became like a Jew to the Jews, to win the Jews and like a Gentile to the Gentiles, to win the Gentiles. Paul's great summary statement challenges every believer: "I have become all things to all men so that by all possible means I might save some" (1 Cor. 9:22).

Like Paul, each of us must seek the common ground with those who do not know Christ. We can respond legalistically and shun harmless practices, but if we do, we risk alienating the very people we want to reach.

One of the most crucial elements foreign missionaries must learn is cultural sensitivity. Such sensitivity means, when possible, not putting obstacles in the way of reaching others for Christ. Knowing how to apply Paul's standard of "all things to all men" requires both spiritual maturity and sensitivity. Ask the Holy Spirit to guide as you build witnessing relationships while maintaining appropriate standards.

Paul met welcome acceptance from some believers in Jerusalem. He met discouraging apprehension from others. Sadly, he also met a third reception.

3. *Paul met accusation.* Now we see the apostle meet another response in Jerusalem. Imagine the moment. Paul and the Asian Jews, who had given him trouble in Ephesus, saw each other (Acts 21:27). I have a feeling Paul thought, *Oh, no!* and the Asian Jews thought, *Oh, yes!*

These were from the same group who had caused the riot in Ephesus (Acts 19:8–9, 33). Now they stirred up the crowd in the temple by shouting: "Men of Israel, help us! This is the man who teaches all men everywhere against our people and our law and this place. And besides, he has brought Greeks into the temple area and defiled this holy place" (Acts 21:28).

The entire city fell into an uproar, and they grabbed Paul and tried to beat him to death. Can you imagine what the apostle was thinking? Surrounded by such a mob, I'm sure he thought he was about to draw his last breath. I can hardly imagine being beaten by one person. What would it be like to be beaten by a gang?

I am sobered when I see how God used pagans or unbelievers to rescue one of His own. The Roman commander arrived and arrested Paul, probably much to the apostle's relief.

Did Paul recall the image of the prophet Agabus tied up with his belt? Paul had expected to be seized, but I'm not sure expectation and preparation are always synonymous. I don't think Paul was prepared for a mob to keep shouting, "Away with such a fellow" (Acts 22:22 KJV). Was he ready for hatred and wholesale rejection by the people he would have given his life for? I'm not sure how adequately a person can prepare for such pain.

Later, in his letter to the Philippians (3:10), Paul made a reference to wanting the fellowship of sharing in Christ's sufferings. Paul received Christ by faith. He knew Christ by name. He came face-to-face with Christ through experience. He spoke to Him through prayer. He grew in Him through the Word. But this particular day, Paul experienced a fellowship in His sufferings unlike any he had ever encountered.

Both Christ and Paul knew suffering was inevitable. Both Christ and Paul knew they would end up giving their lives: One as the Savior of the world, the other as His servant. Both Christ and Paul grieved over Jerusalem. Both Christ and Paul felt compelled to return to the holy city. Both Christ and Paul knew the horror of being swept up in an angry mob. Both Christ and Paul experienced the "newness" of every rejection.

No matter how many times it comes, one can hardly prepare for people who wish you dead. Paul did not know what would happen to him, but he knew Christ. As the apostle fellowshipped in His sufferings, he had never known Jesus better.

■ ■ ■ ■

PART VII
A WALK OF FAITH

■ ■ ■ ■

In the chapters to come we see Paul under very stressful circumstances. God ordained the apostle's ministry before he was born. He prepared Paul with certain assets for ministry under the influence of the Holy Spirit. Paul was a traveling man. Most of us prefer one consistent place of service. The apostle's soul burned for the next assignment and the next venue. Few men would have found imprisonment more difficult than did the apostle Paul. I am sure he did not enjoy having his ministerial wings clipped, yet he maintained his testimony.

We will witness a man of integrity as we try to imagine being on trial for our faith. Stay teachable; bring your imagination as we discuss a faith that endures trials and prospers as a result. Stay sensitive to times when your faith may be tried.

CHAPTER 31
A WILLING WITNESS

Acts 21:37–22:30

*You will be his witness to all men of what
you have seen and heard.*
(ACTS 22:15)

For the next few chapters we will consider
Paul's experiences in Jerusalem. On a human scale we cannot judge his visit a success. Perhaps Paul's experiences in places
like Athens and Jerusalem will teach us to
think differently about success and failure.
Hopefully, we will come to understand that,
in our Christian lives, success is obedience
to God, not results we can measure.

I'm sure Paul wanted to bear fruit in
Jerusalem more than any place on earth. Yet
we see him face greater opposition and
struggle in Jerusalem than virtually anywhere in his ministry. In the holy city Paul
was forced to measure his ministry strictly

on his obedience to the Spirit, not outward results.

The commander mistook Paul for an Egyptian terrorist and ordered him taken to the barracks. Earlier, an Egyptian who claimed to be a prophet persuaded four thousand people to follow him and commit acts of terrorism. He led them to the top of the Mount of Olives, promising that the walls of Jerusalem would collapse at his command. Of course, no such miracle occurred. Instead, the Roman army surrounded them, killing some and capturing others but allowing the Egyptian leader to get away.[1]

Paul was an ambassador of reconciliation (see 2 Cor. 5:19–20). We will never know how he felt when he was mistaken for a leader of terrorists. We do know that he boldly asked for an opportunity to speak to the people. Moments earlier these people beat him with their fists. Paul did not ask God to rain down fire from heaven to consume them. He did not ask God to open the earth and swallow them. He asked nothing but a chance to give his testimony. He desired to overcome their hardened hearts by the word of his testimony (see Rev. 12:11).

Acts 22:3–22 contains Paul's account of

his Damascus-road conversion. His approach contains several elements that build a powerful testimony. We can learn from the following four elements in sharing our own testimonies.

1. *Paul communicated simply and clearly.* Paul spoke in Greek to the commander and in Aramaic to the Jews. Few of us are fluent in several languages, but we can apply his example by learning to communicate more effectively by speaking the language of our hearers.

I grew up going to Sunday school and church. I spent much of my early social life with other Christians, so I had a difficult time learning to speak a language an unchurched person could understand. My speech was so laced with church terms that those unacquainted with church life could hardly understand me. I practically needed an interpreter!

I still have to remind myself to resist assuming every listener knows the lingo. I'm learning to use figures of speech and expressions that lost people will more likely understand. I'm also, like, you know, learning to use more contemporary expressions when speaking to youth. Of course, learning to speak understandably does not mean adopting any level of vulgarity. It means speaking with a greater level of clarity.

2. *Paul honestly described his former conduct.* We lose our listeners the moment they sense an attitude of superiority in us. Paul spoke with honesty and humility. As he explained his background and his persecutions of the church, he related with them as one who had been exactly where they were. Not all of us have a background as dramatically different from our present lifestyles as Paul did, yet we have all been lost. Lost is lost.

Remember an important principle about sharing our former conduct. Generalizations usually are best. I try to avoid becoming specific about ungodly actions in my past. I want the listener to focus on my Savior, not my behavior. Sometimes we glorify ungodly behavior by highlighting how bad we were. This method can dishonor God, and it can dishonor the listener by stirring unnecessary mental images of sin. Share past conduct with caution!

3. *Paul related his experience of conversion.* Few of us have experienced the dramatic conversion Paul described in Acts 22:6–16, but we can tell how we accepted Christ. Don't think your testimony is meaningless if you didn't have a dramatic conversion. Every conversion cost the same

amount of Christ's blood shed on the cross. Yours is just as meaningful as the most dramatic conversion ever told.

In the parable of the prodigal son, the elder brother felt insulted because the father accepted his brother after a season of wild living (Luke 15:29–30). He didn't understand the biggest difference between the two brothers was that the prodigal son had to live with the personal loss and suffering. If your conversion was less sensational than others, praise God for less drama! With it probably came less pain! You don't have to see a bright light from heaven to have a story to tell. The determining factor is not how exciting your conversion was but how excited you are now about your conversion.

4. *Paul shared how he received his commission.* He was very clear that God had a purpose for his life. People we talk to need to know there is life after salvation! Salvation is not only about eternity. Salvation is also the open door to a rich earthly life in which we enjoy the love and direction of an active God. Many unbelievers are repelled by Christianity because they are afraid they will have to give up so much. As we share our testimonies, we can help them see all we've gained. Make your sense of ongoing purpose a part of your testimony. We often

have no idea how much people are struggling to find reason to live and persevere through difficulty.

Unfortunately, the Jews didn't think much of Paul's purpose on this earth. Once he acknowledged the importance of the Gentiles to God, he lost his audience. Sadly, their personal need to feel superior exceeded their spiritual sensibilities.

Paul desperately wanted the Jews to receive Christ. Was he a failure because they rejected him? Was his testimony shared in vain? Absolutely not. God compelled Paul to go to Jerusalem. He warned him of hardships. He gave Paul an opportunity to give his testimony to the very people who had just tried to kill him.

Did they hear Paul's message? Oh, yes. Otherwise, they would not have responded so emotionally. Few of those in hearing distance that day forgot Paul's testimony. We cannot judge effectiveness from immediate results. According to John 14:26, the Holy Spirit can remind a person of truth taught long ago. When we obey God, we find great comfort in leaving the consequences up to Him.

Paul avoided a flogging because God equipped him with Roman citizenship even before his birth. God used every ounce and detail of Paul's past, even his unique citizenship. I want God to use every ounce of me too. Paul poured himself out like a drink offering in Jerusalem. He received little encouragement to preach while he was there — but he continued. Paul's certainty of what he had been called to do was exceeded only by his certainty of who called. Paul considered Him who called worth it all.

Do you have a tendency to rate your own testimony or read your own results? Your personal story about Christ is worth telling. If you are excited about it, others are likely to find your testimony exciting too. However, their reactions are not your responsibility. Sometimes I have to remind myself that I was never called to be the Holy Spirit. He will convict. He will remind. Don't do His job, but faithfully do yours. Go tell your story. No one can tell it like you.

CHAPTER 32
IN ALL GOOD
CONSCIENCE

Acts 23:1–11

*"My brothers, I have fulfilled my duty to
God in all good conscience to this day."*
(ACTS 23:1)

During his stay in Jerusalem, Paul had no
need to make a living. God had already
booked him a room in the city jail. Interestingly, his imprisonment was clearly the
shield God used to keep Paul from being
torn limb from limb by his adversaries. God
did not allow the apostle to be jailed to his
harm but to provide a means of safety for
him while allowing him to share his testimony in the highest courts. In an attempt
to discover the reasons for the accusations
the Jews were making against Paul, the commander ordered all the chief priests and the
Sanhedrin to assemble so Paul could stand
before them. We look at a brief segment in
the Book of Acts in this chapter, but it will

introduce a pertinent topical study.

Acts 23:1–11 leads us to suspect that Paul could spar with the best of them! The scene unfolds with Paul addressing the chief priests and Sanhedrin with the words, "My brothers, I have fulfilled my duty to God in all good conscience to this day" (Acts 23:1). Ananias immediately had Paul struck in the mouth!

Why was Ananias so insulted? Was it because Paul referred to them as "brothers"? Or could it have been because Paul was indirectly suggesting a conscience check for everyone listening?

Unfortunately, we don't have the benefit of hearing Paul's voice inflection. His response instantly following the slap suggests he might have been ready for an altercation. "God will strike you, you whitewashed wall!" (v. 3). I'm quite sure the temperature in the room rose dramatically.

After Paul called Ananias a whitewashed wall, those standing close to him said, " 'You dare to insult God's high priest?' " Don't miss Paul's response. " 'I did not realize that he was the high priest.' "

If we could have heard Paul's voice, I believe his inflection might have contained a little sarcasm. No doubt Paul knew he was insulting the high priest. He was far too knowledgeable not to have recognized Ananias's robes and obvious position of honor. I believe he knew he was insulting the high priest and probably offended him further by saying, in effect, "Sorry, but I never would have recognized this guy as a high priest."

I'm suggesting Paul may have been in an interesting mood, and if I may be so bold, even a touch of an insolent mood. Interestingly, history records this Ananias (not to be confused with the man by the same name in Acts 9) as a very insolent and hot-tempered man. Have you ever noticed our occasional tendency to adopt our foes' tactics? If they lose control of their mouths, sometimes we follow suit.

I mean absolutely no disrespect to the apostle, but I believe he sometimes struggled with a temper. The sight of the false piety of the religious leaders probably made his stomach turn — especially because he had been one of them. I have one more reason for believing Paul might have been in a confrontational mood.

Paul carefully voiced the reason he was on trial as his "hope in the resurrection of the dead" (v. 6). Actually, the greater issue was his belief in someone far superior to Moses. His hope was in the One who had fulfilled all obligations to the Law — the promised Messiah who had died and risen from the dead. Paul had a very distinct motive for bringing up the volatile subject of life after death. He knew the resurrection of the dead was the biggest point of contention between the Pharisees and the Sadducees. Paul manipulated the spotlight off of their grievances with him and onto their grievances with each other. He accomplished two goals:

1. he divided his enemy, diminishing their strength, and
2. he caused the Pharisees to suddenly side with him.

Whether or not Paul planned an altercation, the disagreement got out of hand. The commander was so afraid they would tear Paul "to pieces" that he rushed the apostle back to the barracks. Once again, God used Paul's incarceration as protection.

Whether or not I am right about Paul's mood and motive, one point is unarguable: he wanted the religious leaders to know that his conscience was clear. As we study the life of the apostle, we will learn volumes by noting his priorities. A clear conscience was no doubt one of them, as he spoke often of it in his letters. How important is a clear conscience? Peace of mind cannot exist without it!

The Greek word for "conscience" is *suneidesis,* which means "to be one's own witness, one's own conscience coming forward as a witness. It denotes an abiding consciousness whose nature it is to bear witness to one's own conduct in a moral sense. It is self-awareness." In lay terms we might say the conscience is an inner constituent casting a vote about the rightness of our behaviors. God's Word helps us compile several facts concerning the conscience:

1. *People without a spotless past can enjoy a clear conscience.* What wonderful news! Paul spoke of possessing a clear conscience numerous times, yet he considered himself one of the worst possible offenders. His conscience was clear even though he had wronged many people in the past. A clear conscience is possible for those of us who have sinned.

2. *Good deeds cannot accomplish a clear conscience.* Have you ever tried to worship or serve God when your conscience was bothering you after an unsettled argument with your spouse or a coworker? Or perhaps after telling a lie to someone?

Hebrews 9:9 tells us of two things that

will never clear the conscience of the worshiper: gifts and sacrifices. We've all probably tried to soothe our consciences with good works. God's Word tells us we cannot offer enough gifts or sacrifices to clear a guilty conscience. Take heart! The Bible does give us some steps to a clear conscience.

3. *The Holy Spirit works with the believer's conscience.* The Holy Spirit plays a critical role in creating and maintaining a clear conscience. In Romans 9:1, Paul said the Holy Spirit confirmed his conscience. Once we have received Christ and the Holy Spirit resides within us, the Holy Spirit will work with our consciences. The Spirit works both to confirm a clear conscience and to convict a guilty conscience.

We all naturally prefer to ignore our sin. The one part of us that does not ignore sin is our conscience. For that reason the Holy Spirit deals with conscience first, not with our intellect or emotions. You might think of the relationship this way: the Holy Spirit plants conviction in the soil of the conscience. If ignored, that conviction will usually grow and grow.

4. *The conscience is an indicator, not a transformer.* Only the Holy Spirit can change us and clear our consciences. By itself, all

the conscience can do with a guilty person is condemn. My conscience may lend an awareness of what I ought to do, but it supplies little power to do it. The believer possesses something far greater than a conscience. The Holy Spirit who resides in us supplies abundant power not only to recognize the right thing, but to do it!

Can we really have clear consciences? The Bible says we can. Considering Paul's past, if he can have a clear conscience, any of us can. Like me, you may have discovered that asking God for forgiveness doesn't always make you feel better. Sometimes we know we're forgiven, but we still feel a load of guilt. How can we discover the freedom of a clear conscience? I believe Hebrews 10:22 holds several vital keys: "Let us draw near to God with a sincere heart in full assurance of faith, having our hearts sprinkled to cleanse us from a guilty conscience and having our bodies washed with pure water." Consider these steps to a clear conscience.

1. *Bring your heavy conscience to God.* When we have a guilty conscience, we shy away from the presence of God. We tend to resist what we need most: an awareness of God's love! Draw near to God!

2. *Approach God with absolute sincerity.* Come entirely clean before Him. Spill your heart and confess everything you feel. Tell Him about the guilt that continues to nag at you. You'll not only clear your heart and mind, you'll tattle on the evil one who has no right to keep accusing you after repentance.
3. *Ask God to give you full assurance of His love and acceptance.* In His Word, God tells you over and over how much He loves you. He assures you of forgiveness. He also tells you He forgets your confessed sin. Ask God to give you faith to take Him at His Word. You need not fear rejection or ridicule. Let Him reassure you of His love and forgiveness.

Picture the cross of Christ once more. Really take a good mental look at it. Was Christ's death on the cross enough to cover your sin? Enough to take away your guilt? Yes. He gave everything He had for everything we've said, done, or thought. Then picture yourself at the foot of His cross, close enough to have your heart cleansed by His redemptive blood. No sin is too grievous. No load is too heavy for Christ to carry. Walk away free, and leave with God that old condemning tape you've been playing over and over on your mental "recorder"!

One remaining issue could still bother the conscience. In Acts 24:16, Paul spoke about having a clear conscience before God and man. If my sin has been only against God and no one besides me has been hurt, I should be able to enjoy a clear conscience based on the steps in Hebrews 10:22. If I hurt someone else and I have not tried to make things right with the person, my conscience may still bother me because God wants me to make restitution. If I can possibly make amends, I should try. Caution: Never confess anything that will devastate another person just to unload your conscience; but if the person already knows we have wronged them, we should try to make amends (see Matt. 5:23–24).

Like the apostle Paul, we can enjoy a clear conscience even after a guilty past. Don't wait another moment. "Draw near to God" (Heb. 10:22).

CHAPTER 33
A PECULIAR
DELIVERANCE

Acts 23:11–35

Then he called two of his centurions and ordered them, "Get ready a detachment of two hundred soldiers, seventy horsemen and two hundred spearmen to go to Caesarea at nine tonight. Provide mounts for Paul so that he may be taken safely to Governor Felix."
(ACTS 23:23–24)

Prisons take many forms. Paul was physically imprisoned in Jerusalem. Yet he savored a certain freedom that flowed from a clear conscience. His accusers stood behind no bars. No chains rubbed their wrists raw, for we see them in a different kind of prison. A guilty conscience lived beneath their righteous robes. Outwardly, they were free men. Inwardly, they were in a prison of rage and resentment.

I love God's Word for so many reasons.

One of them is the way it combines different elements. In this chapter we see the touchingly personal and the delightfully humorous woven together in the same account.

We left Paul imprisoned in Jerusalem. Acts 23:11 tells us that "the following night the Lord stood near Paul and said, 'Take courage! As you have testified about me in Jerusalem, so you must also testify in Rome.' "

In the next verse we read of a conspiracy of zealous Jews. More than forty men went to the chief priests with a plan to kill Paul. They had taken "a solemn oath not to eat anything" until they killed Paul (v. 14). Their plan was for the priests to ask for Paul to be brought "on the pretext of wanting more accurate information about his case." They planned to kill him on the way (v. 15).

I can't stifle a little grin as I think of their oath. They must have developed a considerable appetite, for their plan had one flaw. He is called Christ, the eternal God.

We learn a little tidbit about Paul's family. The son of Paul's sister somehow heard about the plot. He came to the barracks to tell Paul. Paul had him taken to the commander. On hearing of the plot, the commander had Paul transferred from Jerusalem to Caesarea under armed guard. A very well-armed guard.

Can't you almost hear Christ saying to the evil one: "OK, I'll see your forty hungry assassins and raise you seventy horsemen and two hundred spearmen." One of the morals? Never play power games with the Lord's Christ.

Think about how Paul perceived all these events. Sometimes we must read between the lines in the Book of Acts to see Paul the man and not just his travels. Acts 23:11 offers us a perfect opportunity to read between the lines without stretching the text. I hope Christ's tenderness toward His willing captive touches you. He stood near Paul and said, "Take courage!"

Why did Christ draw so physically close to Paul at this particular moment? I believe Paul was overcome with fear and may have been convinced he would not live much longer. Paul had looked straight into the eyes of rage. He was separated from his friends. He was imprisoned by strangers. I believe he was terrified.

Later Paul wrote from another prison cell, "My God will meet all your needs according to his glorious riches in Christ Jesus" (Phil. 4:19). He could make such a claim because God had been so faithful to meet his needs. In Acts 23:11 God looked on His servant Paul imprisoned in Jerusalem, and He didn't just see emotions. He saw the need they represented. Paul was afraid. He needed courage. Just like Philippians 4:19 said, God literally met his need in Christ Jesus. That day in Paul's prison cell, Christ stood near and said, "Take courage!" He meant "I'm right here. Take courage from Me!"

The Lord gave Paul great motivation for courage. He said, " 'As you have testified about me in Jerusalem, so you must also testify in Rome' " (Acts 23:11). Paul received his confirmation: he was going to Rome. His life could not be taken until the mission was complete. Paul surely knew that Christ's confirmation did not mean Paul wouldn't suffer or be greatly persecuted. He simply knew he could not be killed until he had testified about Christ in Rome.

God timed Paul's injection of courage perfectly to offset the conspiracy to kill Paul. The Greek word for this conspiracy is *sustophe,* meaning "a turning or spinning together, as in a whirlwind, a gathering together of people, . . . a public tumult." Overnight in Jerusalem, Paul became the center of a dangerous whirlwind of rage that rapidly gained force. By morning, forty men bound themselves with an oath to kill him. The original terminology tells us they were binding themselves to a curse if they didn't carry out their plans. They may not have realized they had bound themselves to a curse already! In the words of Micah the prophet: "Woe to those who plan iniquity, / to those who plot evil on their beds! . . . / Therefore, the LORD says: / 'I am planning disaster against this people . . .'" (Micah 2:1–3).

God did not allow the conspiracy against Paul to be successful. He delivered him from his persecutors. Don't miss Paul's response when his nephew brought him the news of the conspiracy. He sent him to explain the plot to the commander. Remember, God had told Paul he was going to Rome. Paul knew somehow he would be delivered. Notice he didn't sit in his cell and expect another miracle like he and Silas experienced. When his nephew brought the news, he knew God might be planning his escape through natural means. He was right. God delivered him in style.

As Paul rode with the Roman escort, I wonder if he thought, *If my Daddy could see me now,* or *Timothy would love this!* Paul's immediate destination was a cell in Caesarea, but he knew it had to be temporary. The same God who had delivered him from death would deliver him to Rome.

God is the Deliverer (see Ps. 140:7). He can deliver us through peril, or He can deliver us from peril. Like Paul, during the course of our lives, we can probably expect both. We can't put God in a box. We can't assume He will deliver us by the same methods over and over again. God has a wonderful way of keeping things interesting, doesn't He? Remember, deliverance through a natural means is no less the work of God than deliverance through a supernatural means. He can shake the foundations of the prison, or He can employ the Roman cavalry to accompany a servant out of town.

Deliverance through and from peril is undoubtedly one of the themes of Paul's life. We have already had a number of occasions to consider God's creativity in His methods of delivery. When the apostle Paul wrote his second letter to the Corinthians, he had stated his hope to see God continue to deliver him and his associates. "He has delivered us from such a deadly peril, and he will deliver us. On him we have set our hope that he will continue to deliver us, as you help us by your prayers" (2 Cor. 1:10–11).

Never underestimate the effects of intercessory prayer lifted for our deliverance. Never underestimate the effects of prayers for others. The year I began working on this study of Paul, my heart was torn to pieces over a devastating loss. For several months no one outside our family and friends knew we had suffered a loss; because the wound was so fresh, we were not yet able to tell the story. Letters poured in from all over the nation saying something like this: "God has placed a heavy burden on my heart for Beth and her family. I do not know what is wrong, but I'm praying for them." I could hardly believe it. Once we shared more openly about our loss, we learned that literally thousands of people were praying for us. I am absolutely certain those prayers delivered us from the pit of despair. Many times my soul would sink in grief, and I would feel like I was about to descend into depression. Each time I began to slip, I sensed something like a supernatural net disallowing me to descend another inch. I know without a doubt intercessory prayer helped keep me out of the pit.

With great thanksgiving let's acknowledge God as the Deliverer. He can deliver anyone from anything at anytime. He doesn't need any help. Yet He invites us to be part of His great work through prayer. If we don't intercede for one another, we miss opportunities to see His deliverance and thank Him for His faithfulness. I like to call this God's profit sharing plan. When we pray for one another, we share the blessings when deliverance comes because we've been personally involved. Their thanksgiving becomes our thanksgiving.

Many scholars believe Paul wrote 2 Corinthians on his third missionary journey, prior to his arrest in Jerusalem. If so, the Corinthians' prayers were involved in Paul's deliverance. He rode in style to Caesarea, surrounded by soldiers, horsemen, spearmen, and the prayers of the Corinthian Christians.

A thankful heart is not the only result of effective intercessory prayer; our faith in what God can do in our own lives is also strengthened. The believers in Corinth were babes in Christ. Can you imagine how blessed they were to learn that their prayers had helped deliver Paul? God's glory and power does not waver from one child to the next. He can just as surely deliver you as He delivered the apostle Paul. Today may you sense Him near you saying, "Take courage, child — My courage."

CHAPTER 34
AN INCONVENIENT GOSPEL

Acts 24:1–27

As Paul discoursed on righteousness, self-control and the judgment to come, Felix was afraid and said, "That's enough for now! You may leave. When I find it convenient, I will send for you."
(ACTS 24:25)

As we begin this chapter, my mind drifts back over the many stops we've made with the apostle Paul. I suppose none of us wants to trade times, places, and lives with him; but each of us must admit his tenure on this earth was extremely fascinating. He could write about "the breadth, and length, and depth, and height" (Eph. 3:18 KJV) because he experienced each of those extremes. The man we're studying in God's Word was flesh and blood. He bruised. He cried. He got angry. He made mistakes. But he was extraordinary. I am astounded by

311

Paul's courage. Yet we know just where he got it: from a nearby Savior. Let's continue with the events of Acts 24. The scene unfolds with Paul incarcerated in Caesarea after being escorted by a grand cavalry.

Ananias the high priest brought an entourage including a lawyer named Tertullus to Caesarea. Before the governor, Tertullus brought the charges against Paul.

Few things are more disgusting than a political spiel that bears no resemblance to the truth. Tertullus began by flattering Felix, the governor. Judging by the lawyer's words, Felix deserved his own holiday for being a peacemaker, a reformer, a tireless officer, and a noble man! Tertullus knew better. We can't fully appreciate the smoke Tertullus was blowing the governor's direction until we learn more about Felix. He was vile and incompetent. Nero had him recalled only two years later. He was a former slave who had cunningly gained favor with the imperial court. "Felix was known for his violent use of repressive force and corrupt self-aggrandizement."[1]

After blatantly flattering Felix, Tertullus delivered his charges against Paul. He said that Paul was a troublemaker who stirred up riots among the Jews and that he had tried to desecrate the temple (Acts 24:5–8).

Paul responded to the charges with a forthright description of his journey to Jerusalem and the events there. Luke adds the comment that Felix "was well acquainted with the Way" (v. 22).

Felix obviously viewed the conflict as a no-win situation. The size of the Jewish community and the Roman citizenship of Paul left Felix in a dilemma. He lacked the wisdom to make an appropriate decision, so he did nothing. He left Paul in prison. God, however, was clearly up to something. Second Peter 3:9 tells us God doesn't want anyone to perish. He wants all to come to repentance. God loves the most vile offender. He loved Felix, and He sent him a man who was unafraid to preach the truth.

Several days after the hearing, God gave Paul an interesting opportunity. He sent the preacher to a congregation of two: Felix and Drusilla. Drusilla was the third wife of the governor, and both of them had deserted previous spouses to marry. God equipped Paul with a tailor-made lesson for the two. Verse 25 tells us Paul "discoursed," which means "to speak back and forth or alternately, to converse with." Paul didn't just give a sermon. He led Felix and Drusilla in an interactive study. The core of Paul's message was "faith in Christ Jesus" (Acts 24:24).

The apostle's message contained three points: "righteousness, self-control and the judgment to come." We could summarize his message: salvation by grace teaches us to live self-controlled lives. Paul risked bodily harm when he preached such a forceful message to Governor Felix and his wife. Christ had assured the apostle he would go to Rome, so he knew he wouldn't be killed; but torture can be a more difficult prospect than death! You can be sure Paul didn't bring the message Felix was expecting. He and Drusilla, a Jewess, most likely expected a message of mystical divinity. Instead they got a message of practical clarity, and every point stuck.

Felix was not amused by the outspoken preacher. Acts 24:25 tells us that he "was afraid and said, 'That's enough for now! You may leave.' " At least Felix took the message personally enough to be afraid. Felix dismissed Paul. I see some irony in his choice of words. History describes him as a man with a gross lack of self-control.[2] I have a feeling he rarely applied the words "That's enough for now" to himself. Felix told Paul he would send for him at a more convenient time.

I'm not sure confrontation with personal sin is ever convenient. Some of the messages I've needed to hear most were those I wanted to hear least. Like Felix, we in our human natures often resist what is best for us. Unlike Felix, we can dare to accept a truth and find freedom.

While Felix felt fear, Luke tells us of no reaction from Drusilla. We might surmise she was also convicted and frightened, but Scripture only tells us Felix was afraid. I would like to offer a different theory. Perhaps Drusilla simply did not humble herself enough to be afraid. She had quite an interesting heritage — one plagued with pride.

Remember Herod Agrippa I from Acts 12:19–23? He was Drusilla's father. He bestowed on himself the glory due only to God. As a result he was eaten by worms and then died. You might think having a father who was eaten alive by worms would have some impact. Instead, Drusilla led an adulterous life in spite of all she knew about morality and reverence for God from her Jewish heritage. The generational bondage of pride could have been broken with her father's dreadful demise. Instead, she resisted the message, willingly picked up the chain of pride, and carried on.

In His great mercy, God reaches out to the immoral, ill-tempered, and boastful. Many hear but run the other way. Others hear but never apply. But some listen and are set free. God not only sent Felix and Drusilla a fitting message, He sent them a fitting messenger. Paul could not stand before them as one who had never experienced a terrible lack of self-control. He was once puffed with pride. His only righteousness was in the law. Then one day Jesus confronted him in the middle of his sin. He'd been running straight to Him ever since.

CHAPTER 35
MAN ALIVE!

Acts 25–26

"It is because of my hope in what God has promised our fathers that I am on trial today."
(ACTS 26:6)

As our next scene unfolds in the Book of Acts, at least two years have passed since Paul was incarcerated in Caesarea. Acts 24:26 tells us Felix sent for Paul many times after his discourse but solely in hopes that Paul would offer him a bribe. No further word suggests his awareness of sin. Felix may have resisted the Holy Spirit until conviction finally passed. If only he had responded when he felt conviction.

Now we get to listen in as the apostle Paul gives his testimony before a new audience. Acts 25 begins with the arrival of a new leader of the province. Festus replaced Felix, but Paul remained in prison. The Jewish leaders immediately appealed to the new governor to have Paul returned to Jerusalem for trial. Though two years had passed, and they were either very hungry or had abandoned their vow not to eat until Paul was dead, they still harbored such hatred of the apostle that they could think only of killing him. Rather than be returned to Jerusalem, Paul appealed to Caesar.

Why Paul appealed to Caesar rather than return to Jerusalem remains a mystery. After Festus heard Paul's defense, the new governor said in effect, "I would turn him loose but since he appealed to Caesar, I send him to Rome as a prisoner." We cannot judge from the words of Festus whether Paul might have been freed. What we do know is that the apostle is about to travel to Rome at last, but first he had one more chance to present the gospel.

King Agrippa and his wife Bernice came to Caesarea to pay respects to the new governor. Festus told them about Paul, and they decided to hear from the apostle. As Paul had done with Felix and Drusilla, he preached to the new trio.

Festus's response contains a fascinating statement. He "was at a loss how to investigate" Paul's claims that a dead man named Jesus was alive. How would you respond to

Festus's quandary? How do you know Jesus is alive?

Not long ago I shared with a loved one how I know Christ is alive. He said, "I believe in reincarnation," and, "I believe a spiritual presence exists rather than a certain God." He continued by repeating the words "I believe" over and over. Suddenly God gave me such a strange insight, and I was overwhelmed at the difference between my loved one and me. He believed the things he had been taught through New Age philosophers and their materials. I didn't just believe. I knew. With tears in my eyes, I gently said to him, "My God is not just Someone I believe in. He's Someone I know. I've felt His presence. I've seen His activity. I've experienced His deliverance. I've been touched by His healing. I've witnessed answered prayer. I've 'heard' Him speak straight to me through His Word. Yes, I believe. But more than that, I know."

My loved one said nothing more, but I knew he heard my heart. Dead prophets don't save, guide, heal, deliver, answer prayers, or speak through an ancient text with the relevance of this morning's newspaper. My advice to anyone else investigating the matter would probably be twofold:

1. Open your heart to the possibility of Christ's authenticity by coming to church and getting to know Christian people.
2. Ask Christ if He's real, then be honest and open enough to watch for Him to reveal Himself.

I may know that Christ rose from the dead from personal experience, but plenty of other things exercise my faith! Good investigators ask certain questions: Who? What? Where? When? and How? Our present text shows what we may know: who is in control and even what He's doing and where He's leading — but we'll rarely guess when and how! Let's take the Jewish leaders and Paul as an example of our inability to know when and how.

1. *Neither Paul nor the Jewish leaders understood* when. Paul didn't know *when* God would fulfill His promise. Paul knew who had called him and what Christ had called him to do. He even knew where — God was going to send him to Rome. Paul might never have guessed he would still be sitting in jail two years after the promise. He probably asked God many times — When? Time means so much to you and me. When God sheds light on ministries He wants us to

fulfill or promises He plans to keep, we usually assume He means right now! A study of the Jewish patriarchs easily proves that years may separate God's promise and its fulfillment. Not one minute is wasted, but God rarely seems to fulfill His revealed plan when we expect.

Likewise, the Jews didn't know *when* God would fulfill His promise. They believed God would send the Messiah. The Messiah was the answer to *who.* They also knew what He would come to do — bring salvation. They were certain where — Israel, then to all parts of the world. But, you see, they didn't understand *when.* They were still looking for a Messiah, but He had already come. Sometimes we can keep asking when God is going to do something He's already done!

2. *Neither Paul nor the Jewish leaders understood* how. God had assured Paul He was sending him to Rome, but Paul would never have guessed *how.* In Acts 25:25, Festus announced, "I decided to send him to Rome." Actually, God had decided to send Paul to Rome, but He was about to use Festus as the vehicle. Paul may have wondered over and over how he would ever get to Rome while under arrest. He probably asked his associates many times to pray for his release,

so he could fulfill his calling in Rome. I wonder if Paul ever imagined his arrest would be the tool God would use to give him an all-expenses paid trip to his destination.

Recently, I heard a famous actor share his testimony before a secular audience. He said when he was a boy, God revealed to him that he would reach out to thousands and thousands of people. All his life he had waited for God to call him to preach. God never did. Instead, the young man developed into an Academy Award–winning actor. He was thankful for his opportunities to act, but he couldn't understand what had happened to his calling. The evening he was honored he said he realized God had fulfilled His promise. The young boy never would have guessed how God would do what He said.

God is the Deliverer, but we never know how He might deliver us. We see that God always fulfills His promises but not always the way we imagine.

If Paul was occasionally shocked by how God fulfilled His promises, he was not the only one. God had assured the Jews He would send the Messiah, but they never would have guessed how. They were expecting great pomp to accompany their king's arrival. They were not expecting someone who looked so ordinary, so common. They unfortunately wanted a prestigious king more than a servant Savior.

Praise God, He gives us what we need, not what we want. If Christ had come to immediately wear His crown, we would be hopelessly lost. A crown of thorns and a splintered cross had to precede a crown of jewels and a hallowed throne. If they hadn't, Christ would still have a throne but no earthly subjects to approach it.

God calls us to be good investigators. We don't have to be at a loss on how to investigate such matters. When we don't know what, when, where, or how, we can trust in who. We won't always find our answers, but we can always find our God when we seek Him with all our hearts. And He will love and comfort us until all other answers come.

■ ■ ■ ■

Part VIII
The Pathway to Rome

■ ■ ■ ■

Tighten your life jackets. The voyage ahead of us could get a little rocky! Storms in life are inevitable, but how we weather them is always optional. We have quite an adventure ahead. Allow God to capture your imagination completely and involve you in the experiences we are about to study. God is full of surprises — and some of them appear in the worst of storms. God is our refuge: the one plank still floating on the water when the ship around us sinks.

We may never leave our native land or

travel by air or sea; but if we love and serve God, our lives will be a great adventure. He'll never take you anywhere He has not already prepared for your arrival. Keep trusting Him.

CHAPTER 36
AN ANCHOR IN THE STORM

Acts 27:1–26

When neither sun nor stars appeared for many days and the storm continued raging, we finally gave up all hope of being saved.
(ACTS 27:20)

God promised the apostle Paul He would send him to Rome. Paul had no idea when or how. Following his hearing before King Agrippa, both questions were answered. Let's set sail toward Rome with the apostle for an unpleasant journey. It will provide biblical proof that excitement is not synonymous with fun! And you thought going on vacation with three children in a minivan was rough! Give me the air or give me the road, but I think I'll pass on the sea!

Sea travel was the only practical means of making a journey from Caesarea to Rome in Paul's day. At least he had a few good friends along. We know Luke joined him because the terminology of Acts 27 turns once again from *they* to *we*. Another associate by the name of Aristarchus was also named among them. These men were no doubt great support to Paul. Even though God allowed His faithful servant to be in chains for the gospel, He often provoked favor in the hearts of Paul's captors. Julius, a centurion in the Imperial Regiment, showed great kindness toward the apostle during the trek to Rome. Acts 27:3 tells us Julius "allowed [Paul] to go to his friends so they might provide for his needs."

Paul's needs obviously didn't diminish his sensibilities. We ordinarily think of the apostle as deeply spiritual, but Acts 27 reminds us he also could be rather practical. He had spent much time on ships traveling the Mediterranean. Winter was approaching. In ancient days few vessels risked the sea during the winter months.

Although Paul was no expert seaman, he also wasn't a man to keep his opinion to himself. He warned the pilot, the centurion, and the ship's owner, "Men, I can see that our voyage is going to be disastrous" (v. 10). Can you picture this little bearded man licking the end of his index finger and holding it up to check the direction of the wind?

Paul might have been perceived as a know-it-all at times. This was one of those times when someone probably should have listened.

The pilot and owner insisted on sailing regardless of difficulty. Like a plot from a disaster movie, they put profit above safety. They let their ledgers eclipse their good sense. The Alexandrian ship serviced Rome with expensive grain. They took advantage of the first gentle breeze and "sailed along the shore of Crete. Before very long, a wind of hurricane force, called the 'northeaster,' swept down from the island" (Acts 27:13–14). The location of their peril has been called St. Paul's Bay by many for centuries. "Only a few years ago dozens of yachts, some of considerable size, were wrecked here under just such conditions as Luke describes."[1]

This particular peril in the apostle's life struck a chord in my heart for reasons I couldn't quite identify at first. I finally realized why: he and the others met great difficulty because of someone else's poor judgment.

I've gone through storms as a direct result of my own rebellion. I've also gone through storms as a result of spiritual warfare. Others were ordained directly by God for His glory, but sometimes the most difficult storms of all can be those that result from another person's poor judgment. A wrong decision by a business partner, a boss, a driver, a jury, a teacher, a child, or a spouse can have devastating repercussions on other lives.

Of the four origins of personal storms I identified, the one caused by someone else's poor judgment has its own unique difficulty. Why? We have someone else in flesh and blood to blame! We feel much greater potential for bitterness and unforgiveness.

The sailors took steps to deal with the storm that enveloped their ship. In their actions I see practical behaviors we can also apply in our lives for surviving our personal storms. Although the points I am about to make might not apply to a literal ship on an angry sea, they will be helpful in the storms we encounter when someone close to us exercises poor judgment.

1. *Don't pull up the anchor* (see Acts 27:13). The ships masters were ill advised to attempt to sail, but they weighed anchor anyway. Jesus Christ is our anchor beyond the veil (see Heb. 6:19–20). When gentle breezes blow in our lives and all seems calm and peaceful, we often become less attentive to Him. We're not as aware of our need

for the One who secures our lives and holds us steady until the storms begin to rage. Don't let a few calm breezes give you a false sense of security in yourself and your surroundings. Stay anchored in Christ in gentle times too.

2. *Don't give way to the storm* (see Acts 27:15). Peril caused by another person's poor judgment can often cause feelings of immense helplessness. Don't give way to the storm. Give way to the Master of the seas.

3. *Do throw some cargo overboard* (see v. 18). As the storm worsened, the crew began to jettison cargo to keep the ship afloat. Raging storms have ways of identifying some old stuff we're still hanging on to. When we're upset over someone's poor judgment, we have a tendency to drag up memories of other times we've been wronged as well. Storms complicate life enough. Ask God to simplify and clarify a few things in your life by helping you throw some old cargo overboard.

4. *Do throw the tackle overboard* (see v. 19). After jettisoning the cargo, the crew still needed to further lighten the ship. The tackling on a ship included all kinds of gear: ropes, pulleys, spars, masts, and planks. These objects were man-made provisions to

master the storm. Storms are seldom pleasant, but they can serve an important purpose. They help us to see what man-made solutions we are substituting for depending on and getting to know God.

5. *Never give up hope* (see v. 20). Luke uses the word *we* when identifying those who gave up hope. He wrote one of the Gospels! How could he lose hope? He had witnessed miracles! This text reminds us that anyone can lose hope when a storm rages. The original word for "gave up" in verse 20 is the same one translated "cutting loose" in verse 40. We might say Luke and the others cut loose their hope when the storm continued to rage day after day. The psalmist offers us a lifesaver in our raging storms in Psalm 62:5: "Find rest, O my soul, in God alone; / my hope comes from him."

The "hope" in Psalm 62:5 is the word *tiqvah,* which literally means "a cord, as an attachment" *(Strong's).* The psalmist contrasted the disappointment he often experienced in man with the security he found in his faithful God. His cord or rope was attached to God alone. We're all holding on to a rope of some kind for security, but if anyone but God is on the other end, we're hanging on by a thread! Hang on to

Christ for dear life when the waves break harshly against you. He will be your survival no matter what the storm may destroy. Only He can keep you from becoming bitter. Only He can rebuild what gale-force winds tear apart.

6. *Listen for God to speak* (see Acts 27:24). Incline your ear to the Master of the seas when the storms rage. He will not be silent. Just when the passengers and crew had lost hope, Paul stood to testify. He told them, "Last night an angel of the God whose I am and whom I serve stood beside me and said, 'Do not be afraid, Paul. You must stand trial before Caesar; and God has graciously given you the lives of all who sail with you' " (Acts 27:23–24).

God will probably not send an angel from heaven to speak audibly to you, but He may send a fellow believer, a neighbor, a pastor, or friend. You can also hear Him speak through His Word anytime you are willing to open the Bible and receive. Job suffered, for reasons outside his control, in ways we will never experience. He had plenty of places to lay blame. I believe one reason he survived such tragedy was because God proved not to be silent as Job had feared. The place in which He spoke to Job is very applicable to us today. Job 40:6 tells us,

"Then the LORD spoke to Job out of the storm." God will speak to you too — straight to your heart. Sometimes others can make decisions that are devastating to our lives. I cannot promise you everything will be OK. It may be. It may not be. But I promise you based on the faithfulness of God that *you* can be OK. Just don't pull up that anchor. And never let go of the rope.

CHAPTER 37
AN UMBRELLA IN THE STORM

Acts 27:27–44

*"God has graciously given you the lives of
all who sail with you."*
(ACTS 27:24b)

As our story continues to unfold, Paul and
the crew occupy a tossing ship in a terrible
storm. We considered suffering from the
foolishness of another. Now let's look at the
other side of the coin: when blessings result
from someone's faithfulness. Let's allow
God to open our eyes to the importance of
faithfulness and obedience through a study
in contrasts.

Paul's life lends constant proof that the
most outlandish works of God are often
seen in the most difficult circumstances.
This shipwreck was unfortunately not Paul's
first. Second Corinthians 11:25 tells us the
apostle had been shipwrecked three previous times, but this is the only one described

in detail. Paul's voyage to Rome teaches us that one life and one man's decision can dramatically affect many, whether positively or negatively.

Julius, the centurion, was a good man, but he made a foolish decision when he took the advice of the pilot and owner of the ship. The owner gambled everything he had to gain a little more but ended up losing everything. Although the entire crew suffered because of one man's selfish motive and another man's poor judgment, they ultimately kept their lives because of a third man's faithfulness. The angel of God spoke clearly to Paul in Acts 27:24: "God has graciously given you the lives of all who sail with you." Clearly their lives were spared because of Paul. From either viewpoint we can see one moral to the story: The umbrella of protection or destruction in one man's hand can often cover many heads.

Let's think of the effects of one person's actions being like an umbrella over several other heads. One holds the umbrella, but several others are under the influence. What kind of cover these figurative umbrellas provide is not only determined by belief in God versus unbelief but also in faithfulness versus faithlessness. In Acts 27 God gave Paul an umbrella of protection because of

Paul's obedience in ministry. Whether or not they realized it, many were gathered under the umbrella and found safety.

Let's take a look at another kind of umbrella in the storm. Ask God to give you fresh insight into the familiar story of the prophet Jonah. You'll recall that God called the prophet to go preach deliverance to Nineveh, Israel's bitter enemy. Rather than preach to the people of Nineveh, Jonah ran the other way, booked passage to Tarshish, and wound up in a fishy situation.

Consider these similarities between Jonah and Paul:

- Both men were Hebrews. Both had Jewish backgrounds and believed in the one true God.
- Both men were preachers.
- Both men were called to preach unpopular messages in pagan cities. Nineveh and Rome both were powerful cities filled with wickedness.
- Both men boarded a ship.
- Both men experienced a terrible, life-threatening storm.
- Both men greatly impacted the rest of the crew.
- Both men knew the key to the crew's survival.

Paul and Jonah had many similarities, didn't they? We also share common ground with them. We are believers in the one true God. I think we each also realize we've been called to serve Him, but similarities can end dramatically at this point based on individual responses to God's directions. Let's consider a few contrasts between Paul and Jonah. They differed in at least the following ways:

- Paul was compelled by his calling to Rome. Jonah was repelled by his calling to Nineveh!
- Paul faced many obstacles on his way to Rome: imprisonment, many injustices, inclement weather, and other difficulties. Jonah's only obstacle was himself!
- Paul had to sit and wait for the Lord. Jonah stood and ran from the Lord!
- Paul felt a burden of responsibility for the crew, although the calamity was not his fault. Jonah slept while the others worked diligently to survive the calamity he had brought on them.
- Although both men were frightened and probably felt hopeless, Paul received courage from the Lord. Jonah revealed a rather amusing cowardice.

In Jonah 1:12, the fugitive preacher told them, "Pick me up and throw me into the sea. . . . I know that it is my fault." Notice he never offered to jump in! Sadly, heathen men showed more character than God's servant. Jonah 1:13 says, "Instead, the men did their best to row back to land." They did not want to throw him overboard and risk offending Jonah's God.

Paul and Jonah are great characters to compare and contrast because we can relate to both of them! Sometimes we respond with obedience like Paul. Other times we run from God with a sprinter's stride like Jonah. Let's ask a fair question based on their examples: Does prompt obedience really make much difference? When all was said and done, didn't Paul suffer through a terrible storm although he had been entirely obedient? Didn't Jonah get another chance to obey, and an entire city was spared? What difference does prompt obedience or faithfulness make anyway?

God loves us whether or not we are obedient, but the quality of our Christian lives is dramatically affected by our response. Allow me to point out one very big difference between the obedient Christian and the disobedient Christian — between the obedient times and the disobedient times. Jesus said, "If you obey my commands, you will remain in my love, just as I have obeyed my Father's commands and remain in his love. I have told you this so that my joy may be in you and that your joy may be complete" (John 15:10–11).

Although Jonah was ultimately obedient and surprisingly successful, you will search in vain for a single hint of joy in his life. Although Paul seemed to suffer at every turn, he had more to say about joy than any other mouthpiece in the Word of God.

An attitude of obedience makes a difference to the servant and to those close by. Servants of God can dramatically affect the lives of others positively or negatively. Under Jonah's umbrella in the storm many experienced calamity. Under Paul's umbrella many found safety. Is the sky rumbling? Are clouds darkening? Is a storm rising in the horizon? If you are a child of God, you will hold an umbrella in the storm. You will not be under the umbrella alone. Neither will I. Our children will be under there with us. Our coworkers may be too. The flocks God has entrusted to us will be there. Even the lost are often drawn to people of faith when hurricane winds begin to blow. Child of God, you and I are centered on the bow of the ship when storms come and the waves crash. May the rest of the crew find an umbrella of blessing in our midst.

CHAPTER 38
ISLAND WONDERS

Acts 28:1–10

Once safely on shore, we found out that the island was called Malta. The islanders showed us unusual kindness. They built a fire and welcomed us all because it was raining and cold.
(ACTS 28:1–2)

After fourteen days of stomach-turning terror, the ship ran aground on an unexpected island. Some swam to shore, but others paddled their way on planks and pieces of the ship. I would have been the one clinging to the biggest piece of the ship and hollering for Keith.

I've had my own terror in the tropics: a snorkeling expedition off the coast of Maui in 1995. I assure you Keith will never forget it either. Fifteen minutes after everyone else jumped in the water with all their gear, I was still standing on the back of the boat.

The captain found the tragic scene rather amusing.

The trouble really began once I got into the water. They told us simply to breathe normally and enjoy the scenery. I really tried. But I couldn't see a single fish for the fog in my mask. Keith swam over to me and said, "Elizabeth, every swimmer within ten nautical miles can hear you breathing all the way under the water." He appeared to be losing patience with me. We were supposed to have snorkeling buddies, so Keith had to swim close to me. Every time I turned my head, I accidentally smacked him in the face with the breathing tube sticking out in the back. After three or four rounds, I looked up and my buddy was nowhere to be found. We didn't meet again until the captain pulled me back into the boat. Keith and I have shared some great laughs over parting waters in the deep, and in case you're concerned, we're still buddies!

As Paul and his coworkers paddled their way from the sinking ship to shore, they must have wondered what they would find. On the island of Malta they made at least six discoveries:

1. *"Unusual kindness"* (Acts 28:2). Paul and the crew could have easily stumbled on unhappy natives. Instead, God prepared a

safe haven for them among kind and civilized people. Luke tells us the people of Malta were not just kind; they were "unusually kind." This was not always the case. Ancient islanders often considered visitors to be unwelcome intruders.

Every day I pray for a different country specified in a prayer guide. Not long ago I was to pray for missionaries in the Pacific Islands. My first thought was, *What an easy life, serving on some beautiful tropical island.* Then the first two sentences grabbed my attention: "The Pacific was one of the first areas to be evangelized in the modern Protestant missionary era. Few areas of the world have claimed more missionary lives through disease, violent death and cannibalism."[1] Numerous believers exist on those islands today because many missionaries suffered to take them the message.

Can you think of a time when you were shipwrecked, in a manner of speaking, and encountered unusual kindness? If so maybe you'd like to send a thank-you note to the person or people who cared for you. At the time did you recognize God as the source of the unusual kindness for you? Maybe you'd like to send Him a thank-you also.

2. *Warmth.* The water was cold! Furthermore, rain was falling. I don't mind being

cold for a few minutes if I can then put on a warm coat, but I don't like to be cold and wet! Just as Paul promised, not one hair was lost — but you can be sure each was standing on end! When you're wet and cold, few things are more comforting than a warm fire. In fact, you can't truly appreciate warmth until you've experienced cold. Picture the crew huddled tightly around the campfire, warming their trembling hands. God met their most immediate need — warmth — first.

Another detail catches my attention and, if possible, raises my esteem for the apostle even more. Verse 3 tells us that Paul gathered a pile of brushwood for the fire. After enduring the many days on the sea and the wintry swim to shore, surely Paul had earned a break, but the apostle's servant heart showed in everything he did. His act of servanthood not only demonstrated his heart, it led to the next discovery.

3. *Snakes!* A viper indigenous to this region is a small but poisonous snake. Interestingly, it looks similar to a dead branch when immobile, so in all likelihood Paul picked up the snake as he was gathering brushwood. (Doesn't that give you the creeps?) When he put the branches in the fire, the viper took the first way out: Paul's

hand. Can you imagine what Paul was thinking as the snake dangled from his hand? "Five times I received . . . forty lashes minus one. Three times I was beaten with rods, once I was stoned, three times I was shipwrecked" (2 Cor. 11:24–25) and now this! God used the creature, however, to reveal the beliefs of the islanders.

4. *Limited knowledge.* The response of the islanders to Paul's snakebite was, "This man must be a murderer; for though he escaped from the sea, Justice has not allowed him to live" (Acts 28:4). Even though their assumption was incorrect, they revealed a limited knowledge of the one true God. If you have a New International Version of the Bible, you may have noticed the word *justice* was capitalized as a proper noun. I discovered the reason when I researched the original Greek word. The word *dikastes* actually means "a judge. One who executes justice. One who maintains law and equity." Although the island of Malta had presumably never been evangelized, they revealed an awareness of a divine judge who maintains justice.

Out of love for the world, God makes Himself known even in the most remote places on earth. Some call this self-disclosure "natural revelation." He desires for people to seek the unknown through the known and discover a greater knowledge leading to salvation. Paul penned the clear words verifying God's universal declaration of His existence: "For since the creation of the world God's invisible qualities — his eternal power and divine nature — have been clearly seen, being understood from what has been made, so that men are without excuse" (Rom. 1:20).

Through physical nature and perhaps human nature, the islanders of Malta perceived the existence of a divine Judge who ultimately enforced justice — even on those who thought they had escaped.

God is so merciful, isn't He? He doesn't just want people to be without excuse. He doesn't want people to be without a Savior. Justice was the natural light through which the people of Malta first perceived the one true God.

5. *Spiritual need.* The people of Malta were walking in the natural light they had received. They believed in justice and equity, but their knowledge was incomplete. When Paul shook off the snake and suffered no ill effects, they changed their minds and said he was a god. Although they believed in a divine Judge, they also believed in other gods. Many peoples of the world have

received enough natural light to recognize the existence of deity, but they do not realize only One is truly God. They are dependent on missionaries, preachers, and teachers to come and be used of God to bring supernatural light. Paul and his associates didn't just happen on the island of Malta. God sent them to bring the Word of God.

6. *Physical need.* Something unique happened on the island of Malta. All the sick were healed. Through this awesome, miraculous work, I believe God still placed the priority on their spiritual need. Three details suggest God worked in the physical realm for spiritual reasons.

First, Paul prayed before he healed the chief official's father. Paul did not want the people of Malta to think he was a god. Prayer helped redirect their attention to the source of all healing — Jesus Christ, the Great Physician.

The second detail that suggests God used physical needs to shed light on spiritual realities was His means of healing. He used Paul to heal, yet Luke was a physician. Why? I believe God wanted the people of Malta to recognize God, instead of some well-educated professional, as the source of their healing. No doubt God used Luke many times to tend the sick, but when He wanted to leave no room for doubt, He used someone with no knowledge of medicine.

The last detail that suggests God was up to something spiritual is wholesale healing. Sadly, an evangelist may not pack the house with good preaching and Spirit-filled worship, but he can draw large crowds with rumors of healing. Yes, God cares about the sick. He cares deeply. And He often heals physical illnesses, but seldom in Scripture did He use a servant to bring physical healing to an entire land. I believe God used the physical needs of those in Malta to draw attention to the only One who could meet their spiritual needs. He trusted Paul not to take credit for a work only God can do.

We must also be careful to give God the glory when He uses us to accomplish things only He can do. Every time you lead someone to the Lord, the Holy Spirit is accomplishing His work through you. Every time you exercise a spiritual gift, God is accomplishing His work through you. If you are a servant of God and you have known Him long, He has used you to do something only He can do.

Think of a work He has accomplished through you. If you're uncomfortable with this request, you still may be taking too much credit. I'm asking you to boast in God, not in yourself.

If you sense the direction of the Holy Spirit now, take time to pray about your availability for any work He might use you to accomplish. Then commit to give Him the glory.

God used the apostle Paul to do something only God could do. He will use you and me too, but we must be trustworthy. Acts 28:11 tells us God allowed Paul and his coworkers to remain on the island for three months. You can be sure those islanders heard more preaching in a few short months than most people hear in a lifetime! When Paul revitalized the crew by saying, "We must run aground on some island" (Acts 27:26), little did he know he would run aground on an island called Malta where God had a glorious agenda planned.

CHAPTER 39
BROTHERS AMONG
STRANGERS

Acts 28:11–16

There we found some brothers who
invited us to spend a week with them.
And so we came to Rome.
(ACTS 28:14)

In the early spring of A.D. 61, God fulfilled His promise to Paul. The apostle arrived in Rome. Our text in Acts is very brief and may leave some of us yearning for details. Although Luke wrote about the shipwreck in detail, he did not include Paul's reaction when he reached Rome. Surely, he was overwhelmed by the imposing sight, yet more so by his faithful God.

Another Alexandrian ship had docked for the winter in Malta before the sea became so treacherous. When winter had passed, Paul and his crew boarded this ship bound for Rome.

A number of Christians from Rome traveled to meet Paul as far as the Forum of Appius (43 miles away) and the Three Taverns (33 miles away). They were not old acquaintances of Paul's. They had never met him, but they were brothers in Christ.

Paul had never seen anything like Rome. At the time of his arrival, Rome was inhabited by one million citizens and approximately the same number of slaves. By even today's standards the city was gigantic. Rome shared a number of characteristics with many current overcrowded inner cities. Although magnificent buildings and luxurious villas begged to steal the onlooker's attention, he would have to tear his focus from the seas of tenements on the verge of collapse. These four- to five-story insulae, with no running water or sanitary restrictions, housed most of the city's population. "Like many modern cities, Rome had an urban police force and firefighters, and prostitutes, who registered with the courts and paid their tax, wandered the streets in identifying clothing."[1] Even though Claudius formerly ordered all Jews to leave Rome, the edict either lapsed under Nero's rule or was rescinded. At the time Paul entered Rome, a large number of Jews once again had populated the city.

As Paul approached the gargantuan city, I believe God knew he would be overwhelmed by a great sea of strangers and the certainty of enemies. Not coincidentally, God met him at each stepping-stone to Rome with brothers; therefore, the concept of brotherhood in Christ will occupy our attention as we study this season in the apostle's life. Keep in mind that *brotherhood* in Christ is not a term related to masculinity. It rather refers to the unique fellowship shared by brothers and sisters in Christ.

How important was brotherhood in Christ to the apostle Paul? Scripture refers to a natural sibling of Paul's only once, yet I counted ninety-nine times in his epistles when the apostle referred to other Christians as brothers. The Greek word for "brothers" is *adelphos.* In reference to fellow believers in Christ, the term "came to designate a fellowship of love equivalent to or bringing with it a community of life." As Paul approached Rome, God knew he needed "a fellowship of love" or "a community of life."

Paul's need was not unique. People are desperate for a sense of community today. We all want to feel like we belong somewhere. God recognizes our need for community and desires to meet the need through His church — the body of believers God organized to offer a community of life.

Paul obviously sensed a strong bond of brotherhood with other believers. Many Christians lived in Rome probably as a result of the outpouring of the Holy Spirit on the Day of Pentecost. Obviously many believed in Christ, returned to Rome, and were used by God to bring a greater harvest. Paul presumably had never met the Christians in Rome, yet he clearly considered them his siblings in the faith (see Rom. 1:13). Paul's strong bond of brotherhood with other believers was not accidental nor was it the automatic outcome of his salvation.

Many people believe in Christ as Savior yet never sense a brotherhood or sisterhood with other Christians. I believe that imitating Paul's approach to other Christians would lend the same sense of community for any of us who dared. In preparing for his visit to Rome, Paul wrote the Romans a letter. In the opening verses of that letter, I see three strands that formed the cord of brotherhood he felt toward believers in Rome. Those three cords are: Paul's constant practice of intercessory prayer, his powerful sense of obligation to fellow believers, and his strong commitment to equality.

1. *Paul believed in the power of prayer and in our spiritual poverty without it.* His intercession on behalf of the Romans was certainly no exception. He wrote, "Constantly I remember you in my prayers at all times" (Rom. 1:9–10). Over and over in his letters, Paul assured churches of his prayers. He didn't just ask God to bless them. Paul jealously sought God's best for them.

Paul asked big things of God because he knew God had big things to give. Paul had experienced the riches of an intimate relationship with Christ. He wanted other believers to experience those same riches.

Be bold in your prayers! Ask for the riches Christ intends for you and ask for them in behalf of others too! As a result of Paul's constant prayers for other believers, he had a strong bond of brotherhood with them. His unceasing intercession fueled a sense of camaraderie and unity in his heart. Likewise, our sincere intercession for others will also result in a sense of closeness, strengthening our family ties in Christ. Without a doubt, one primary reason why such a strong cord of brotherhood tied Paul to fellow believers was his faithful practice of intercession.

Many of us feel or have felt alienated from others in our church family. Think of the impact that interceding for brothers and sisters in your congregation could make in your sense of belonging and bondedness.

2. *Paul believed that part of his calling was to share his gifts and faith with other Christians.* He truly believed Christians have an obligation to one another as well as to the lost. In 1 Corinthians 12:12 he said, "The body is a unit, though it is made up of many parts; and though all its parts are many, they form one body. So it is with Christ."

Without apology, Paul instructed believers, as "parts" of the "body" of Christ, to recognize their obligation to one another — and their need for one another. Generally speaking, my spiritual gifts were given for your edification. Your spiritual gifts were given for mine. Paul presented our mutual encouragement more as an obligation than an invitation. Paul's sense of obligation didn't result in resentment toward the body of Christ as some might imagine. Rather, his sense of obligation resulted in strong bonds of brotherhood.

3. *Paul desired to see all people come to Christ: Jews and Gentiles, wise and foolish.* He preached to anyone who would listen, and he considered any convert a brother or sister. All were equally in need of salvation, and all were equally loved by God.

At first consideration, we may fully believe we share his attitude; but sometimes we struggle with the equality of all believers. We may desire to see all people saved regardless of race and position, but we don't necessarily want them to attend church with us. The status struggle is still alive and active in the church. We tend to be selective about those we want to associate with as brothers and sisters. We often think a sense of community comes from others accepting us. Paul's sense of community came from his acceptance of others.

As Paul reached the Forum of Appius and the Three Taverns on his way to Rome, he was greatly encouraged by a group of strangers who met him there because they were his brothers. Their faces were unfamiliar, but they each had been washed in the blood of Jesus Christ. They were family. God used prayer, a sense of mutual obligation, and a sense of equality to bind their hearts.

Paul's example teaches us that a sense of brotherhood and community is not derived from the actions and attitudes of others toward us, but our actions and attitudes toward them. As we imitate his approach to other believers, we will form cords of love not quickly broken.

CHAPTER 40
EARS, EYES, AND HEARTS

Acts 28:17–31

For this people's heart has become calloused; they hardly hear with their ears, and they have closed their eyes. Otherwise they might see with their eyes, hear with their ears, understand with their hearts and turn, and I would heal them.
(ACTS 28:27)

We now conclude our studies in the fascinating Book of Acts. I've relished every second of our journey. In a blinding light on the Damascus road, I saw God's mercy. In a midnight song from a dungeon, I heard authentic worship. In every miracle on the island of Malta, I felt hope. The Book of Acts has quickened my senses and involved me. I pray that you've also gotten involved. Much more awaits us; but not from the pen of Luke. Our remaining chapters take us to the letters Paul wrote during the last six years of his earthly life. Luke's final account of the apostle Paul provides a fitting conclusion to the Book of Acts.

Recently a friend asked me what impressed me most from my research about the apostle. I didn't hesitate to answer. God used Paul's unparalleled passion for Christ to woo me into the study and his inconceivable perseverance to sustain me. When I was a child, someone gave my brother an inflatable clown with sand in the base. No matter how we socked that clown, he always came back up for more. The apostle was no clown, but, every time he got hit, he bounced back up for more. Of course, the reason for his perseverance was his deep passion for Christ.

Paul hardly had time to brush his teeth in Rome before he assembled the leaders of the Jews. Ordinarily when he arrived at a new city, he made a beeline for the synagogue, but his new living arrangements necessitated others coming to him. No matter how many times he had been rejected by the Jews, he bounced back up and tried again. He approached them with the same method and the same message. He tried to convince them about Jesus from the law of Moses and from the prophets. Based on Old Testament prophecy, Jesus was unmistakably the Messiah. Paul tried to make the Jews see the obvious fulfillment too.

When Paul realized that many were intentionally closing their eyes to the truth, he responded with an updated application of Isaiah's revelation:

"Go to this people and say,
'You will be ever hearing but never
    understanding;
    you will be ever seeing but never
    perceiving.'
For this people's heart has become
    calloused;
    they hardly hear with their ears,
    and they have closed their eyes.
Otherwise they might see with their eyes,
    hear with their ears,
    understand with their hearts
and turn, and I would heal them." (Acts
    28:26–27)

Be careful not to miss one of the most tragic elements of the Jews' rejection: Paul was not trying to take anything away from them. He had something more to give them. He never asked them not to be Jews. He simply pleaded with them to receive their Messiah.

How terribly we cheat ourselves when we

have as much as we want from God. Although many of us have received the gift of salvation, in other ways, we are not unlike some of the Jews Paul encountered. We mimic the words of Felix and sometimes hold up our hand to God and say, "That's enough. That's all I'm comfortable with" (see Acts 24:25). In our previous lesson we discovered a host of extraordinary blessings available to us as we considered Paul's intercessory prayers. Each of us is probably aware that God offers more than we accept.

God's gift of salvation is complete. Although we can't accept more salvation, we can receive on a daily basis

- a greater filling of the Holy Spirit (Acts 4:31),
- a deeper wisdom (1 Cor. 12:8),
- a more obvious disclosure of God's activity (John 14:21),
- more effectiveness in service (Ps. 127:1),
- character more conformed to Christ (Rom. 8:29), and best of all
- a more intimate relationship with Christ (Phil. 3:10).

Whatever the reason for our resistance, we may suffer from our own rendition of

Paul's diagnosis of many Jews. Is it possible we could resist what God is trying to tell us, give us, and work in us? We need to be aware of the possible outcome: our spiritual ears don't hear as well, our spiritual eyes don't see as well, and our hearts develop a toughness. Based on my own experience, I recognize the danger. At times I've resisted what God wanted to do in me or through me. I seemed to hear Him less, see His activity less, and, tragically, love Him less. Thankfully, when I finally relented and became receptive, my spiritual abilities to hear, see, and love were restored to me.

Let's examine the expressions Paul used and consider the abilities at risk when God desires to give and we continue to resist. Those who continue to resist God will be

- ever hearing but never understanding,
- ever seeing but never perceiving, and
- developing calloused hearts.

1. *"Ever hearing but never understanding"* (Acts 28:26). By the word *hearing,* Paul referred to the basic physical ability. By the phrase *never understanding,* he referred to a crippling inability. The Greek word for "understanding" is *suniemi,* meaning "the assembling of individual facts into an

organized whole, as collecting the pieces of a puzzle and putting them together." *Suniemi* is exercised when "the mind grasps concepts and sees the proper relationship between them." Do you see the tragedy at stake?

When we continue to resist what God has for us, we may cripple our ability to understand how the pieces of our puzzle fit together. We will constantly single out our experiences rather than understand them as parts of a whole. The things we go through may never make any sense to us. Preachers and teachers may tell us God is at work in our lives; but, although we physically hear, we have little ability to understand. Although we will not understand *everything* until we see Christ face-to-face, God often blesses us by letting many things make sense during our lifetimes. Most things I've encountered eventually made sense as I developed a more cooperative spirit and a greater understanding of God's purposes. Many of those experiences still hurt, but I find comfort in seeing their eventual usefulness as parts of the whole. You might think of the process this way: God is faithfully putting a puzzle together in each life so that the final picture will resemble Christ (see Rom. 8:28–29). If we continue to resist this further work, we will be less likely to see the pieces fit.

Can you see how difficult life would be without some ability to understand? God's working an awesome puzzle in you and me. We don't want to miss the blessing of seeing pieces fit together.

2. *"Ever seeing but never perceiving"* (Acts 28:26). Again Paul referred to a basic physical ability as he used the word *seeing. Perceiving* is translated from the Greek word *eido,* which merges the ability to see with the ability to know. *Eido* is "not the mere act of seeing, but the actual perception of some object." If we continue to resist the further blessings and works of God in our lives, we may lose some ability to see past the obvious and the physical. Those who allow God to unleash His Holy Spirit in their lives are those who often perceive spiritual and eternal works in the physical and temporal realm. People who never see with spiritual eyes can't comprehend how others claim to see God at work.

I'll never forget the time Amanda's seat belt in our old station wagon would not fasten. Five years old at the time, she pushed and pushed on it to no avail, so I finally told her to crawl into the front seat. Seconds later, the window where she had been sitting unexplainably imploded and pieces of glass imbedded into the seat she had just left. I exclaimed, "Thank you, dear God!"

Later she asked, "Do you really think that was God?"

I said, "No, baby. I know that was God." Every now and then God blesses us with a good dose of *eidos.* We not only see, but we know. When Paul tried to point out Christ's fulfillment of Old Testament prophecy, many Jews chose to close their eyes and refuse to see. God wants to give us supernatural sight. Let's not resist Him. Our lives are so much richer when we not only see but we also perceive!

3. *Developing calloused hearts* (see Acts 28:27). I was surprised when I discovered the meaning of the word *calloused.* You may be too! The original word is *pachuno,* meaning "to make fat . . . calloused as if from fat." According to Acts 28:27, people who continue to resist God can develop fat around their hearts. In the physical realm, one reason fat develops around the heart is a lack of exercise. In spiritual matters many of the Jews had ceased exercising their hearts. Religion for them involved more of a state of mind and intellect than the heart.

At one time or another, we've all been

hurt in love relationships. But if we cease to exercise our hearts by loving God and loving others, getting involved, and taking risks, our hearts will become diseased and hardened.

Through the prophet Isaiah and the apostle Paul, God revealed three dangers and three opposite blessings. By heeding Paul's warning, we can have ears willing to hear, eyes willing to see, and hearts willing to be exercised. In this final portion of the Book of Acts, we discover three gains that can accompany a receptive attitude toward God: understanding, perception, and an uncalloused heart.

1. *Understanding:* the ability to put puzzle pieces together.
2. *Perception:* the ability to see past the obvious and "know" God is at work.
3. *An uncalloused heart:* the willingness to remain tender and open to God and others.

God has so much to give us. We've just gotten a glimpse of the risk humans take when we put our hand up to God and say, "No more. I'm comfortable this way." We've also realized what we have to gain by remaining receptive to God. His greatest riches are those things that are conformable, not comfortable.

As we conclude the Book of Acts, I pray we've each had our eyes unveiled to the extraordinary works God can do in ordinary lives. As we've sojourned from chapter to chapter in Luke's wonderful book, we've met Stephen, Paul, Barnabas, John Mark, Timothy, Silas, Aquila, Priscilla, Philip the evangelist, his four daughters, and many more. They all shared one thing in common: they were simple flesh and blood infiltrated by the awesome power of the Holy Spirit. All because they didn't resist.

The Book of Acts concludes with the information that for two years Paul remained under house arrest in Rome. Unfortunately, the spiritual imprisonment of too many of his countrymen remains to this day.

■ ■ ■ ■

PART IX
LETTERS BRIDGING THE MILES

■ ■ ■ ■

As we approach the end of our study, I am struck by how many remaining riches we won't have time or space to discover! God appointed the great apostle to pen thirteen books of the Bible. I have chosen to emphasize his life and passion for Christ rather than his writings; however, now we will seize an opportunity to glance at four letters believed to have been written during Paul's house arrest in Rome. Each of them is like a buffet overflowing with rich foods. We will only get to sample and taste, but I pray our appetites will be kindled to return to them after our study.

Paul's incarceration took away his ministry of traveling and preaching, but it necessitated his second method of ministry — letter writing. We have four significant reasons to be thankful for Paul's first imprisonment in Rome: Colossians, Ephesians, Philemon, and Philippians. Ultimately, Paul was imprisoned a second time in Rome, but we will focus on his first imprisonment.

CHAPTER 41
DON'T BE
KIDNAPPED!

Colossians 2–4

*See to it that no one takes you captive
through hollow and deceptive philosophy,
which depends on human tradition and
the basic principles of this world rather
than on Christ.*
(COL. 2:8)

During Paul's first imprisonment in Rome
the apostle was under what we would call
house arrest. Acts 28:30 tells us that "for
two whole years Paul stayed there in his own
rented house and welcomed all who came
to see him." The openness of Paul's first
imprisonment in Rome enabled him to
receive ample information about the
churches. One of the letters he wrote during this two-year period became the Book
of Colossians. Though as far as we know
Paul never visited the Asian city of Colosse,
he obviously received word about the false

371

teaching there and wrote his epistle as both a warning and an encouragement. You would benefit most by reading all four chapters of Colossians. If you choose one chapter, the primary purpose for Paul's epistle appears in Colossians 2.

Paul made one primary purpose for the letter clear in verse 4: "So that no one may deceive you." Have you, or someone you know, ever been "taken captive" through some "deceptive philosophy"? Our world is replete with those who seek to control others through false and deceptive beliefs.

Try to capture Paul's frame of mind as he wrote the Christians in Colosse. He described himself as struggling (v. 1). The Greek word is *agon,* from which we derive the English word *agony. Agon* means "strife, contention, contest for victory or mastery such as was used in the Greek games of running, boxing, wrestling, and so forth." By using the word *agon,* Paul implied he was figuratively boxing or wrestling with Satan for the minds and hearts of the Colossians and Laodiceans. No sooner had the people of Colosse and Laodicea received the Word than Satan began infiltrating them with deceptive doctrines. Satan used at least four "isms." Let's briefly consider each one.

1. *Gnosticism.* The word *gnosis* means

knowledge. Followers of the gnostic belief system believed that knowledge, rather than faith, led to salvation. We risk something of the same problem if we focus on knowledge instead of Christ. We need to study the Bible to know and glorify Jesus rather than to impress others with our knowledge. I once heard a friend utter a prayer I have not forgotten. She said, "Lord, we know you desire followers who have hearts like a cathedral rather than minds like a concordance."

Since the gnostics prioritized intellect and reason, they tried to force God into humanly understandable form. They could not accept both the deity and the humanity of Christ, so they tried to reduce Him to the status of an angel. Paul responded to gnosticism clearly in verse 9: "For in Christ all the fullness of the Deity lives in bodily form."

2. *Legalism.* In verses 11–17, Paul addressed the fruitlessness of keeping endless laws that condemn rather than liberate the believer to pursue godliness. We humans constantly attempt to replace a love relationship with legalistic requirements such as

- seeking to be more "spiritual" by keeping man-made, extra-biblical rules,

373

- believing that God requires harsh treatment of the body,
- elevating one Christian above another based on keeping rules,
- refusing to accept those who have committed certain sins, and
- attempting to restrain sin by making lists of do's and don'ts.

No matter how ingeniously humans pursue legalism, it still will never work. Only a love relationship with Christ can change the human heart and bring about genuine piety.

3. *Mysticism* is the belief that we can obtain direct knowledge of God from our internal thoughts, feelings, or experiences. It conflicts with biblical faith because Jesus Christ is the source of our knowledge about God. In verses 18 and 19, Paul addressed a mystical belief that has recently infiltrated our own society — the worship of angels. Angels have important positions in God's creation, but Paul helps us find the balance. Angels were created to praise God and act as messengers and ministering servants. We worship angels when we disconnect them from their original purpose and focus on them.

4. *Asceticism.* In verses 20 through 23, Paul addressed the practice of denying the

body and treating it harshly in an attempt to achieve holiness. Followers of asceticism do not stop at the wise denial of dangerous, perverse, or unhealthy practices. Ascetics deny the body unnecessarily. In Paul's day, as in ours, some people branded, burned, starved, or cut themselves in an attempt to force the body into submission. Most of us have discovered that unnecessary denial arouses more desires.

We still battle many of the same destructive philosophies faced by the early believers. Though the list of "isms" may change, Satan is still up to the same old tricks. He seeks always to infiltrate the church with false teaching. Paul instructed the believers in Colosse: "See to it that no one takes you captive through hollow and deceptive philosophy" (v. 8). The Greek word for "captive" is *sulagogeo,* meaning "to lead off as prey, carry off as booty, rob, or kidnap." Recently my community was devastated over the kidnapping of a thirteen-year-old girl. I cannot imagine anything worse than the agony of one of my children being kidnapped. Paul responded with agony *(agon)* when he felt a kidnapper (Satan) was after some of his children in the faith.

Paul was addressing believers, faithful believers. Not even the faithful are completely immune to deceptive doctrine. Had Paul's recipients not been Christians, he would not have referred to the act as a kidnapping. Kidnapping takes place when someone steals a person who belongs to another.

No matter what a kidnapper does, he cannot make a child no longer belong to her family. The same is true spiritually. Once we accept Christ as Savior, we become joint heirs with Christ (see Rom. 8:17), and God becomes our Father (see John 20:17). Satan may try to kidnap us by enticing us away from the truth, but no matter what he does he cannot make us his. My security in God's family comforts me, but I don't ever want to be kidnapped, do you? The safeguards Paul taught the believers at Colosse will also help protect us. Based on Colossians 2:6–7, let's discover how to protect ourselves from being kidnapped by "hollow and deceptive philosophy."

1. *Remember how you received Christ.* None of us entered God's family through our own effort. We received Christ as a gift of grace. Now Paul tells us "the way we got in is the way we go on." We must not believe any teaching or philosophy that replaces God's grace with our performance.

2. *Continue to live in Christ.* The best way

for a child of God to avoid being kidnapped is to stay close to home. Children in natural families cannot live their entire lives in their yards, but children in the spiritual family of God can! Continuing to live in Christ means remaining close to Him and retaining a focus on Him. Any other focus can lead to deceptive doctrine, even if the focus is a biblical concept. Satan's favorite trick is to twist the Word of God (see Gen. 3). Remember, any doctrine that loses connection with the Head has been twisted into deception.

Many of us have probably let something under a religious umbrella temporarily become a greater focus than Christ Himself. I've seen people make a specific belief or detail of doctrine such a focus. We are less likely to be kidnapped when we stay close to home by staying focused on the Head, Jesus Christ.

3. *Grow deep roots in Christ.* The more we feel like family the less likely we'll be enticed. An important part of feeling like family is knowing your family history and the belief systems handed down through the generations. Spiritually, we have difficulty growing up until we've grown down. We form deep roots by knowing the basics of our faith. We can receive Christ and be

enthusiastic and still fall into confusion the first time someone confronts us with strange doctrine. Our roots are our basics.

4. *Grow up in Christ.* In Colossians 2:7, the apostle exhorted believers to be "rooted and built up in him." After we've grown roots, we're ready to grow up. Hebrews 6:1 strongly exhorts believers to a progression in Christ: "Therefore let us leave the elementary teachings about Christ and go on to maturity."

The Hebrew Christians knew the basics, and the writer knew they were ready for more. Paul suggested the same progression by a different analogy. In 1 Corinthians 3:2, he wrote, "I gave you milk, not solid food, for you were not yet ready for it." Paul was not implying infants in Christ should start with anything but milk. He was frustrated because people who should have been mature were still infants.

What will be the result if we "continue to live in him, rooted and built up in him"? We will be "strengthened in the faith" (Col. 2:6–7). Savor the definition of the Greek word for "strengthened": *bebaioo* means "to make firm or reliable so as to warrant security and inspire confidence." Satan is looking for victims. As we stay close to Christ, grow deep roots in the basics of our

378

faith, and press on to maturity to become Spirit-filled, power-packed believers, we won't be easy targets.

I understand that attackers target vulnerable-looking people. Being confident provides protection. The more you know about Christ, His Word, and His ways, the more confident you will feel. You will be the dread of those peddling strange doctrines.

A kidnapper is on the loose. If he tries to get his grasp on you or someone you love, Paul's exhortations can be easily summed up in the words of Christ in John 8:32: "Then you will know the truth, and the truth will set you free."

CHAPTER 42
A PROFOUND
MYSTERY

Ephesians 5

Wives, submit to your husbands as to the Lord. . . . Husbands, love your wives, just as Christ loved the church.
(EPH. 5:22, 25)

For the next two chapters we will concentrate on the letter to the Ephesians. Most scholars believe Colossians and Ephesians were written early in Paul's two-year imprisonment because he never hinted of a possible release as he did in Philemon (see v. 22) and Philippians (see 1:19–26).

The letter to the Ephesians differs from his letter to the Colossians. He never warned of deceptive philosophy; rather, Paul wrote about a greater knowledge and experience in Christ. We can easily deduce the reason for the omission of several basics. Remember, the Christians at Colosse had never met Paul, while the people of Ephesus had benefited from his teaching and an unparalleled demonstration of power for several years.

Paul found receptive soil in Ephesus, even in the midst of terrible hardships. His lengthy and effective ministry in Ephesus not only resulted in deep bonds of love (see Acts 20:37–38); it also freed him to proceed to great depths in his letter. If you have a translation with chapter or paragraph headings, turn to Ephesians and look at the subjects Paul explored in his letter.

Space limits me to choose only two subjects from the Book of Ephesians. We will examine the subject of marriage now and spiritual warfare in the next chapter. (Perhaps you thought marriage and warfare were synonymous!)

Ephesians 5:22–33 revolves around the biblical roles of three distinct figures intimately involved in marriage: wives, husbands, and Christ. We will approach each role individually. Ladies, let's get the painful part over first!

Part 1: The Role of Christian Wives

First, notice verse 21: "Submit to one another out of reverence for Christ." The attitude of all Christians is to be submissive to one another. No discussion of this topic can stay on track apart from that spirit.

How does the principle of mutual submission play itself out in marriage? The way I see it, Keith has to worry about things I don't. He sometimes has to come up with answers when I can't. He's responsible for things I'm not. Many times, I'm very happy to pass the proverbial buck. Keith would say the same about me. He really doesn't want to drive a carload of teenagers all over the city or sit for hours on the end of our daughters' beds discussing matters of the heart. Usually we defer to each other on our "turf issues." When I'm not in agreement with Keith, I usually speak up, and we pray and work it out — at times less easily than others! This spirit of praying things through until we can come to consensus on important issues is the essence of mutual respect and the opposite of "lording it over one another."

Paul's primary directive to women dealt with submission, while his primary directive to men dealt with love. Could it be that he was targeting the areas most likely to be our weaknesses? Before we learn what submission means for Christian wives, let's learn what it does not mean:

1. *Submission does not mean women are under the authority of men in general.* I love

the King James Version's rendition of Ephesians 5:22: "Wives, submit yourselves unto your own husbands." Guess what? Wives aren't asked to submit to anyone else's husband! Just their own! While I make this point somewhat tongue-in-cheek, many women assume the Bible teaches their general inferiority and subjection to men. Untrue. Paul is talking about marriage as a matter between each husband and wife.

2. *Submission does not mean inequality.* Paul, the same man who taught submission, made a statement in Galatians 3:28 pertinent to our subject: "There is neither Jew nor Greek, slave nor free, male nor female, for you are all one in Christ Jesus."

Spiros Zodhiates' definition of the Greek word *hupotasso* explains that submission "is not due to her being inferior to her husband, for they are both equal before God."

3. *Submission does not mean wives are to treat their husbands like God.* The Bible Knowledge Commentary explains: " 'As to the Lord' does not mean that a wife is to submit to her husband in the same way she submits to the Lord, but rather that her submission to her husband is her service rendered 'to the Lord.' "[1] I think most husbands are relieved they are not called on to be God to their wives!

4. *Submission does not mean slavery.* Let's release a few old notions and fears! Paul uses an entirely different word in Ephesians 6:5 when he instructs slaves to obey their masters. This Greek word for "obey," *hupakouo,* embraces more of the meaning people often mistakenly associate with marital submission. *Hupakouo* means "to obey, to yield to a superior command or force (without necessarily being willing)." The term draws a picture of a soldier saluting his commander, not a wife submitting to her husband!

Now that we've learned a few things submission does not mean, just exactly what does it mean? The Greek word for "submit" is *hupotasso. Hupo* means "under" and *tasso* means "to place in order." The compound word *hupotasso* means "to place under or in an orderly fashion." Paul didn't dislike women, he liked *order!* He advocated order in the church, order in government, order in business, and, yes, order in the home. I'm convinced he even kept his cell in order! Galatians 3:28 and Ephesians 5:22 could spill from the same man's pen because Paul regarded husbands and wives as spiritual equals but with functional differences.

The concept of a submissive wife really used to go against my grain until I began to learn more about God. Two realizations have changed my entire attitude:

1. *God is good and loving.* He would never give approval to meanness or abuse. Any misuse of submission by either the husband or wife is sin.
2. *God granted women a measure of freedom in submission that we can learn to enjoy.* It is a relief to know that as a wife and mother I am not totally responsible for my family. I have a husband to look to for counsel and direction. I can rely on his toughness when I am too soft and his logic when I am too emotional.

Certainly, I haven't just delivered the definitive dissertation on submission, but I believe I'm offering you sound doctrine. I hope it helps. Now, let's take a brief look at the role of husbands, according to Ephesians 5:25–31.

Part 2: The Role of Christian Husbands

Thus far Paul probably had the Ephesian Christians nodding their heads in agreement. Submission of the wife to the husband was codified Hebraic law. Nothing new here. Now Paul raised eyebrows in a hurry.

He told husbands to love their wives. The Greek word for "love" is *agapao,* meaning "to esteem, love, indicating a direction of the will and finding one's joy in something or someone." Notice the phrase "indicating a direction of the will." A husband is called by God to exercise his will to love his wife. Love is not simply an emotion or a feeling. Love is a willingness to continue in devotion and goodness toward the spouse.

For a society where women were little more than property, passed from father to husband, the command to love their wives was a radical idea. Paul knew few role models existed for the men to follow. He gave them the best role model possible: Jesus Christ.

1. *Husbands should love their wives sacrificially "as Christ loved the church and gave himself up for her"* (v. 25). Just as a husband must be careful not to abuse his wife's exhortation to submission, a wife must not abuse her husband's exhortation to sacrifice. Some men work several jobs sacrificing time at home in a continual effort to raise the standard of living for their families.

2. *Husbands should love their wives in ways that encourage purity.* Christ encourages purity in His bride, the church, desiring for her to be holy and without stain. God calls

upon husbands to treat their wives as pure vessels even in physical intimacy.

3. *Husbands should "love their wives as their own bodies"* (v. 28). I have to snicker when I think about verses 28 and 29. I wonder if Paul might have been thinking, "If you love yourself at all, Mister, then love your wife — because life will be far more pleasant under the same roof with a well-loved woman!" I also have to wonder if Paul's reference to a man treating his wife as he does his own body, such as feeding and caring for it, implies that husbands are supposed to cook for their wives. I'm not certain about that interpretation, but I would submit to my husband's cooking any day!

I would like to suggest one last responsibility for both husbands and wives based on the final phrase in Ephesians 5:31: "And the two will become one flesh." The Greek word for "flesh" in this passage is *sarx,* which means "flesh of a living creature in distinction from that of a dead one." Our marriages were meant to be alive, not dead. Is your marriage more like romance or road-kill?

Think of marriage as a three-legged stool. The legs are a submissive wife, a loving husband, and Christ. All three legs must be in place for marriage to work as God intended. A wife submitting to an unloving husband is as lopsided as a loving husband sacrificing for a domineering wife. When Christ is not the head of the marriage relationship, the stool falls indeed. Paul pictures for us God's ideal marriage relationship. Sadly, many Christian women are trying to keep their stools balanced with only one leg in place — their submission.

Over the course of the last twenty years, my marriage has been at both extremes and everywhere in between, but Keith and I have never been the types who could tolerate dull for very long. God has always been faithful to restore the life, passion, and active care to our marriage, and we have worked very hard to cooperate. You may need help from a real marriage expert like we have at times. I'd like to recommend the one who saved our marriage. His name is Wonderful Counselor, and His office is open twenty-four hours a day. He also uses human Christian counselors to help with His caseload!

Part 3: The Role of Christ in Marriage
Not only has Christ set the standard for a good marriage and the example of a loving husband, He offers sound counsel. Then

He supplies every ounce of power necessary to make a marriage work.

"For by him all things were created" (Col. 1:16). Beloved, God created marriage (Gen. 2:21–24). Figuratively speaking, before Adam and Eve said, "I do," God did. No one helped Him. Only God created marriage, and only He can hold it together. Many people live in the same home and share a joint checking account under the same name, but they don't have a clue about the true covenant of marriage. Marriage as the institution and wonderful mystery God created cannot exist or hold together without Him.

I want to conclude with a poem I wrote for Keith a number of years ago after a difficult season of our marriage. I pray God will use it to speak to you or encourage you.

Too

We were much too young
Much too selfish
Much too blind
To make it

Much too wounded
Much too frightened

Much too hurt
To take it

Too much we said
When love seemed dead
To go on
And forget

Too little learned
From anger burned
Too much
We both regret

Yet God's been

Much too good
Much too faithful
Much too kind
To walk away

Much too patient
Much too present
Much too able
Not to stay

Too much harm
To children's charms
To tear our home apart

Too much time
For nursery rhymes
To give away our hearts

Too much we've shared
With no one else
To go on and forget

Too many years
Of drying tears
To do what we'd regret

Too many laughs
when thinking back
Remind me what is true
I find that I still love you
And I think you love me,
Too.

CHAPTER 43
A READY WARRIOR

Ephesians 6

Put on the full armor of God so that you can take your stand against the devil's schemes.
(EPH. 6:11)

In the last chapter we looked at "Helps for War in the Home," so now let's consider "Helps for War in the Heavenlies." We'll approach this chapter as a battalion of soldiers in the middle of a heavenly war. Lives are at risk. Casualties may be high. Our Commander in Chief issues orders. The victory is sure, but the fight will be difficult. Hear the voice of your Commander in Ephesians 6:10–20 as He exhorts you to do the following:

1. *Realize your natural limitations.* We cannot enjoy spiritual victory without actively calling on the power of God. We are only strong when we are "in the Lord and in his

mighty power" (v. 10).

2. *Remember the "full armor"* ("put on the full armor of God," v. 11). Paul exhorted us to use every weapon available. Picture your Commander in Chief standing behind a table displaying six tools or weapons. He says, "I've tailor-made each of these for you. You may take only some of them if you choose, but they were designed to work together. Your safety and effectiveness are only guaranteed if you use them all."

Don't underestimate the enemy's ability. He is an expert archer. He's had at least six thousand years of practice on human targets. He won't waste arrows on well-armed places. He will aim for the spots you and I leave uncovered. Trust me, I know.

3. *Recognize your real enemies* ("our struggle is not against flesh and blood," v. 12). The struggles of warfare you and I experience do not originate in spouses, in-laws, neighbors, coworkers, or even our earthly foes. Spiritual forces of evil exist. The original word for "struggle" in verse 12 is *pale,* which was "used of the wrestling of athletes and of the hand-to-hand combat of soldiers."

Not every problem we have is warfare. Yes, Satan is ultimately at the origin of every temptation, but we're not perpetually going hand-to-hand with principalities of darkness. Some of my problems have resulted from personal rebellion. Sometimes I sense Satan is actively opposing my life. Other times I sense he is more passive because he sees me doing a fine job of getting myself into difficulty! We are wise to pray for discernment to know the nature of our problems. Sometimes the prescription is repentance. Other times it is fortification against the evil one.

4. *Realize our enemies' limitations* ("you may be able to stand your ground," v. 13). Satan and his powers and principalities cannot do anything they want with us. They have certain limitations. One is absolutely crucial for believers to understand: Demons cannot possess Christians. They can oppress, but they cannot possess. In his letter the apostle assured the Ephesians of their security in Christ before he ever warned them about warfare. "Having believed, you were marked in him with a seal, the promised Holy Spirit" (Eph. 1:13). "You were sealed for the day of redemption" (Eph. 4:30).

The Greek word for "seal" is *sphragizo,* meaning "to seal, close up and make fast with a seal signet such as letters or books so that they may not be read; generally to seal . . . for the sake of security." When you and I received Christ, God dropped His Holy Spirit into us, slammed on the lid, and tightened the cap. We've been closed and sealed every moment since. Nothing can get in.

Did you notice? Satan cannot read our minds. Check the definition once more. The kind of seal to which Paul referred closed a document so it could not be read. You may be thinking, "Satan sure seems to read my mind at times." My children used to think I could read their minds too. In reality, I simply knew them so well that I sometimes guessed what they were thinking. In the same way, because of our past behavior, Satan can often guess what we are thinking.

5. *Retain an active stance.* The word *stand* appears twice in verse 13: "Put on the full armor of God, so that when the day of evil comes, you may be able to stand your ground, and after you have done everything, to stand" (Eph. 6:13).

Paul uses two different Greek words for stand. The first appearance of the word *stand* means "to stand your ground." A more accurate translation of the word is "withstand." The second appearance of the word is rendered accurately as "stand."

The word *withstand* draws an image of a

soldier occupying his own piece of land and an enemy threatening to take it from him. Ephesians 4:27 warns us not to "give the devil a foothold." The original term for "stand" paints the picture of the evil one trying to grab a believer's foot to pull him off the ground he is occupying.

In the years we have known Christ, hopefully we have gained some ground. We're beginning to occupy some of the victorious space God desires for us. Satan wants to force us off our property and make us feel like we've gone nowhere. Believer, you are getting somewhere! Your dedication to study God's Word is proof! You and I must actively guard the gains we've made in Christ. Paul exhorts us to stand our ground!

6. *Reject personal hypocrisy.* The "belt of truth" (v. 14) represents not living a lie in any part of our lives, living free of secret areas of hypocrisy. Satan loves to blackmail believers who have a secret they want to keep hidden.

7. *Resist snares of unrighteousness.* "The breastplate of righteousness" (v. 14) is the protection we receive when we choose the right thing even when we feel like choosing the wrong thing. Not only will we find protection from disaster, God will honor our obedience by changing our hearts if

we'll let Him. We will find great protection in learning to pray Psalm 141:4: "Let not my heart be drawn to what is evil."

8. *Remain balanced!* Good soldiers have their "feet fitted with the readiness that comes from the gospel of peace" (v. 15). The word for "readiness" is *hetoimasia,* meaning "firm footing." Roman soldiers' boots had cleats on the soles to give them firm footing. Our feet give our bodies balance. We can remain balanced because, although we are at war with Satan, we are at peace with God. Sink your feet into "the gospel of peace"!

9. *Refuse unbelief.* "The shield of faith" (v. 16) is our protection when Satan tempts us to disbelieve God. A big difference separates doubting what God may do and doubting God. Even when you have no idea what God is doing, your protection is in never doubting God is God. We're not called to have faith in our faith. We are called to have faith in God and never doubt Him.

10. *Reinforce your mind.* "The helmet of salvation" (v. 17) protects our minds. The best way to protect our minds is to fill it with the Word of God and things pertaining to godliness. We need to deliberately avoid destructive influences.

11. *Raise your sword.* You've probably noticed the defensive nature of all five previous weapons. "The sword of the Spirit" (v. 17) is our only offensive weapon against the evil one. Christ demonstrated how to be an expert swordsman. In His wilderness temptation Jesus attacked Satan with "the Word of God" until the enemy gave up. Know and use "the Word of God" persistently!

12. *Retain an active prayer life* ("pray in the Spirit on all occasions," v. 18). Prayerless lives are powerless lives. Active prayer lives equip us with the power and motivation to put on the full armor of God. Because Paul mentioned praying for others next, I believe this first exhortation was primarily about praying for ourselves.

13. *Remember one another in warfare prayer* ("always keep on praying for all the saints," v. 18). Power results from collective prayer. God delights in our petitions for each other. Soldiers depend on one another to watch their backs! Not long ago I realized I was having an internal problem with anger. I was caught off guard because ordinarily I do not struggle with anger. I prayed many times; finally I shared my struggles with a friend. She began to join me in prayer, and the anger ceased immediately. I cannot explain why. I only know

that Satan's secret was out, prayer doubled, and God acted.

14. *Remember spiritual leaders in warfare prayer.* Notice Paul ended by asking for prayer ("pray also for me," v. 19). Again, I believe he was talking about warfare prayer, because he asked specifically for intercession regarding fearlessness. According to 2 Timothy 1:7, God does not give us a spirit of fear (KJV). Satan is the one who fuels fear in an attempt to keep people from serving God effectively. If the great apostle needed prayer to fulfill his calling fearlessly, we all need prayer! Our missionaries, pastors, leaders, and teachers need our prayers. The enemy wants to destroy ministries. Our prayers help build a hedge of protection around them.

The following list includes each of Paul's fourteen exhortations about warfare. As you read the list, mentally evaluate yourself on each of the actions.

- I realize my natural limitations.
- I remember (keep in mind) the importance of the full armor.
- I recognize my real enemies.
- I realize my enemies' limitations.
- I retain an active stance.
- I reject personal hypocrisy.

- I resist snares of unrighteousness.
- I remain balanced.
- I refuse unbelief.
- I reinforce my mind.
- I raise my sword.
- I retain an active prayer life.
- I remember others in warfare prayer.
- I specifically remember spiritual leaders in warfare prayer.

What a set of goals! Would you consider making each of these part of your daily walk with Christ? Warfare is a reality for the Christian life. We can do nothing to change that. We can, however, decide whether to be victims or victors.

CHAPTER 44
A MORE EXCELLENT WAY

Philemon

I appeal to you on the basis of love.
(PHILEM. 9)

By this time, Paul had written the following epistles, probably in this order: Galatians, 1 and 2 Thessalonians, 1 and 2 Corinthians, Romans, Colossians, and Ephesians. In the last years of the apostle's life, four out of five of his letters were written to individuals rather than to bodies of believers. Philemon was the first of Paul's personal letters divinely chosen to be part of Scripture. Philemon was a believer from Colosse whom Paul probably met while ministering in a nearby city. Quite possibly Paul had personally introduced Philemon to the Savior.

Philemon owned a slave whose name was Onesimus. Onesimus ran away from Philemon and by the providence of God found himself in Rome, where he met Paul. Paul told Onesimus about Christ, and the runaway slave became a brother. Then Paul sent Onesimus back to Philemon with the letter that bears his name.

I am a hopeless romantic. I hate conflict, and I love happy endings. Of all the chapters of this study, the conflict between Paul and Barnabas was one of the most difficult. I had grown to love the partnership between them so much. My heart ached over their disagreement over John Mark. Twelve years passed. Paul was placed under house arrest in Rome. Now we see Mark with him once again. Time heals and, if we're the least bit cooperative, matures us. Praise God, sometimes we live and learn.

You may be wondering why I am focusing on Paul and Mark when the letter is obviously about Paul and Onesimus. I think Mark may have been Paul's inspiration for seeking restoration between Philemon and Onesimus. A dozen years earlier Paul had been hard and unyielding. Perhaps he had since learned a more excellent way.

Let's compile a few facts and assumptions about the letter. Based on his statement in verse 19, Paul apparently led Philemon to Christ. They developed a friendship, and Paul saw Philemon become an active worker for the gospel. Philemon must have been a wealthy man to be a slave owner and own a home large enough to serve as a meeting place for the church. At some point Onesimus, one of his slaves, ran away. Verse 18 indicates he also may have stolen something from Philemon: "If he has done you any wrong or owes you anything, charge it to me."

We have no way of knowing for certain, but while he was on the run, Onesimus may have stolen again and been incarcerated with Paul. Imagine how strange their meeting must have been once they realized they both knew Philemon. You can be sure their meeting wasn't a coincidence. No doubt, God ordained the fugitive slave to have a heart-to-heart collision with the most well-known slave of grace in Christendom.

Paul could have dealt with the situation in one of several different ways, but the wise apostle chose the most excellent way. He portrayed a beautiful example of Micah 6:8: "He has showed you, O man, what is good. / And what does the LORD require of you? / To act justly and to love mercy / and to walk humbly with your God."

More than sacrifices or offerings, God desires three things from us: to act justly, love mercy, and walk humbly with Him. The solution Paul sought in the conflict between Philemon and his fugitive slave, Onesimus, met all three requirements.

1. *Paul acted justly.* One easy way Paul might have handled the situation was to consider Onesimus absolved from all responsibility after he repented and accepted Christ. However, Onesimus had wronged Philemon in several ways. He ran away from his legal owner, and possibly he stole from him. In Paul's estimation the restoration of two Christian men was priority. The issue could not be resolved fully unless Onesimus returned to Philemon and unless Philemon was repaid for all Onesimus owed.

For justice to prevail, someone had to take responsibility for Onesimus's actions, and someone had to pay his debt. Paul responded with great wisdom. Paul insisted that Onesimus take responsibility for wrongdoing, yet he took on the debt. Likewise we must take responsibility for our sins; but, thankfully, Christ has paid the debt!

2. *Paul loved mercy.* Paul did more than preach to people. He lived the concepts he taught. When he met Onesimus, he saw a man in need of a Savior; Paul didn't just preach to him about the mercy of God, he showed it to him. He took Onesimus's debt not only out of justice, because the debt

needed to be paid, but out of mercy, because a sinner needed grace. Paul wanted Philemon to show mercy as well. According to the original language, Onesimus was a slave bound to permanent servitude to Philemon. His return to Philemon would mean the return to slavery.

Critics of God's Word often protest that the Bible seems to support evils like slavery, but in fact the opposite is true. Jesus and Paul could have come preaching against the specific evils of their day, such as slavery. If they had done so, the message of heart transformation through forgiveness of sin would have been lost. Instead both Christ and Paul concentrated on getting people into a right relationship with God. They knew that evil social institutions would fall before the force of people with the heart of the Father beating in their chests.

Though Paul did not spend his time battling issues like slavery, he left no doubt how he viewed the institution. "There is neither Jew nor Greek, slave nor free, male nor female, for you are all one in Christ Jesus" (Gal. 3:28). If he spoke in our churches today, he would say, "How can you who belong to Christ treat others as anything but brothers and sisters in Him?"

You see, although Paul had to deal with

slavery realistically as a part of his society, he believed in absolute equality. He believed that slaves must be obedient to their masters just like citizens must obey the law, but he was definitely not an advocate of slavery. He told Philemon he was returning Onesimus to him but "no longer as a slave, but better than a slave, as a dear brother" (Philem. 16).

God has strong feelings about mercy. In the Old Testament God demanded mercy on slaves. God required His people to remember they also had been slaves and to have mercy on others. As Christ's ambassador, Paul did not violate the Old Testament principle. He had the full cooperation of Onesimus, who was willing to return so restoration would ensue. Paul also asked Philemon to be an ambassador of Christ by abolishing Onesimus's slavery and receiving him as a brother. Paul's proposal was to let mercy reign.

3. *Paul walked humbly with God.* Anyone who truly walks with God, walks humbly. The closer we draw near to Him and the more we behold His majesty, the more we relate to the psalmist who said, "What is man that you are mindful of him?" (Ps. 8:4). Like the psalmist, Paul recognized the pit from which God had pulled him. Both men

enjoyed an intimate relationship with God, yet neither of them viewed Him as a chum or a running buddy. They each knew grace had bridged the wide gulf fixed between them. To walk with God is to walk humbly. We cannot help but confront His holiness. Paul's proposal for restoration between Philemon and Onesimus required both men to walk humbly with God.

Paul also had to humble himself by resisting the temptation to be bold and order Philemon to do what he ought to do (vv. 8–9). Instead, he appealed to him on another basis, which brings us to our final point.

When God sent His Son to be an atoning sacrifice for our sins, He showed mankind a more excellent way: He fulfilled the law with love (see Rom. 5:8). Paul could have demanded certain actions from Philemon, but he appealed to him on the basis of love.

Paul learned the hard way how meaningless gifts, talents, and sacrifices were without love. In his earlier years Paul attempted to exercise his gifts and make extreme sacrifices without love.

The hollowness of works without love becomes evident to all who seek to serve God. We cannot serve God wholeheartedly without the whole heart. Even though many years earlier Paul and Barnabas had probably made the right decision to divide and multiply, I'm not sure Paul responded to the conflict with John Mark in love. I think a hollowness accompanied Paul everywhere he went until the gulf was bridged with grace. Somewhere along the way, Paul learned the most "excellent way." And he showed it by personal example to others like Philemon and us.

The rich Book of Philemon ends with Paul's request for Philemon to prepare a guest room for him in hopes that he would be there soon. I grin as I imagine Philemon receiving his runaway slave as a brother, just as Paul asked. After all, Paul might be on his way.

CHAPTER 45
A RARE GEM

Philippians 4

*I know what it is to be in need, and I
know what it is to have plenty. I have
learned the secret of being content in any
and every situation, whether well fed or
hungry, whether living in plenty or in want.*
(PHIL. 4:12)

In this chapter we conclude the letters Paul
wrote during his house arrest in Rome. Our
thoughts will center on the glorious Book of
Philippians. Most scholars assume Colossians and Ephesians were written earlier in
the two-year period. Both Philemon and
Philippians refer to the possibility of Paul's
release, leading us to believe they were written in the latter part of his house arrest.

I consider the entire Book of Philippians a
discourse on the higher life in Christ. Every
precept he taught the Christians in Philippi
can be a reality for any believer; but we

must have open hearts and cooperative wills to truly proclaim, "For to me, to live is Christ and to die is gain" (Phil. 1:21). Philippians 4 contains many treasures. If you sift through the treasures, you will find one of the rarest of all gems: contentment.

How many truly contented people do you know? They are rare gems, aren't they? The enemy loves to see our discontentment. Why? Contented Christians live a powerful and effective testimony. Their lives are walking witnesses, proving that Christ can deliver what the gods of this world can't. You can be sure of this: Wherever a rare gem exists, a jewel thief is lurking close by. We can identify five thieves of contentment based on Philippians 4.

1. *Pettiness.* To everyone who thought the apostle Paul did not believe in women in ministry — allow me to introduce Euodia and Syntyche: "I plead with Euodia and I plead with Syntyche to agree with each other in the Lord . . . help these women who have contended at my side in the cause of the gospel" (Phil. 4:2–3).

Someone dubbed them "Odious" and "Soon Touchy." They worked right beside him. They were fellow workers! They had just one little problem: they couldn't get along. Let's admit it: people can be petty!

410

God intentionally made women sensitive. I believe the counterfeit of sensitivity is pettiness. We tend to get our feelings hurt easily and take things personally. God gave us a special tenderness and sensitivity to lend a sweetness to our service. Pettiness sours a servant's heart and steals contentment. Next notice the second thief of contentment.

2. *Anxiety.* Does anything rob us of contentment more than anxiety? I personally can't think of a more successful jewel thief. "Do not be anxious about anything, but in everything, by prayer and petition, with thanksgiving, present your requests to God" (Phil. 4:6).

No anxiety — what a thought! How do we turn off the valve that is pumping anxiety into our souls? Paul proposes an answer: prayer. You might say, "A better solution to fighting anxiety must exist. I've prayed — and still been anxious." I want to suggest gently that you haven't necessarily been practicing the kind of prayer Paul was describing as a prescription for anxiety.

Verse 6 describes an intimate and active prayer life. Notice Paul's words for prayer and supplication. The word *prayer* refers to a very general kind of prayer. The word *supplication* is translated from the Greek word

411

deesis describing a very personal kind of prayer. *Deesis* is "the petition for specific individual needs and wants." Paul exhorted believers to come to God with general requests and needs as well as the details that cause us anxiety. Then don't give up! Persist until peace comes.

Keep praying not only about your critical needs but also about everything! An open line of communication with God reminds you He is real and active in your life. Peace overflowing from an active prayer life lends contentment.

3. *Destructive thinking.* Proverbs 23:7 describes man with the words, "For as he thinketh in his heart, so is he" (KJV). We might apply the proverb this way: A person feels like he or she thinks. Our human natures tend toward negative and destructive thoughts. If ten people complimented you today and one person criticized, which would you go to bed thinking about tonight? Probably the criticism!

Destructive, negative thinking is a habit that can be broken, but this thief takes diligence to overcome. God knows the tendency of the mind to meditate on things. Meditation is simply the thinking and rethinking of certain subject matter. Paul gave us a wonderful checklist for determining whether our thoughts are worth thinking! "Whatever is true, whatever is noble, whatever is right, whatever is pure, whatever is lovely, whatever is admirable — if anything is excellent or praise-worthy — think about such things" (Phil. 4:8).

I struggle with destructive thinking just like you do. In my journey, God has used Scripture memory and Bible study to set me free. I continue to make a priority of His Word daily, but He also blesses refreshment I gain from school events, an occasional decent movie, a wholesome magazine, a good documentary, or a funny book. Worthy thought patterns are a key to contentment.

4. *Resistance to learn.* In verse 11 Paul wrote, "I have learned to be content whatever the circumstances." We do not suddenly get contentment. We learn it. No one was born with contentment. Paul learned from experience that God was faithful no matter what circumstance he met. Had he never been in want, He never would have learned! Often we're in no mood to learn when we're in difficult circumstances, but God desires to show us that we can't meet a circumstance He can't handle. We handcuff a sly thief of contentment when we ask God to give us hearts willing to learn.

413

5. *Independence.* We now unmask the fifth thief that steals the rare gem of contentment. Refusing to rely on God robs us of some of God's most priceless riches. Through countless ups and downs, Paul learned he could do everything God called him to do, but only "through him [Christ] who gives me strength" (Phil. 4:13). Through the multitude of needs Paul encountered, he learned that "God will meet all your needs . . . in Christ Jesus" (Phil. 4:19).

I believe Paul considered reliance on God a secret because everyone has to discover it for themselves. I can tell you God will meet your every need. I can say that you can do all things through Christ; but until you find out for yourself, it's still a secret. I can tell you, but He will show you. Let Him. He is so faithful.

Contentment is a rare gem. Because Paul ceased letting thieves steal his contentment, his testimony was powerful. Even many who belonged to Caesar's household were compelled to know Christ! (see Phil. 4:22). My guess is, Paul had a secret they wanted to know.

■ ■ ■ ■

PART X
GOING HOME

■ ■ ■ ■

I told you I've been a fan of the apostle Paul for years. As we prepare for our final chapters, I must confess; my "fan-dom" has grown. I'm a greater fan not only in spite of his frailties and weaknesses but in some ways because of them. He gives me hope. He reminds me that none of us is beyond grace, beyond use. Only God can make the common sacred. We've learned so much about this man who once persecuted the people of Christ with such vengeance; yet, to me, the best of him is yet to come. Finishing the race is not all that matters.

How we finish the race is sometimes our most powerful testimony.

Withhold nothing from God during the homestretch of our study. Stop and pray right now for Him to have full access to do anything still lacking among His goals for you in this journey. Let God's Word break every chain and loosen you to be a mighty servant of God. He is life — and life more abundant.

CHAPTER 46
A SHARP MEMORY

1 Timothy 1

> *I was once a blasphemer and a persecutor.*
> (1 TIM. 1:13)

I can hardly believe we are beginning the final lap of our journey. The apostle Paul has occupied my thoughts for more than a year. His experiences have permeated every circumstance I met. Each sermon I hear sparks thoughts of one of Paul's. Virtually every prayer I raise is now marked with phrases and concepts I learned from his petitions.

Each time I approach the end of a study, I have the same overwhelming feeling: "Lord, keep the truths I've learned in this journey as fresh on my heart as they are at this moment. Never let me forget!" Today I realize why refusing to forget the glorious works of God is so important. As we will soon see,

417

Paul's refusal to forget brought great benefit.

Let's recapture our context. Our previous chapters carried us through the two-year period Paul spent under house arrest in Rome in A.D. 61–62. We believe during this time he wrote the books of Colossians, Ephesians, Philemon, and Philippians. In this final portion our focus is on the last five years of his life.

This portion of the study unfolds with Paul's release from house arrest and his presumed freedom for about four years. Scholars debate his exact whereabouts during his last season of freedom and whether he finally made it to Spain. We do know that Paul wrote three personal letters to a couple of young preachers during his last five years. He wrote to Timothy and Titus during his season of freedom, and he penned a second letter to Timothy during his final imprisonment. We will look first at 1 Timothy.

Although many fellow workers endeared themselves to Paul, I'm not sure anyone ever shared Timothy's place in the apostle's heart. He referred to several people as sons in the faith, but no one seemed to compare to Timothy. One reason Timothy was so dear to Paul was his young age when Paul met him. All Jewish men longed to be fathers and deeply desired to have sons. Perhaps Timothy filled a gap in Paul's life at a crucial time. He deeply loved this young man and felt an obvious freedom to both praise and correct him.

Paul and Timothy spent years together, yet oddly the apostle hardly greeted the young preacher before he repeated his testimony (1 Tim. 1:12–17). Paul recounted how he had come to Christ and served Him with an emphasis on two points. Paul emphasized his own unworthiness and Christ's grace. Twenty-six years had passed since a blinding light had opened the eyes of a persecutor named Saul. He was still repeating his testimony because he never forgot. He remembered like it was yesterday.

I don't know how you feel about Paul or the journey we've shared, but I know I want his unquenchable passion! Fortunately, it's contagious. We catch it by imitating what he did to get it. The apostle retained his spiritual passion through a roller-coaster existence. I see at least six reasons in 1 Timothy 1:12–17.

1. *He never forgot the privilege of ministry* (v. 12). Decades later, Paul was still amazed to have been appointed to Christ's service. When Jesus first appointed him, He said to Ananias, "This man is my chosen instru-

ment. . . . I will show him how much he must suffer for my name" (Acts 9:15–16). Paul's life obviously fulfilled Christ's testimony. Unlike most of us, Paul's conversion and subsequent ministry took him from a life of relative ease to almost constant pressure and turmoil. He was beaten, stoned, whipped, jailed, and starved in the course of his ministry; yet he considered his calling to serve God to be the greatest privilege anyone could receive.

A host of reasons probably existed for Paul's continued gratitude. One possibility stands out most in my mind. His chief desire was "to know Christ" (Phil. 3:10). I believe the more he knew Christ, the more he saw His greatness. The more Paul saw His greatness, the more amazed he was to have the privilege to serve Him. We will also become more amazed over our privilege to serve as we seek to know Christ better.

2. *He never forgot who he had been* (v. 13). God used Paul to perform more wonders and birth more churches than any other human in the New Testament. In a quarter of a century, Paul had plenty of time to forget who he had been and take pride in his powerful ministry. One reason God leaves our memories of past repented sin intact is because a twinge of memory is indeed

profitable to us. Pride is the archenemy of ministry.

I think one reason Paul continued to remember who he had been was because his love for Christ continued to grow. The more he loved Christ, the more he wondered how he could have sinned against Him so horrendously in his past. I've personally experienced this. Even though I know I am fully forgiven, the deeper my love for Christ has grown, the more I regret past sins.

In his final letter to Timothy, Paul would write, "Nevertheless, God's solid foundation stands firm, sealed with this inscription: 'The Lord knows those who are his,' " (2 Tim. 2:19). We are wise never to forget who we were. God never forgets who we are. Never forgetting who we were lends a far greater appreciation for who we now are!

3. *He never forgot the abundance of God* (v. 14). Paul discovered God's intent was not just for us to get by. He is not the God of barely enough. Paul encountered a God who supergave! Paul wrote, "The grace of our Lord was poured out on me abundantly, along with the faith and love that are in Christ Jesus." The word *abundantly* means to "superabound" *(Strong's)*. Paul never forgot the abundance of God. Greater still,

God never forgets the abundance of our need.

Isaiah described God's devotion to His children: "Can a mother forget the baby at her breast / and have no compassion on the child she has borne? / Though she may forget, I will not forget you!" (Isa. 49:15). He sees our needs like a mother sees her helpless infant's needs. Like a loving mother, He will never forget one of His children.

4. *He never forgot the basics* (v. 15). Can you imagine the wealth of knowledge Paul gained in his quest for God? Still he never lost sight of the most important truth he ever learned: "Christ Jesus came into the world to save sinners." May we also never forget! We don't have to lose touch with our most basic belief to press on to maturity.

How long has it been since tears stung your eyes when someone received Christ? Or how long has it been since you felt deep gratitude for the simplicity of your salvation? I beg you, never stop thanking Christ for coming into the world specifically to save you.

5. *He never forgot his primary role* (v. 16). According to the apostle, God saved "the worst of sinners," to "display His unlimited patience as an example." The Greek word

for "example" means "to draw a sketch or first draft as painters when they begin a picture." Paul saw himself drawn in that picture. You are painted in the portrait. I am painted in. The worst of sinners — the spiritually blind, lame, and lost — find unlimited patience in our God! If we look on the era of Paul's life and his contemporaries to be the last great movement of God, then we have tragically misunderstood. If our conclusion is "Wow! Those were the days," we missed the point. God is still painting the portrait of His church. Paul was only an example of what God can do with one repentant life. God hasn't finished the picture — but one day He will.

6. *He never forgot the wonder of God* (v. 17). Twenty-six years after he fell to his knees, Paul still felt so overwhelmed by the awesome work of God that he exclaimed, "Now to the King eternal, immortal, invisible, the only God, be honor and glory for ever and ever." I wish I could have seen Timothy's face reading Paul's words. Perhaps he thought, *How has he kept his wonder?* The answer? He never forgot who he had been. He relished the abundance of God. He never lost sight of the basics.

When my oldest daughter was little and I offered her a treat that had lost its luster to her, she responded politely, "No, thank you, Mommy. I'm used to that." The apostle Paul had known Christ for twenty-six years. Still he looked back on his salvation and the privilege to serve and never got "used to that." May God grant us a memory like Paul's.

CHAPTER 47
SPIRITUAL FITNESS IN MINISTRY

1 Timothy 4

Train yourself to be godly. For physical training is of some value, but godliness has value for all things, holding promise for both the present life and the life to come.
(1 TIM. 4:7–8)

If you glance through the Book of 1 Timothy, you will notice a continuing exhortation for order in the churches. Paul wrote about servants (deacons), overseers, widows, elders, and slaves. In stressing order in the church, he made some statements about women that raise controversy. Although these statements are not my focus, I do not want to be charged with cowardice by omitting any mention of them. We are wise to view Paul's exhortations in context. He used far more ink to address deacons and overseers.

In 1 Timothy 2:11–12, Paul wrote, "A woman should learn in quietness and full submission. I do not permit a woman to teach or to have authority over a man; she must be silent." When he said, "A woman should learn in quietness" and "be silent," he did not use a Greek word that meant "complete silence or no talking. [He used a word] used elsewhere to mean settled down, undisturbed, not unruly."[1] Remember, Paul's primary ministry was geared toward Gentiles who had never been trained to have respect and reverence in worship. Paul encouraged women to observe traditional customs lest the young churches suffer a bad reputation.

Consider a traditional Jewish worship service. Men sat on the lower floor of the synagogue while women sat in the balcony or at the back of the room. Women were not allowed to utter a word; they merely listened. Contrast this picture with a Christian worship service in the New Testament world. The men and women were together in a private home. The worship centered around praising God, singing, fellowshipping, eating together, sharing testimonies, and receiving instruction in their new faith. Women were included as never before. Talk about a radical idea!

The Christian movement was new and fragile. Any taint of adverse publicity could greatly hinder the mission of the church and mean persecution for believers. Women had to restrain their new freedom in Christ (Gal. 3:28) so as not to impede the progress of the gospel. Paul's "weaker brother" principle (1 Cor. 8:9) applies. He said, "Be careful, however, that the exercise of your freedom does not become a stumbling block to the weak." Thus, women were to learn quietly, without calling attention to themselves.

In regard to instructing women not to teach men, you must understand that most women in Paul's day were illiterate. They were not taught in synagogue schools or trained by a rabbi. Paul goes on to say in verse 12 that women should not usurp authority over men. The Greek word *authenteo,* "one who claims authority," is used only this one time in the Greek translation of the Bible. This word refers to an autocrat or dictator. Paul says women were not to come in and take over!

We cannot regard verses 11 and 12 as a prohibition against women opening their mouths in church or men learning anything biblical from women. Paul gave instructions for how women are to pray and prophesy (1 Cor. 11:5). He was fully aware of Priscilla's role in teaching Apollos in Ephesus (Acts 18:26). Paul issued differing instructions for churches based on their cultural settings and his desire for order in the church.

Our focus today is on Paul's personal exhortations to Timothy, his son in the faith. Midway through my preparation for this study, I began to realize that one of God's priority goals is to raise up and encourage passionate, persevering servants who are completely abandoned to His will. Paul's exhortations to Timothy stand as timeless words of advice to every servant of the living God, regardless of generation or gender.

In chapters 4, 5, and 6 of this letter to Timothy, we can identify six imperatives for strong ministry. Look with me at Paul's instruction to his son in the faith.

1. *"Train yourself to be godly"* (4:7). Godliness does not instantly accompany salvation. Remember, salvation is a gift. Godliness is a pursuit. The word meaning "to train" is *gumnazo,* from which we derive the word *gymnasium.* The apostle drew a parallel between an athlete's preparing for the Greek games and a believer's pursuing godliness. An athlete who is preparing for intense competition makes frequent visits to the gym.

2. *"Set an example"* (4:12). Although Tim-

othy was young, Paul exhorted him not to let others who were older intimidate him. Rather, he should "set an example . . . in speech, in life, in love, in faith and in purity." God is practical. His Word works. He wants us to be living proof by our example. The apostle expressed the principle clearly in Philippians 3:17: "Join with others in following my example, brothers, and take note of those who live according to the pattern we gave you."

How could Paul have enough nerve to invite people to follow his example? The key was his obvious philosophy on Christian leadership. Years before, in 1 Corinthians 11:1, he had written, "Follow my example, as I follow the example of Christ." This verse defines the single most important characteristic for all church leaders. If we're leading but we're not closely following Christ, we are misleading.

3. *"Do not neglect your gift"* (4:14). Spiritual gifts must be cared for, cultivated, and developed. Paul felt so strongly about this exhortation to Timothy, he gave it even greater emphasis in his second letter. In 2 Timothy 1:6, Paul told Timothy "to fan into flame the gift of God."

When we receive Christ, God gives us spiritual gifts, but they must be developed.

For example, I received Christ as a young child, but I did not use the gift of teaching until I became an adult. Then God opened a door for me to teach Sunday school. Although He gave me the spiritual gift and opened the door for me to use it, God expected me to accept the opportunity and fan the gift into a flame. Every week I had to study. I also spent numerous hours listening to other teachers. I asked one to disciple me personally. I had to develop a consistent prayer life. I also had to learn from my blunders and lessons that flopped! Still I kept asking God to teach me His Word so I could be obedient. These are a few ways God directed me to "fan into flame" one gift He gave me. God honors a beautiful blend of gift and grit! He gives the gift, and He expects us to have the grit to practice and learn how to use it effectively.

4. *"Watch your life and doctrine closely"* (4:16). The Greek word for "watch" is *epecho,* meaning "to hold upon" *(Strong's).* Paul exhorted Timothy to keep tight reins on how he lived and what he taught. Remember, Timothy was a young preacher. We can never overemphasize the importance of preachers and teachers keeping tight reins on what they teach. Teaching is a tremendous responsibility because we risk

compromising the truth. God intends for teachers and preachers to instruct soberly with an ongoing sense of reverence for God and responsibility toward man. James warns us that teaching and preaching call for a stricter judgment due to the great responsibility involved (James 3:1).

5. *"Keep yourself pure"* (5:22). Paul exhorted Timothy to watch his life closely. He then became more specific by directing Timothy to keep himself pure. Nothing marks the erosion of character or has the potential to destroy ministries and testimonies like impurity. Paul told Timothy to keep himself pure. The original word for "keep" comes from the word *teros,* meaning "a warden or guard." Paul told Timothy to stand as a guard over purity in his own life. I must take responsibility for purity in my life. You must take responsibility for purity in your life.

If you are trying to keep yourself pure but you continue to fall, please seek godly counsel. A mature and discerning believer can help you identify reasons you continue to be drawn to impurity. It is not too late to consecrate your life to God and find victory.

6. *"Turn away from godless chatter"* (6:20). The word for "godless" is *bebelos,* which

431

speaks of "a threshold, particularly of a temple." This "threshold" separates the profane from the holy. If we are believers in Christ, we are sacred temples of His Holy Spirit. We have a choice what crosses the threshold and finds a place in our temples. Paul exhorts believers to discern a line in conversation that should not be crossed.

Sometimes we have to think of ways to turn away from godless chatter without deeply offending another person or disrespecting someone in authority. Pursuing godliness isn't always pleasant. Sometimes we are forced to make difficult decisions. He will direct us how to turn away appropriately. If we turn away proudly and self-righteously, we ourselves have crossed an important threshold. Humility is the earmark of God's genuine servant. Even when we turn away, we should be humble.

The apostle Paul spoke to Timothy from experience about safe and strong ministry. He knew the pitfalls. He knew how quickly lives could be shipwrecked. Paul knew that integrity is more easily maintained than regained. I believe Paul would offer us the same advice today: "Train yourself to be godly" (1 Tim. 4:7). Set an example! Don't neglect your gift! Watch what you teach!

Keep yourself pure! Turn away from profanity!

I pray that Paul's life has compelled you to be an active part of God's agenda. I hope you will never again be satisfied to sit on the sidelines. I pray that you desire your life to leave footprints someone else could follow straight to Christ. None of these things will happen accidentally or coincidentally. Godliness and effective ministry take attention, but nothing you could pour your energies into will ever have a greater payoff.

CHAPTER 48
PERSON TO PERSON

Titus 2

*Then they can train the younger women
to love their husbands and children.*
(TITUS 2:4)

The second epistle Paul wrote during his
final five years was to another young
preacher he nurtured in ministry. This
youthful Gentile was named Titus. When
Paul wrote the letter, Titus was a busy
preacher on the island of Crete. Paul introduced a wonderful concept to Titus that we
don't want to miss. It's tucked into chapter
2: mentoring.

First, let's check out Paul's instruction to
men; then we'll focus on the biblical relationship between older and younger women.
I believe he prioritized some of the instructions each needed most. We tend to think
Paul picked on women, but please notice
his priorities for older men. He urged the

young preacher to "teach the older men to be temperate, worthy of respect, self-controlled, and sound in faith, in love and in endurance" (Titus 2:2). The word *sound* means "healthy." Through his letter to Titus, Paul charged preachers with teaching men healthy ways to live, exercise authority and faith, and love others. All of us need to be taught not only what is God's will, but how to do it!

Now consider Paul's instruction to Titus for teaching young men in 2:6. He only gave one instruction. He charged Titus with the responsibility for setting an example for young men. In essence he said, "Don't just command it. Show it!" Titus was also a young man. Nothing would be a more effective teaching tool than his own example. Paul called Titus to be living proof.

Now let's turn our thoughts to the wonderful concept of mentorship. I wish I had the space to share about the older women who have mentored me as a Christian woman, wife, mother, and servant of God. Instead, I will ask you also to remember those who have mentored you. If you happen to be a male, don't tune Paul out here. Men need older men as mentors just as women need older women.

If you are fortunate to have benefited from

some godly mentors, think of what they have taught you. You know, none of those mentors were in your life accidentally. God brought you into their sphere of influence purposely to fulfill His purposes. Let's look at Paul's charge to older women. Notice he began by pointing out certain qualifications for a mentor to younger women in verse 3:

1. *Reverent in the way she lives.* Her actions are to be those of a woman who respects God. Each of the women who have mentored me were quite different in personality, but they all shared one common denominator: their lives were replete with a reverence for God. Those I respect most are those who respect God.

2. *Not slanderous.* I believe older women may have more opportunities to remain active today than in Paul's day. One of my eighty-three-year-old friends told me the other day she was too busy to die! Still, for some who have grown idle, slanderous talk can become a means to keep life interesting. Younger women struggle with temptation to slander too. Slanderous people thrive on conflict and division. The godly mentor sets an example by edifying others through her speech — rejoicing over their victories and hurting with them in defeat.

3. *Not addicted to much wine.* The original

word for "addicted" is *douloo,* meaning "to enslave" *(Strong's).* In Paul's generation wine was the primary substance to which a woman might become addicted. Today we could fill a grocery aisle with potentially enslaving substances.

I have two very dear friends whose mothers were alcoholics. They still struggle with the painful results. So many people in our society are enslaved to different substances. Alcohol, prescription and nonprescription drugs, diet pills, sleeping pills, and illegal drugs are readily available to anyone the least bit desperate or vulnerable.

The general purpose for older women mentoring younger women is stated at the end of Titus 2:3: "to teach what is good." The original Greek word for "good" is *kalos,* which "expresses beauty as a harmonious completeness, balance, proportion." Older women are to teach younger women about genuine beauty: God's idea of a beautiful woman.

Allow me to emphasize three areas from Titus 2:3–6 in which older women are to help younger women.

1. *Love their husbands.* Interestingly, the original word used for "love" is not *agape* this time. It's *philandros,* which speaks of "loving [someone] as a friend." Romantic

love is so important in a marriage but, in addition, Titus 2:4 expresses our need to learn to be a friend to our mates. Women often have several good friends, but men tend to have fewer close friendships. A man often needs his wife to be a friend as well as a lover. Not long ago, Keith said to me so sweetly, "Elizabeth, you're my best friend." Keith is my husband and my love for him is totally unique, but I have so many close girlfriends that I didn't think of him as my best friend. I nearly cried and prayed silently, *Oh, God, help me be a good best friend to my husband — and make him mine.*

Phileo love, which is central to *philandros,* grows from "common interests." By our feminine natures, women don't often share the same interests as men. But we can learn to share their interests! I'm intimidated by deep water, so I rarely fish with my husband. But we've spent many nights by the fire at the deer lease, and we love to watch basketball together. One common bond that Keith and I share is humor. Rarely a day goes by that we don't share a rousing belly laugh. A good laugh has healed many hurts in our home! We make an effort to spend lots of time together and share each other's worlds. I want to be a better friend to my husband. If you're married, let's make this commitment together. We can be a friend to our spouses. Let's start working on it right away.

2. *Love their children.* You may be thinking, *Who needs to be taught how to love her children?* Lots of wounded people, that's who. As recently as three days ago a woman at a conference whispered in my ear, "I don't know how to love my children." I've heard those words a staggering number of times over the course of my ministry.

I had the great blessing of a family where children are virtual royalty. My mother mentored me to love children. Many women haven't had a mentor like my mom. I would make four heartfelt suggestions to those who have difficulty loving their children: (1) Seek a mentor who can help train you to be a loving parent. (2) Seek sound, godly counsel to discover why your heart is hindered and how you can find freedom in Christ. (3) Do the right things until you feel the right things. In other words, hug your children and tell them you love them whether or not these actions are easy for you. They so much need hugs and reassurance. (4) Take up their interests. Attend their school functions, go to their games, have their friends over for pizza! Whether or not parenting comes naturally to you, it's hard work! Nothing has ever drained me or thrilled me more on this earth than motherhood. Hang in there and seek some good support!

3. *Be busy at home.* The original word for "busy" means "one who looks after domestic affairs with prudence and care." I believe Paul wanted older women to teach younger women that homes and families do not take care of themselves. Someone has to watch over the priorities. Children don't raise themselves. Someone has to watch over them and be involved. A marriage doesn't improve itself. Someone has to watch over it and encourage growth and intimacy. Even if we work, wise women still remain very involved in their homes and families. The wife and mother has something to give her home and family that no one else can supply as effectively: tenderness, nurturing, a personal touch.

CHAPTER 49
COME BEFORE
WINTER

2 Timothy 1–2

Do your best to come to me quickly.
(2 TIM. 4:9)

The year was A.D. 67, the place was Rome, and the conditions inhumane. A crazed emperor named Nero ruled the Roman Empire. The horrors began when a fire broke out in the Circus Maximus in Rome on July 18, A.D. 64, burning for nine days and consuming two-thirds of the city. Rumors began to circulate that Nero had ordered the fire so he could rebuild Rome in his own honor. With his last shreds of sound mind, Nero realized he had to offer a scapegoat. He chose a despised group of people commonly called *Chrestiani,* or Christians.

Numbers only Christ Himself could count were put to death. Nero applied every ounce of his creativity to appoint means of death. Many were nailed to crosses. Others were covered with animal skins, tied down, and devoured by dogs. Still others were doused with flammable fluids and set on fire as torches in the night.[1] Nero exercised such unimaginable cruelty toward Christians that many believed he must be the Antichrist.[2]

Peter lost his life in this terrible wave of persecution.[3] We have no idea whether officials captured and brought him to Rome or whether he came to help. We can, however, be reasonably sure that Paul was Nero's prime trophy. Nero could not tolerate the zealous apostle, but the emperor would have to be careful how this Christian would meet his death. After all, Paul was a Roman citizen.

We now approach the final letter from the pen of the apostle Paul. He wrote his second letter to Timothy during his last imprisonment in Rome, shortly before his death. Our goal is to capture the state of mind and physical conditions of the great apostle in the final season of his life.

I encourage you to read 2 Timothy in its entirety. The letter reveals several descriptions of Paul's condition and state of mind during his final imprisonment:

1. *He was in physical discomfort.* Some

criminals were simply incarcerated behind locked doors with no chains. Paul was held under conditions like those of a convicted killer. He was bound by heavy chains — the type that bruise and lacerate the skin. He was almost sixty years old and had taken enough beatings to make him quite arthritic. The lack of mobility greatly intensified any ailments or illnesses. He most likely was reduced to skin and bones. The cells where the worst prisoners were chained were usually filthy, wet, and rodent-infested dungeons. Paul was cold. He wanted his cloak and begged Timothy to do everything he could to come before winter.

Think of a time when you were physically miserable. You probably had great difficulty concentrating, didn't you? Severe physical conditions such as extreme temperatures, chronic pain, or hunger are quite consuming. The beauty and articulation of Paul's final letter cannot be fully appreciated without realizing how physically uncomfortable he must have been when he wrote it.

2. *He was probably humiliated.* In ancient prisons captors often thought of ways to shame their captives. Perhaps the least of their inhumanities was not allowing prisoners to wash and dress themselves adequately. Their confines doubled as bedroom and

bathroom. In 2 Timothy 1:12, Paul said, "That is why I am suffering as I am. Yet I am not ashamed." Paul's words may hint at the attempts of his captors to shame him. He told Timothy several times not to be ashamed of him (see v. 8). As much as Paul had suffered, he was unaccustomed to the treatment he received in the final season of his life.

3. *He felt deserted and lonely.* Some deserted him. Others, like Onesiphorus, had trouble finding him. Paul told Timothy in 2 Timothy 4:16 that everyone deserted him at his first defense. Since he was a Roman citizen, he had a hearing. People could come forward in his defense. No one came forward at Paul's first hearing. Can you imagine the loneliness he must have experienced as the bailiff called for defense witnesses, and silence fell over the courtroom? I don't believe they deserted him because they didn't love him. Many probably grieved because they did not come to his defense, but they were frightened for their lives. As far as most of them were concerned, Paul was on death row anyway. They couldn't save him. After all, he was certainly guilty of denying the deity of Nero. Even in these extreme straits Paul still said, "May it not be held against them" (4:16).

I keep staring at the words "only Luke is with me" (2 Tim. 4:11). Sometimes I think nothing is dearer than an enduring friendship between two men. Maybe because it's rarer than those among women. Now do you see why God appointed Luke to tell Paul's story in the Book of Acts? Who on earth loved him more? Who was more devoted?

Picturing these two men in a rancid cell moves me. One was bound to the floor with chains, the other chained to his friend with heartstrings. You can be fairly certain whatever wrap Luke had, he draped around the frail shoulders of his friend. I wonder if the Paul of the old days was hardly recognizable. Paul had been so fiery, so temperamental. Luke had watched the great apostle speak with indescribable authority. He saw him perform wonders and woo people to Christ. In that prison cell in A.D. 67, he saw a frail man, cold and lonely. I think perhaps Luke would rather have seen his friend dead than chained like an animal and humiliated.

God was gracious to sustain Dr. Luke's life so he could care for Paul in his last days. Luke was an old man by this time, with few tools to take care of his beloved patient. But perhaps most important of all, as the weakening apostle struggled in the blackness of a dungeon night, his old friend could say, "I'm here, Paul. Right here."

4. *He longed for normalcy.* Although Paul's life was seldom normal in our terms, in his last season I believe he longed for things that were normal to him. Notice how he wanted his oldest friends. He asked for Mark (see 2 Tim. 4:11). He spoke of Luke at his side. He sent greetings to Priscilla and Aquila. He begged Timothy to come quickly. His request for his scrolls, especially the parchments, also tenders my heart. His scrolls were probably copies of Old Testament Scriptures. Very likely he had also recorded on parchments facts about the earthly life of Christ, based on the stories of Peter and Luke. I can't begin to put myself in Paul's position, but if I were away from loved ones and facing certain death, I would want several things.

I have stacks of journals recording prayers too private to allow anyone to read, yet I cannot bring myself to throw them away. During uncertain times when I am called to walk by faith, I can turn back to personal records of God's faithfulness and find strength again. My Bible and my journals are my most treasured tangible belongings. During difficult days, even holding my Bible close to my chest brings me comfort. No doubt Paul longed for these things.

A person confined and facing death inevitably turns the mental pages of the past. Surely Paul was no different. He must have thought about Tarsus. His mother's face. His father's voice. His childhood in a Jewish community. His first impressions of Jerusalem. The classroom debates he enjoyed. The way people whispered about his genius behind his back. His bright future. His return to Tarsus and the respect he commanded. His drive to persecute the people of the Way. The blinding light that sent him to his knees. He traded a life of respect and honor for one of rejection and tribulation. If his childhood friends could have seen him in that horrendous dungeon, they might have surmised that he had traded everything for nothing.

So, what do you have when you have nothing left? You have what you know. Faced with humiliation, Paul proclaimed, "Yet I am not ashamed, because I know whom I have believed, and am convinced that he is able to guard what I have entrusted to him for that day" (2 Tim. 1:12). Paul's sanity was protected by his certainty. He knew the One in whom he believed.

Paul had entrusted everything to Christ.

No matter how difficult circumstances grew, he never tried to take it back. As the chains gripped his hands and feet and the stench of death assailed him, he recalled everything he had entrusted to his Savior and said, "[I] am convinced that he is able to guard what I have entrusted to him" (2 Tim. 1:12).

Paul used a terminology that painted a graphic image. The original term used for "guard" is *phulasso*. The noun form of the word is *phulakterion*. Do you know what this word meant? Phylacteries! Paul's father wore phylacteries. As a young rabbi, Paul wore phylacteries. Years later, his thoughts obviously returned to the many experiences leading him to this place where he was bound in chains, and he said, "Christ is safely keeping everything I've entrusted to Him. Every record is kept like words on a scroll — every trust tucked safely in His care. He will not forget." With chained hands, Paul could still touch the face of God.

CHAPTER 50
FINISHING THE RACE

2 Timothy 3–4

*I have fought the good fight, I have
finished the race, I have kept the faith.*
(2 TIM. 4:7)

We have journeyed with the apostle through
many years and across many seas. We've met
many interesting characters. We've been
thrown out of cities, boarded boats, and
battled waves. We've been in and out of
prison. We've been to the heights and to the
depths. We've walked next to one of the
most influential men in Christendom. He
was far from perfect. Indeed, we've seen
ourselves in him. But more than anything,
we've seen Christ in him.

I've prayed so for you on this trip. I've
asked God over and over to reveal Himself
to you at every stop. As we conclude, I am
reminded of my earliest prayer when I
began this study. I asked God to meet each

of us on our roads to Damascus and cause the scales to fall from our eyes. I've prayed that we would live the rest of our lives with new vision. Not because of my feeble prayers but because of the faithfulness of God.

I do not want this journey to end. I don't want to unpack and go back to life as I knew it before this trip. I want where I've been to impact where I'm going. Too many times we've said farewell with the words, "God be with you." He's already promised He would. My farewell wish is, "Go with God," suitcase packed and ready to go. In the spirit of the apostle Paul, go wherever Christ may lead.

Before we continue our own journeys, let's join a certain sinner saved by grace on his final flight. I sense a fatherly tone in Paul's instructions to Timothy. An urgency is evident in Paul's words to his dear son in the faith.

The apostle knew without a doubt he was about to die. Paul probably prayed for God to release him once again to minister in the midst of chaotic Rome. Paul may have believed his death at that exact time was totally illogical, yet he also had surrendered his life to God's perfect will. God's glory was the issue in every situation he encountered (see 2 Cor. 4). Whether he felt the timing of his death was logical, clearly he realized it was inevitable.

Paul was no masochist. We don't find him striking a martyr's pose or singing "Nobody Knows the Troubles I've Seen." He wasn't begging for the guillotine. He simply looked at life through the window of Philippians 1:21: "For to me, to live is Christ and to die is gain." Our entire journey has been an effort to study the heart of a man who could sincerely make such a statement. Christ had profoundly transformed Paul's attitude toward life and death. Having spent his adult life in pursuit of Christ, Paul had a unique view of death:

1. *Paul saw death as a departure.* He did not say, "The time has come for my death." He said, "The time has come for my departure." His entire life was a series of departures. He followed the leading of the Holy Spirit through Judea, Syria, Cilicia, Galatia, Pamphylia, Asia, Macedonia, Achaia, and Italy. He never knew what awaited him as he entered a city, but one result was inevitable — as surely as he arrived, he would depart. God never let him hang his hat for long. "Our citizenship is in heaven," Paul said in Philippians 3:20. To him, settling in would be pointless until then. Paul had faithfully done his time in Rome and,

predictably, another departure awaited him. This time, he was going home.

2. *Paul saw death as a rescue.* He wrote, "The Lord will rescue me from every evil attack and will bring me safely to his heavenly kingdom" (2Tim. 4:18). Paul didn't see death as a defeat. He did not believe the enemy finally had his way. He saw death as a rescue! We tend to define the word *rescue* an entirely different way. God certainly rescued Paul many times on this earth, just as He has rescued us, yet Paul knew the greatest rescue of all awaited him. Death was not God's refusal to act. Death was God's ultimate rescue. Oh, if we could only understand this difficult truth, how different our perspectives would be. Paul not only saw death as the ultimate rescue from evil, he saw death as a rescue from frail, limited bodies.

3. *Paul saw death as a safe passage.* Remember the words of 2 Timothy 4:18. God will not only rescue us, but He will bring us safely to His heavenly kingdom. Earlier we learned the original Greek meaning for the word *rescue. Rhuomai* means "to draw or snatch from danger, rescue, deliver. This is more with the meaning of drawing to oneself than merely rescuing for someone or something." God is not simply trying to

snatch us from danger. He desires to draw us to Himself spiritually, then one day physically. When our ultimate rescue comes, God's purpose is to deliver us to Himself — safely.

In our most vulnerable moments, all of us fear death. When the time comes, God will deliver us safely. You may say, "But what if we die a violent death?" Paul was about to die a violent death — yet God would deliver him safely.

Each nightfall in that dark dungeon in Rome, Paul knew he was one day closer to certain execution. The only reason he was spared so long was the problem of his Roman citizenship. Many Christians were fed to lions in an amphitheater packed with spectators. Nero could not legally sentence Paul to such a death; hence, Paul's literal expression in 2 Timothy 4:17: "I was delivered from the lion's mouth" — not by Nero but by God. I believe the crazy emperor incited more anger and revulsion than fear in Paul. Paul had grown and changed in so many ways during his lifetime with Christ. He grew less harsh and more understanding. Yet some things never changed — like Paul's propensity to have the last word. Let me show you something absolutely vintage Paul as we draw our study to a close. He wrote, "I have fought the good fight, I have finished the race, I have kept the faith. Now there is in store for me the crown of righteousness, which the Lord, the righteous Judge, will award to me on that day — and not only to me, but also to all who have longed for his appearing" (2 Tim. 4:7–8).

Paul wasn't just pulling a word picture out of a hat. Anyone in the Roman Empire would know exactly what he was talking about. I wouldn't be the least surprised if these words spread and ultimately hastened his death. In A.D. 67, the year of Paul's death, Nero had the audacity to enter himself in the Olympic games. Mind you, Olympic athletes trained all their lives for the games. The thirty-year-old, soft-bellied emperor used medications to induce vomiting rather than exercise to control his weight.[1] He was in pitiful shape and ill prepared, but who would dare tell him he could not compete? He cast himself on a chariot at Olympia and drove a ten-horse team. "He fell from the chariot and had to be helped in again; but, though he failed to stay the course and retired before the finish, the judges nevertheless awarded him the prize."[2]

Nero did not finish the race. Nevertheless, a wreath was placed on his head, and he was hailed the victor. He showed his gratitude for their cooperation in the ridiculous scam by exempting Greece from taxation. For his processional entry into Rome he chose the chariot Augustus had used in his triumph in a former age, and he wore a Greek mantle spangled with gold stars over a purple robe. The Olympic wreath was on his head. "Victims were sacrificed in his honour all along the route."[3] You can be fairly certain they were *Chrestiani.*

Needless to say, word of the humiliating victory spread faster than the fire of A.D. 64. Soon after Nero returned to Rome, the apostle wrote his stirring final testimony: "I have fought the good fight, I have finished the race, I have kept the faith. Now there is in store for me the crown of righteousness, which the Lord, the righteous Judge, will award to me" (2 Tim. 4:7–8). The edict was signed for his execution. The apostle Paul desired one thing of his death. The same thing he desired in his life, to "have sufficient courage so that now as always Christ will be exalted in my body, whether by life or by death" (Phil. 1:20).

God did not allow the deaths of His beloved apostles to overshadow their lives. Their departures were intimate encounters between themselves and the One for whom they laid down their lives. Traditional teaching handed down through the ages tells us two soldiers by the name of Ferega and Parthemius brought Paul word of his death. They approached him and asked for his prayers that they might also believe in his Christ. Having received life from his instruction, they then led Paul out of the city to his death.[4] Traditional teaching claims he prayed just before his execution. At this point I would have trouble believing anything different. Wouldn't you?

After praying, the apostle Paul gave his neck to the sword. Before his earthly tent had time to collapse to the ground, his feet stood on holy ground. His eyes, possibly scarred and blurred from a glorious light on a Damascus road, saw their first crystal-clear vision in thirty years. Paul, himself, had written, "Now we see but a poor reflection as in a mirror; then we shall see face to face" (1 Cor. 13:12). Faith became sight, and the raptured saint saw His face. He beheld the ultimate surpassing glory.

No thought of beatings. No questions of timing. No pleas for vengeance. No list of requests. Just the sight of unabashed, unhindered, unveiled glory. And he had not yet looked past His face. "The glory of God in the face of Christ" (2 Cor. 4:6). He was seeing the face he had waited thirty years to see.

The Righteous Judge raised a wreath of righteousness and placed it on the head of His faithful servant. He had finished the race. More impressively, he had kept the faith. Never doubt the difference.

Paul once wrote, "Now I know in part; then I shall know fully, even as I am fully known" (1 Cor. 13:12). The partial knowledge of Christ Paul had acquired in his lifetime was the same knowledge he claimed to be worth every loss (see Phil. 3:8–10). Oh, my friend, if partial knowledge of the Lord Jesus is worth every loss, what will full knowledge be like? "Oh, the depth of the riches of the wisdom and knowledge of God!" (Rom. 11:33). One day the prayer of the apostle will be answered for all of us. We will indeed "grasp how wide and long and high and deep is the love of Christ, . . . and know this love that surpasses knowledge" (Eph. 3:18–19).

Until then, may God find us faithful, unstoppable servants of the One who saved us, waiting to hang our hats on heaven's door. "For I am convinced that neither death nor life, neither angels nor demons, neither the present nor the future, nor any powers, neither height nor depth, nor anything else in all creation, will be able to separate us from the love of God that is in Christ Jesus our Lord" (Rom. 8:38).

Most Worthy Lord,
make me a drink offering
and take me not home
until the cup is overturned
the glass broken
and every drop loosed
for Your glory.

STUDY QUESTIONS

Chapter 1

1. How would you describe the events surrounding the circumcision of an infant boy in an ancient Hebrew home?
2. Why were family and community particularly important to Jews in the Gentile world?
3. What were the positive aspects of the highly ritualized lifestyle of the Pharisees? What were the negative aspects?
4. How do you think the Pharisee's expectation of the coming of Messiah compares to your expectation of Christ's Second Coming?

Chapter 2

1. What are a few ways the ancient Hebrew home emphasized Scripture in the life of a young boy?
2. What was the Jewish attitude toward children?

3. What part did Scripture memorization play in the Pharisee's home? How has Scripture memorization benefitted you?

4. How would you describe a childhood like Saul's?

Chapter 3

1. How would you describe Gamaliel, Saul's primary teacher in Jerusalem?

2. How do you imagine Saul felt as he left home to go to Jerusalem?

3. What feelings did the Jews harbor for the city of David?

4. What places have particular spiritual significance for you and your family?

5. What does the torn-down wall of partition mean to you?

Chapter 4

1. What would you imagine Saul's life was like as he attempted to live by the law faultlessly?

2. How do you think Paul responded to the hypocrisy of the Jews in Jerusalem? How have you been disillusioned by Christians?

3. Why do we have such difficulty honestly facing our areas of sin, weakness, and failure?

4. What was Jesus' attitude toward the hypocritical Pharisees?

Chapter 5

1. What important event occurred in Jerusalem in the years following Saul's assumed departure?
2. Put yourself in the place of the Pharisees of Jesus' day. How would you feel toward John the Baptist and Jesus?
3. Have you ever failed to speak up for Christ because of what you feared your testimony could cost you?
4. In what ways have you experienced "religion gone sour"?
5. In what ways does Satan seek to use self-interest against you?

Chapter 6

1. What was the connection and contrast between Saul and Stephen?
2. Why did you first believe in the resurrection of Jesus? Why do you believe now?
3. What about Stephen do you think infuriated the religious leaders?
4. How difficult do you find it to pray for those who persecute you?

Chapter 7

1. What was most significant to you about Saul's conversion?
2. What thoughts and feelings do you think went through Saul's mind on the Damas-

cus road? During the days of blindness?

3. Has God had to teach you black and white, or gray? What kinds of lessons has He taught?

4. Can you think of a personal opinion or a devout belief you used to have that you ultimately, based on God's Word, realized was incomplete or misguided?

Chapter 8

1. When Saul set out to prove to the Jews that Jesus was the Christ, what was his method?

2. What characteristics are admirable about Barnabas?

3. Who has been particularly encouraging to you at a time when you needed the help?

4. What difference did Barnabas's encouragement make in Paul's life?

Chapter 9

1. How did God speak to Peter about prejudice?

2. How has God opened your mind about some prejudice that you had in your life?

3. How has God used the tool of repetition to get through to you about something?

4. How have you experienced God's giving similar visions to different people?

5. What are you doing to prepare yourself to be a recipient of a word from God?

Chapter 10

1. How did Barnabas and Saul begin their ministry together?
2. What experiences have you had with "mold breakers"?
3. What difference does it make when you plan in advance to remain faithful to the Lord?

Chapter 11

1. Who was Bar-Jesus?
2. What can you do to strengthen Christian leadership? To strengthen yourself as a Christian leader?
3. Have you gone through one or more times of spiritual flatness? If so, what has helped you to come through such times?

Chapter 12

1. What does being "appointed for eternal life" mean?
2. How was Satan able to stir up persecution against Paul and Barnabas?
3. How have you used the power of influence in a positive way recently? In a negative way?

4. What is it like to obey God but still not get the results you wanted or expected?

Chapter 13

1. Why was Paul stoned?
2. How should a person determine when to trust God to protect and when to run for his or her life?
3. Why do you think God chooses either to work a miracle or to withhold a miracle?
4. Can you think of a situation when you have been tempted to take God's glory for yourself?
5. Can you describe a time when God used a difficult situation to draw you with loving kindness to Himself?

Chapter 14

1. How were the Gentiles who were turning to Christ being wrongly burdened?
2. What should be the relationship between evangelism and discipleship?
3. Why is hardship inevitable in the nature of things?
4. Can you describe someone who has been to you a living example of surviving hardships with victory and joy?

Chapter 15

1. How does Acts 14:21–22 refute many popular prosperity gospels?
2. What is the difference between legalism and healthy belief?
3. Why must we be cautious about drawing a universal standard from our personal experience?
4. What can we learn from the practice of eating meat sacrificed to idols?

Chapter 16

1. Why did Paul and Barnabas go their separate ways?
2. Why do we tend to judge and take sides in disputes?
3. How should we deal with situations when we strongly differ with someone about matters related to church or ministry?

Chapter 17

1. How would you describe Timothy?
2. Why did Paul invest his life in so many other disciples?
3. What problems result from being unequally yoked?
4. For what are you most grateful in your spiritual family tree?

Chapter 18

1. How can we be best equipped to discern God's redirection in our lives?
2. Describe a time when you properly followed the leadership of the Holy Spirit. Describe a time when you missed the leadership of the Spirit.
3. Why is peace one of the most obvious earmarks of the authority of Christ?
4. What is it like to have to deal with feelings of spiritual inferiority?

Chapter 19

1. How did God use the imprisonment of Silas and Paul for His glory?
2. How does it feel to see someone you love suffer?
3. Can you describe a situation in which you learned to sing praises through your pain?

Chapter 20

1. Why were the Bereans of more noble character than the Thessalonians?
2. Why do you suppose Paul followed the same pattern wherever he went: preaching first in the synagogue and seeking to prove that Jesus was the Christ with the Old Testament Scripture?
3. Why is it so important to cross-check with

the other Scriptures any message we receive?

Chapter 21

1. How was Paul's visit to Athens particularly unique?
2. Why did the Athenians reject the idea of a resurrection?
3. How would you explain to a skeptic why God is completely different from the gods of this world?
4. Which do you find more difficult to deal with: opposition or apathy?

Chapter 22

1. What was Paul's apparent state of mind when he came to Corinth?
2. Have you ever had a lengthy time alone in which your mind "ran away with you" with negative thoughts?
3. What important lesson did God teach Paul through the Athens experience?
4. How does seeing Paul's experience of struggle affect your ability to relate to him as a fellow struggler on the road to serve Christ?

Chapter 23

1. Why did Paul take extra measures to consecrate himself to God in Corinth?

2. How have you learned to prepare yourself for times of temptation?

3. What are the advantages of ministering as a "tentmaker"? The disadvantages?

Chapter 24

1. How would you describe Apollos?

2. How do you feel about opening your home for ministry?

3. Can you think of a time when an opportunity to serve seemed so rational for you, but you realized later it was not God's will for your life?

4. What lessons do you draw from the situation with Paul and Apollos?

Chapter 25

1. What extraordinary miracles did God perform through Paul in Ephesus?

2. What do you think causes the name of the Lord Jesus to be held in high honor today?

3. Why do you think God made such a point of the arrival of the Spirit in certain specific cases?

4. How has God come to you and met you right at the point of your need?

Chapter 26

1. What prompted Paul to leave Ephesus?

2. What significance do you see to the fact that Paul "decided" to go to Rome?

3. How do you complete the sentence: "God has allowed me to decide to do a number of things for His sake, but beyond all other things I feel I must _____"?

4. How does Paul's willingness to bow to the wisdom of others impact your thinking about the apostle?

Chapter 27

1. What prompted an eye-opening miracle during one of Paul's long-winded sermons?

2. Why do you think we sometimes have difficulty knowing when to stop talking?

3. How many people are basing their opinion of God on how they see you act in time of stress or trouble?

4. How do you think you would react if your child were suddenly killed by accident or disease?

Chapter 28

1. How would you describe the farewell between Paul and the Ephesian elders?

2. What kind of bonds develop between believers who serve together for an ex-

tended period of time as did Paul and the Ephesian elders?

3. How do you feel about finishing strong in your Christian journey?

4. What kind of "flock" has God given you to care for and keep watch over?

Chapter 29

1. Who was Agabus and how did God use him?

2. What blessings has God brought into your life during "unscheduled stops" along the way?

3. How does this study impact your idea about Paul and women, particularly women in ministry?

4. How do you suppose Paul felt when his friends tried to get him to refrain from going on to Jerusalem?

Chapter 30

1. How did Paul fellowship in Christ's sufferings in Jerusalem?

2. How does it feel to be caught in the middle of anger and disagreement between people you care about?

3. How difficult is it for you to seek the common ground with those who do not know Christ without compromising Christian truth?

4. Do you tend to go overboard on stressing truth or on seeking common ground?
5. What does the "fellowship of Christ's sufferings" mean to you?

Chapter 31

1. What were several elements of Paul's powerful testimony in Acts 22?
2. Why might we assume we have stepped outside God's will when persecution comes?
3. How does it feel to desperately want to reach a person or group of people but seemingly without success?
4. Why is our personal testimony so important?

Chapter 32

1. What did you learn about the conscience?
2. How have you tried in the past to soothe your conscience?
3. What can the Holy Spirit do that our consciences can never accomplish?
4. How can we enjoy a clear conscience even after a guilty past?

Chapter 33

1. How and why was Paul transported to Caesarea?
2. How has God given you courage at a time

when you needed it?

3. What is the difference between being delivered *from* peril and being delivered *through* peril?

4. What part does intercessory prayer play in the deliverance of God?

Chapter 34

1. What subjects did Paul preach to Felix?

2. Of what crimes did the Jews accuse Paul?

3. To what lengths did both God and Paul go in order to witness to Felix and Drusilla?

4. Why do you think God is willing to go so far to present the gospel even to those who will not respond?

Chapter 35

1. How can a person investigate whether Christ is alive today?

2. How did you come to "know" Christ is real?

3. How has God worked in your life in some way that you could never have imagined?

4. Have you had to wait a long time for some promise of God to appear?

Chapter 36

1. How would you describe Paul's voyage toward Rome?

2. Why do you think it is particularly difficult to deal with trouble that comes as a result of someone else's poor judgment?
3. Have you ever been in a storm due to another person's poor judgment?
4. What cargo or tackle do you presently need to throw overboard?

Chapter 37

1. Why do you think all the passengers' lives were spared?
2. What sort of protection have you experienced because of someone else's faithfulness?
3. Whom do you relate to more, Jonah or Paul? Why?
4. What difference does prompt obedience or faithfulness make?

Chapter 38

1. What did the shipwrecked crew discover while in Malta?
2. Can you think of a time when you were shipwrecked, in a manner of speaking, and encountered unusual kindness?
3. How did the islanders respond to Paul's encounter with the snake?
4. How has God made Himself apparent to all people even if they have not encountered the gospel?

Chapter 39

1. How do you suppose Paul felt as he approached the city of Rome?
2. What ties bind Christians together as brothers and sisters?
3. What benefits have you seen come from someone's faithful practice of intercession?
4. Do you believe Christians have an obligation to one another as well as to the lost? Why?

Chapter 40

1. According to the original language, how can a person hear but never understand?
2. What impresses you most about the apostle Paul?
3. Have you ever held up your hand to God and said, "That's enough. That's all I'm comfortable with"?
4. What happens when we resist what God is trying to tell us, give us, and work in us?

Chapter 41

1. How can we protect ourselves from being kidnapped by hollow and deceptive philosophy?
2. Have you encountered the belief that

knowledge, rather than faith, leads to salvation?

3. Why do you think legalism has such appeal to us?

4. Can you think of a time when Satan tempted you to misappropriate a biblical concept, giving it priority over Christ?

Chapter 42

1. What are a few things submission does not mean?

2. How does the principle of mutual submission play itself out in marriage?

3. How has Paul's command for men to love their wives changed society?

Chapter 43

1. Which exhortation spoke most clearly to you in your battle against an unseen enemy?

2. What difference does it make to remind ourselves that the enemy is Satan, not our spouses, in-laws, neighbors, coworkers, or even our earthly foes?

3. How can you actively guard the gains you've made in Christ?

4. What part does prayer play in your life?

5. What goals have you set to grow in your effectiveness, furthering Christ's kingdom and resisting Satan's?

Chapter 44

1. How did Paul demonstrate wisdom as he sought reconciliation between Philemon and Onesimus?
2. Why did Paul choose not to consider Onesimus absolved from all responsibility after he repented and accepted Christ?
3. What does the story of Onesimus say to our "me first" and "freedom at all costs" culture?
4. Why is the approach Paul took to slavery the only method that would eventually end the practice?

Chapter 45

1. What are the thieves of contentment?
2. How do we turn off the valve that pumps anxiety into our souls?
3. Why do our human natures tend toward negative and destructive thinking?
4. How do we learn to develop contentment?

Chapter 46

1. How was the apostle Paul able to retain his spiritual passion through so many years and experiences?
2. How do you feel about your calling to serve Christ?
3. In what ways has God shown Himself to

be a superabundant giver in your life?

4. How long has it been since you felt deep gratitude for the simplicity of your salvation?

Chapter 47

1. What are several imperatives for strong ministry?

2. Why do you think godliness must be a pursuit?

3. How can you "fan into flame" the gifts God has given you?

4. In what ways are you tempted to engage in "godless chatter"?

Chapter 48

1. What are several characteristics of an effective mentor?

2. Can you think of a way in which someone could exercise unhealthy faith?

3. Why are good mentors so important?

4. How does Paul's concept of learning to love your mate differ from our culture's idea of love as a feeling or something you fall in?

Chapter 49

1. How did Paul's second imprisonment in Rome differ from his first?

2. What impacts you most about Paul dur-

ing this final season of his life?

3. What have you entrusted to Christ for the final days of your life?

Chapter 50

1. How did Nero's experience in an Olympic race contrast so vividly with Paul's experience in life's most important race?

2. In what way is death God's ultimate rescue?

3. What do you think the scene looked like in heaven when Paul made his entrance following his execution here?

4. What one thing most impacts you from this study of the life of Paul?

NOTES

Chapter 1

1. Rabbi Solomon Ganzfield, trans. Hyman E. Goldin, *Code of Jewish Law* (New York: Hebrew Publishing Company, 1993).
2. Ibid., I, 1.
3. Ibid., IV, 43.
4. Ibid., IV, 44.
5. Ibid., II, 62.

Chapter 2

1. Ganzfield, trans. Goldin, *Code of Jewish Law,* IV, 47.
2. F. B. Meyer, *Paul, A Servant of Jesus Christ* (Fort Washington, Penn.: Christian Literature Crusade, 1995), 17.
3. E. K. R. Johnsen, *Paul of Tarsus* (Minneapolis: Augsburg Publishing House, 1919), 20.
4. Ganzfield, trans. Goldin, *Code of Jewish Law,* IV, 47.
5. Ibid., I, 27.

6. To see some of the benedictions required of the faithful Jew, see ibid., 6.

Chapter 3

1. Meyer, *Paul,* 26.
2. Ernle Bradford, *Paul the Traveller* (New York: Barnes & Noble, 1993), 35.
3. Ibid., 35.
4. Ibid., 36.

Chapter 8

1. Cited in Joan Comay, *Who's Who in the Old Testament* (New York: Crown Publishers, 1980), 322.

Chapter 11

1. Patrick Johnstone, *Operation World* (Grand Rapids, Mich.: Zondervan Publishing House, 1993), 643.

Chapter 14

1. Trent C. Butler et al., eds., *Holman Bible Dictionary* (Nashville: Holman Bible Publishers, 1991), 406.

Chapter 18

1. Butler et al., eds., *Holman Bible Dictionary,* 899.

Chapter 25

1. Bradford, *Paul the Traveller,* 196.
2. Ibid., 197.

Chapter 31

1. John F. Walvoord and Roy B. Zuck, eds., *The Bible Knowledge Commentary New Testament* (Wheaton, Ill.: Victor Books, 1983), 417.

Chapter 34

1. Walvoord et al., eds., *The Bible Knowledge Commentary New Testament,* 421.
2. Ibid., 422.

Chapter 36

1. Bradford, *Paul the Traveller,* 226.

Chapter 38

1. Johnstone, *Operation World,* 81.

Chapter 39

1. *The Revell Bible Dictionary* (Old Tappan, N.J.: Fleming H. Revell Company, 1990), 871.

Chapter 42

1. Walvoord et al., eds., *The Bible Knowledge Commentary New Testament,* 640.

Chapter 47

1. Walvoord et al., eds., *The Bible Knowledge Commentary,* 735.

Chapter 49

1. Will Durant, *Ceasar and Christ* (New York: Simon & Schuster, 1944), 280–81.
2. John Foxe, *Foxe's Book of Martyrs* (New Kensington, Penn.: Whitaker House, 1981), 12.
3. *The Revell Bible Dictionary,* 775.

Chapter 50

1. Robert Graves, *The Twelve Caesars* (New York: Penguin Books, 1957), 222.
2. Ibid., 226.
3. Ibid.
4. Foxe, *Book of Martyrs,* 12.

ABOUT THE AUTHOR

Beth Moore is a writer and teacher of best-selling Bible studies whose public speaking engagements carry her all over the United States. A dedicated wife and mother of two, Moore lives in Houston, Texas, where she serves on the pastor's council of First Baptist Church, teaches a weeknight inter-denominational women's Bible study, and teaches a coed adult Sunday school class with an attendance of over three hundred.

Beth loves the Lord, loves to laugh, and loves to be with His people. No doubt you will be compelled to a greater intimacy with the Savior through her writing. Her previous books include *Feathers from My Nest, A Heart Like His, Praying God's Word, Breaking Free,* and *Things Pondered.*